D0221494

Dorothy Thompson and Rose Wilder Lane

DOROTHY THOMPSON

AND

ROSE WILDER LANE

Forty Years of Friendship

Letters, 1921–1960
edited by William Holtz

University of Missouri Press
Columbia and London

University of Missouri Press, Columbia, Missouri 65201
Printed and bound in the United States of America

5 4 3 2 1 95 94 93 92 91

Library of Congress Cataloging-in-Publication Data

Thompson, Dorothy, 1893–1961.
Dorothy Thompson and Rose Wilder Lane : Forty Years of Friendship.
Includes index.
1. Thompson, Dorothy, 1893–1961—Correspondence.
2. Lane, Rose Wilder, 1886–1968—Correspondence.
3. Authors, American—20th century—Correspondence.
4. Journalists—United States—Correspondence.
I. Lane, Rose Wilder, 1886–1968. II. Holtz, William V.
III. Title.
PS3539.H649Z487 1987 070.4'092'4 [B] 86-30876
ISBN 0-8262-0646-8 (alk. paper)

∞™ This paper meets the minimum requirements of the American National Standard for Permanence of Paper for Printed Library Materials, Z39.48, 1984.

Typesetter: Connell-Zeko Type & Graphics
Printer: Thomson-Shore, Inc.
Binder: Thomson-Shore, Inc.
Typeface: Baskerville

For my mother

Contents

Preface

This book is an attempt to rescue from obscurity the voices of two brilliant and articulate women—to bring into history some measure of the dialogue that occupied them over the course of forty years. Neither is a household name today, although in her time one was second, perhaps, only to Eleanor Roosevelt among American women in the attention she commanded from the public. The other achieved no such stature; rather, she moved at the margins of the world of greater figures, and her finest accomplishment consisted in making her mother famous.[1] To the extent that history is a roll of names remembered beyond their time, neither rises from obscurity in the backward glance from our day. It has been their fate to be identified merely by their attachment to those we do remember: Dorothy Thompson as the wife of Sinclair Lewis, the first American writer to win the Nobel Prize; Rose Wilder Lane as the daughter of Laura Ingalls Wilder, the author and heroine of the "Little House" pioneer books for children.

Biographical studies of both women are either narrow or superficial. Dorothy Thompson has been the subject of one responsible but cursory biography, and partial portraits have appeared in the standard life of Sinclair Lewis and in a privileged reminiscence of the Lewis-Thompson marriage by one of their friends. But as the most recent summary of her career concludes, "There is no fully satisfactory biography."[2] Even more is this the case for

1. See the Introduction to Part 4.

2. This book was in proof when a new biography of Dorothy Thompson appeared: Peter Kurth, *American Cassandra: The Life of Dorothy Thompson* (Boston: Little, Brown, 1990). Kurth's biography promises to remedy many of the deficiencies of the sources I have drawn on: Marion K. Sanders, *Dorothy Thompson: A Legend in Her Time* (Boston: Houghton Mifflin, 1973); Mark Schorer, *Sinclair Lewis: An American Life* (New York: McGraw-Hill, 1961); Vincent Sheean, *Dorothy and Red* (Boston: Houghton Mifflin, 1963); Paul Boyer, "Dorothy Thompson," in *Notable American Women: The Modern Period* (Cambridge: Harvard University Press, 1980), p. 686.

Rose Wilder Lane. Beyond a few standard handbook entries, her career is recorded only in a pamphlet justified by her connection with her mother and in the partial perspectives of a few specialized essays. Most of the biographical detail in this volume has been drawn from diaries and letters in the Hoover Library.[3]

This book does not pretend to remedy these major deficiencies, nor does it seek to emulate what has been achieved already. It attempts neither an overview nor a narrowly focused analysis; rather, it merely traces the thread of a friendship through a correspondence of forty years' continuance. In the simplest sense, it is personal history; but to the extent that these women participated in the greater world around them, it is history made personal. In the first respect, certainly, the characters of these women shine through their letters: Dorothy the more self-centered, the less attentive, probably with less emotional investment in the friendship, coarser-grained in both style and sensibility, yet accepting, as such people often do, the tribute of Rose's friendship as the natural due of one fated to lead, organize, and dominate. For her, the relationship with Rose was apparently grounded in a narrow zone of private comfort in a life all but wholly dedicated to public affairs. Rose seems clearly the more giving and the more demanding in the duties of friendship, and to her fall the major burdens of acceptance and forgiveness. More private and more reflective than Dorothy, hers is the more complex sensibility, one that gradually adopted a more rigid and idiosyncratic stance toward the public realm. The older by six years, she was early a guide and mentor, and there is much in her regard for Dorothy of the devotion to a gifted younger sister. Of the two, she is certainly the better letter-writer—probably one of the best of our time.

Inevitably, however, personal history is a partial account of

3. William T. Anderson, *Laura's Rose: The Story of Rose Wilder Lane* (Mansfield, Mo.: Laura Ingalls Wilder–Rose Wilder Lane Home Association, 1976); Rosa Ann Moore, "The Little House Books: Rose-Colored Classics," *Children's Literature* 7 (1978): 7–16, and "Laura Ingalls Wilder and Rose Wilder Lane: The Chemistry of Collaboration," *Children's Literature in Education* 11 (1980): 101–9; William Holtz, "The Little House on the Desert," *Aramco World Magazine* 25 (Nov.–Dec. 1984): 28–33, and "Sherwood Anderson and Rose Wilder Lane: Source and Method in *Dark Laughter*," *Journal of Modern Literature* 12 (March 1985): 131–52. The papers of Rose Wilder Lane were donated to the Herbert Hoover Presidential Library in 1980; for a description, see William Holtz, "The Rose Wilder Lane Papers," *The Annals of Iowa* 47 (Winter 1985): 646–53.

public history. These women led full and active lives through the first half of our century, and their friendship spans most of this period. Often their private concerns are intelligible only in wider perspectives, and where this has been the case I have tried to provide the necessary background. The result is a series of momentary glimpses into history as it conditions the affairs of daily life. No rigorous attempt is made to connect episode with episode; the continuity is that of private lives, not that of public affairs, and the larger realm must stand as footnote to the smaller. There is no "history of our times" here except as these women participated in it; and they are offered not as representative figures but as extraordinary ones.

A certain reciprocal imbalance follows from this intermittent attention to world and national affairs: the obscure and parochial life of Rose Wilder Lane is amplified at each touch, while the continuously public and international career of Dorothy Thompson is correspondingly diminished by occasional and partial views. Each distortion, however, pursues a degree of truth; and the two distortions complement one another in framing this picture of the friendship of two remarkable women.

Acknowledgments

I must first acknowledge the heirs of the estate of Dorothy Thompson, and Roger Lea MacBride, heir of Rose Wilder Lane, for permission to publish these letters. I am indebted to my colleagues in the Department of English and to the Research Council of the University of Missouri–Columbia for a leave during which much of my work was completed. Dwight M. Miller of the Herbert Hoover Presidential Library and Carolyn A. Davis of the George Arents Research Library of Syracuse University cheerfully helped me in my work with the manuscripts. Each of the following has assisted me in specific ways: Edzard Baumann, James Curtis, Marilynn Keil, the late Isaac Don Levine, Ruth Levine, Paula L. MacNeill, Greg Michalson, Carolyn Perry, Robert Sattelmeyer, Donald Soucy, and Robert O. Stephens. Rick Boland of the University of Missouri Press offered good counsel and saved me from some embarrassing errors, while Jane Lago saw the book finally through the press. Linda Webster compiled the index. Inevitably, I levied upon my family for aid: my daughters Victoria, Erica, and Sigrid all answered the call; as did my wife, whose enjoyment of these letters during repeated readings has reassured me of their value.

Bibliographical Note

This gathering of letters is drawn from the resources of two libraries. The larger portion comes from the George Arents Research Library of Syracuse University, which upon the death of Dorothy Thompson in 1961 became the repository of most of her papers. The slightly smaller remainder became available in 1980, when the Rose Wilder Lane papers were given to the Herbert Hoover Presidential Library in West Branch, Iowa, in recognition of Lane's association with Hoover. The letters in neither collection form a significant series; but together—despite some gaps—the two collections afford the gathering of a coherent sequence upon which this book is based.

Most of the letters are originals in one collection or the other. Some, however, are represented only by carbon copies or drafts. Several exist as originals in one collection and as copies or drafts in the other. The following list indicates the location and status of each letter.

Syracuse University Library: Letters 1–16, 19, 21, 25, 27, 30–32, 35, 37, 38 (draft), 39, 40, 41 (copy), 42–45, 46 (copy), 47–50, 51 (copy).

Herbert Hoover Presidential Library: Letters 9 (copy), 10 (copy), 17, 18, 19 (copy), 20, 22 (copy), 23 (copy), 24, 26 (copy), 28, 29, 33, 34, 36 (copy), 38, 40 (copy), 41, 42 (copy), 46.

Unless otherwise specified, Thompson items cited are from the Syracuse Library and Lane items from the Hoover Library. Occasional misspellings have been corrected silently, and in a few instances punctuation has been brought into conformity with current conventions. Where dates can be inferred, they have been inserted in brackets.

Dorothy Thompson and Rose Wilder Lane

Prologue

The friendship between Dorothy Thompson and Rose Wilder Lane began in November of 1920 in the publicity office of the American Red Cross in Paris. Rose was thirty-three, Dorothy six years younger.

Both women had come to Europe in that year to join the hundreds of other writers who had gathered to bear witness to the wreckage of the old world and the efforts toward its reconstruction. Rose was already an established journalist. She had worked as a feature-writer for the *San Francisco Bulletin* and had published popular biographies of Jack London, Henry Ford, and Herbert Hoover.[1] Her earlier background included the American pioneer heritage that her mother, Laura Ingalls Wilder, would write of in her "Little House" books for children. Dorothy was still a neophyte. Daughter of a Methodist minister, she had graduated from Syracuse University in 1914 and had spent the intervening years as an organizer and publicist in the women's suffrage movement and as a worker in an experimental social reform program.[2] Once in Europe, publicity work for the American Red Cross was for both a kind of anchor to the wind. Rose had come with a contract for a regular series of articles which still allowed her time for other writing; Dorothy had arrived simply with an introduction that might serve to get her some similar work—which she fell back on in November of 1920 as her free-lance efforts for American newspapers seemed unlikely to sustain her.

Dorothy felt herself above such work, which Rose was turning out with a journeyman competence. The aim of their writing was to keep American emotions alive to the misery of a shattered Europe and to highlight the good that contributions to the Red

1. "Life and Jack London" appeared serially in *Sunset* (Oct. 1917–May 1918); *Henry Ford's Own Story* (Forest Hills, N.J.: E. O. Jones, 1917); *The Making of Herbert Hoover* (New York: Century, 1920).

2. Sanders, *Dorothy Thompson,* I. 1–5.

Dorothy Thompson (circa 1922)

Rose Wilder Lane (circa 1926)

Cross had done. On November 27, 1920, Dorothy recorded her impressions in her diary:

> Oh, I wish that I were either more talented or less intelligent. The whole place is cluttered up with almost successful people. . . . They know their job well. Do it. Make a "good living." But oh, their shallowness. Appalling! Rose Wilder Lane their chiefest writer with her sob stuff. . . . if I stay here for months I shall never make friends with them.

But Rose improved with acquaintance, and in the next month their friendship flourished. Dorothy's closest friend had just married, leaving Dorothy lonely and depressed at her lack of success; in Rose she found a worldly wise, tough-minded mentor. Rose apparently found in this strikingly beautiful, energetic, and articulate young woman a version of an ideal self she had longed to be; "a song, a poem, flame in the sunlight,"[3] she would say later of Dorothy, acknowledging a kind of incandescent energy that compensated for other failings. And in each other, both women found a talent for good talk that bonded them in a natural affinity and affection.

Rose first recorded their acquaintance in a diary entry noting a dinner party on December 17. On December 30 she made a similar entry, and the entries for January 1–2 of the new year note briefly a walking trip from Blois to Ambois with Dorothy and Kate Horton, another Red Cross writer. This walking trip through the valley of the Loire would be the charmed center of their history, a moment when each was at her best for the other: it becomes a leitmotif in the correspondence. The following months marked a growing intimacy. There was a vague plan to travel together to China in the fall.[4] And there was the Mardi Gras celebration that Rose reported in a letter to a friend in the States:

> I had a box at the Bal Bullier, and wore my famous gypsy costume with some glittering additions; a crowd of the girls I know were there—Kit van Buskirk and Helen Boylston who are down from Poland, and Dorothy Thompson of the Manchester Guardian, and Kate Horton—the last two are the ones I went walking with through

3. See Letter 27.

4. Rose Wilder Lane to Elmer and Berta Hader, May 18, 1921 (University of Oregon Library).

> the chateau country—Kit was absolutely stunning in an Albanian harem costume—she has another that she's going to give me—enormous wide trousers of rose silk, with six-inch cuffs of solid gold embroidery, and a jacket of the same solid stiff golden, and a sash of bright blue and a golden chiffon-cloth veil. Dorothy went as the stunningest of Paris students, in corduroy trousers, a silk shirt open at the neck, a Roman-striped sash, a blue tam, a mustache and a pipe. We collected a dozen eager admirers, a tall and absolutely charming Indian Prince in white and silver with a tall turban, and an Apache or two, and several unimaginative evening-dressers, but they could dance, and a Roumanian peasant, and champagne popped on every hand, and the two orchestras relieved each other without a pause, and the floor was something I can't describe—a million costumes, all more colorful and witty than the ones you'd seen a minute ago. We came home at five o'clock in the morning, with blistered feet, and sang all down the boulevards, while the dawn was just coming up the sky.[5]

The trip to China did not materialize. Dorothy escaped the humiliation of the Red Cross office by posting herself to Vienna, where she worked as an unsalaried stringer for the Paris bureau of the *Philadelphia Public Ledger.* She was also to continue work for the Red Cross operations in Budapest. Her work in Vienna was so exceptional that within a few months she felt justified in applying to the Paris bureau for a salaried position. Rose met her in Paris and waited in a tea shop while Dorothy presented her case. Her success was celebrated with champagne in the Cafe de la Paix and a dinner in Rose's apartment. The date was May 6, 1921.[6] Dorothy's career was launched, and as a journalist, at least, she would no longer need a mentor.

5. Rose Wilder Lane to Elmer and Berta Hader, Feb. 11, 1921 (University of Oregon Library). The Bal Bullier was a well-known place of entertainment. Rose overstates Dorothy's connection with the *Manchester Guardian,* which was in fact the employer of Dorothy's sometime partner Marcel Fodor.

6. Sanders, *Dorothy Thompson,* p. 70.

Part I

Letters 1–5 (1921)

Introduction to Part I

The first group of letters are all Dorothy's from 1921. Rose's side of the correspondence has been lost, although she saved these letters from Dorothy and returned them to her in 1960.[1]

This is the period in which Dorothy began to make her name as an international journalist. This side of her life, however, is incidental to the main theme that runs through these letters—that is, love and marriage. For these talented and hard-working women, among the first generation to come of age in the twentieth century, there were no easy answers. In her diary entry for October 3, 1920, Dorothy had contemplated writing a novel that would present "the tragedy of the modern young woman of 27: how genuinely limited (by her own discrimination and maturity) are her opportunities for marriage, but how difficult and unsatisfactory is the other mode of life." The dilemma would be dramatically embodied in her own experience as she met the man who would become her first lover and husband, Josef Bard.

As Dorothy struggled with the problem, Rose became her adviser and sounding board. Rose had already put behind her a failed marriage and a subsequent love affair in San Francisco; since arriving in Europe, she had been involved with a literary agent named Arthur Griggs, an affair that at its end, she had said, had left her emotionally "beaten and sore"; and she was just now to begin the longest relationship with a man in her life, a romance with newspaperman Guy Moyston.[2] Rose could find little good to say about marriage for a woman like Dorothy, but Dorothy would nonetheless end by marrying Josef Bard early in 1922.

1. See Letter 45.

2. Her marriage to Gillette Lane lasted from 1909 to 1918. For the later San Francisco relationship, see Letter 1, note 10. The romance with Arthur Griggs can be traced through her diaries and journals for 1920–1921. The phrase "beaten and sore" is from Dorothy's Letter 5, but she seems to be echoing Rose's own language. For Guy Moyston, see Holtz, "Sherwood Anderson and Rose Wilder Lane," pp. 140, 142–43. Rose's journals, diaries, and letters indicate that the relationship with Moyston ran from 1921 through 1927.

Letter 1

We enter this series of letters in medias res, as Dorothy replies to one of Rose's. Rose is in Paris, writing and putting behind her the ill-fated romance with Arthur Griggs. Dorothy, in Vienna, is busy as a working journalist and is about to commence the first real love affair of her life. The ostensible subject of her letter to Rose is the conference of the "peace ladies," but the real concern is the appropriate stance toward love, sex, and marriage. Dorothy tries to pick her way between equally repellent alternatives: on the one hand are the one-dimensional, unrealistic idealogues whose humanity has been sapped by devotion to causes; on the other are the self-indulgent and self-consciously sexual libertines, here identified vaguely with the fictional women of D. H. Lawrence and more specifically with scantily clad swimmers and the frankly sexual conversations of certain acquaintances. Freudian theory is in the background, as Dorothy notes the "compensatory striving" of the peace delegates; but her deeper allegiance is to a balanced independence and decorum that she associates with George Meredith and Rudyard Kipling.

Rechte Wienzeile 31
Wien IV
July 15 [1921]

Rose:-

We just came in from an afternoon of swimming in Gauselhaufel and dining in the Prater[1] with Maud Swartz, the Secretary of the Women's Trade Union League of the U.S. Maud blew in to the women's peace conference in session here,[2] and I fell on her neck and lured her away from feeding-kitchens to swim in the Danube and enjoy the sights of the *real* Vienna. She was titillated with delighted horror! My dear, you *should* see the Austrian beaches. As my little sister[3] would say, "These women ain't got no shame." This (see sketch) is the maximum clothing ever worn by a Viennese. Anyhow, Maud enjoyed it and chortled with glee, swearing to drag Mrs. Henry Villard[4] thither if it cost her her life. I said it wouldn't because the lady was a non-resistant. I'd heard her say so that afternoon.

Rose, your letters are the chief joys of my life. The clock which faces me announces it's 12 midnight, but I *must* talk to you. . . .

This women's peace conference now going on—oh *Rose*! They

are dreadful, these "peace" women. As Maud said, "I travelled on the boat with 'em and wanted to start a war." They argue like this: "Wars are caused by trade competition. We must institute free trade and abolish competition. Some countries can manufacture dolls, and the United States steel." Happy idea. Smiles all around. Resolution introduced. Passed amid cheers. I have bitten off all my fingernails in a rage at being one of the asinine sex whose praises you and I have mutually sung.

Indeed, I am in a mood to say, "Yes, there *must* be a man—always. And *men*!" Have you ever noticed how hideously depressing large assembled groups of women are? So much of their enthusiasm is "compensatory striving." It seems to me that they release suppressed desires with every resolution. Jane Addams[5] is presiding—all the glamour of her eradicated by the sight of her tired face and edgy, irritated and irritating voice. Emily Balch[6] moves hectically, amid them all, sustained by her unquenchable and quite esoteric idealism. Rosika Schwimmer[7]—odious old fake—harangues the crowd in demagogic banalities in three languages and they applaud vigorously. Mary Winsor[8] waylays you in the hall to tell you, while her gaze wanders palely, of the terrible hours she spent in jail for women's freedom. "Each hour a pearl, each pearl a prayer—" etc. etc. *ad nauseam.* Maud, who has *her* feet solidly in the good brown earth of vulgarity and realism is a huge relief, and I lugged her off for lunch and a talk chiefly regarding her and my superiority to the rest of these females.

I haven't read D. H. Lawrence's *Women in Love* or *The Lost Girl* or anything else—but *a priori,* I am all with you. As for "wild, overweening backbone"—I'd like to hear Katherine Fullerton Gerould on it.[9] I don't *like* eroticism. I don't *like* wallowy, mucky love. I don't *like* to be squashed by my own emotions or anyone else's. I like love on which the comic spirit can look without shooting his oblique light and his volleys of silvery laughter.[10] I like love which is illuminated all through by humor. Perhaps I am the victim of inhibitions—but I do not think so!

Yes, of course there must always be a man. I have been a "wild cat walking by my wild lone self"[11] most of my life since 16—but—

but—. Still, the sensation of falling *out* of love is a wonderful one. I remember once I was very much *in* love—quite overpoweringly so—and there were things—circumstances—which made it hard and me unhappy.[12] We could not be real lovers and I thought I couldn't live without him. And then one day I was with him, calling on a friend, and there was a conversation, peculiarly revealing, and as they sat there talking and I sat listening, suddenly, like a flash, I noticed things about him—absurd things—a certain smugness, and conceit—it doesn't matter what. Only then, just like that, I knew I *could* live without him. Quite well. And when we went out in the street I could have sung for joy and waltzed in the street because I knew I was I and I was free again. Of course there was a relapse—still it was a great moment.

What is vulgar about revulsions of feeling? What is vulgar about anything that is swift and sincere? To be fearful and grasping is vulgar.

Sex *is* life. I suppose—the life of the worm and the fly. I don't suppose of itself it's odious. But in the atmosphere of this day and generation—subjective, over-emphasized, perfumed, refined, saturated—much of it is very odious indeed. "A little breeze—a little air—*please*! And now let us be quiet and walk for a while and forget we are *in* love with each other and remember only that we love each other." . . . which is a quite different thing.

I can't be like Doris Stevens—or Jane Burr[13]—discussing my life's intimacies.

But if you come to Vienna, I hope you will meet Josef[14]—he is not always here. He is a gentle and remote soul, interested in abstract philosophy. He does *not* crush my personality. He approaches with courtly bow and humorous eyes.

Dorothy

Sanders mentions two letters to RWL regarding the "peace Ladies" (*Dorothy Thompson,* p. 382, n. 75). Proper collation of these letters, I believe, reveals that they are together one letter of July 15, 1921.

1. Gauselhaufel is a swimming area on the Danube; the Prater is a large wooded park and pleasure-garden.

2. The conference referred to was the Third Congress of the Women's International League for Peace and Freedom. Twenty-eight nations were represented by members and visitors from affiliated groups, such as Maud Swartz's Women's International Labor Congress. The proceedings of the conference are conve-

niently summarized in Florence Kelley, "The Women's Congress in Vienna," *Survey* 46 (Sept. 1, 1921): 627–29; for a history of the league, see Gertrude Bussey and Margaret Tims, *Women's International League for Peace and Freedom* (London: Allen & Unwin, 1965). Dorothy perhaps knew Maud Swartz from her days in the U.S. as a campaigner for women's suffrage and social reforms (Sanders, *Dorothy Thompson,* I. 4–5).

3. Her younger sister "Peg" (later Margaret Thompson Wilson) was always a close friend.

4. Mrs. Henry Villard (1844–1928), an eminent pacifist, attended the congress as representative of the U.S. Women's Peace Society (Kelley, "The Women's Congress in Vienna," p. 627). Her career is conveniently summarized in *Notable American Women.*

5. Jane Addams (1860–1935) of the famed Hull House in Chicago. See Kelley, "The Women's Congress in Vienna," and the *New York Times,* July 14, 1921, 14:8. She had helped to found the league in 1915 and served as international president until her death in 1935. See her *Peace and Bread in Time of War* (1922; rpt. New York: King's Crown Press, 1945). In 1931 she was awarded the Nobel Peace Prize.

6. Emily Greene Balch (1867–1961), a well-known pacifist and defrocked faculty member of Wellesley College, was secretary of the congress. In 1946 she was awarded the Nobel Peace Prize. See *Notable American Women.*

7. Rosika Schwimmer (1877–1948), a noted pacifist, had been instrumental in persuading Henry Ford to launch his "peace ship" in 1916. The plan for "neutral mediation" that had captured Ford's mind had come from the first congress at the Hague in 1915 and had been largely conceived by Schwimmer. See *Notable American Women.*

8. Mary Winsor (1869?–1956), according to her *New York Times* obituary, was frequently jailed during the women's suffrage movement.

9. D. H. Lawrence's *The Lost Girl* (1920) and *Women in Love* (1921) were fictional treatments of the difficult choices women faced reconciling love, sexuality, freedom, and marriage. In chapter 3 of *The Lost Girl,* the heroine is described in terms of "her isolate self-sufficiency . . . , her wild, overweening backbone," which preserves her integrity in the face of sexual harassment by the men she works with. Katherine Fullerton Gerould (1869–1944) was a well-known American periodical and fiction writer in the 1920s. According to the entry in *American Women Writers,* "her attitudes were influenced by the clerical and academic puritanism of the privileged classes" and were characterized by "too-frequent displays of snobbishness."

10. The reference here is probably to something Rose has said about the self-conscious sexuality of Lawrence's work. Over against it, Dorothy sets an allusion to George Meredith's well-known essay on comedy (1877), which stresses the common sense, civilized basis of the comic spirit. For the significant passage, see "Essay on the Idea of Comedy and the Uses of the Comic Spirit," in *The Works of George Meredith* (29 vols.; New York: Russell and Russell, 1968; rpt. of Memorial Edition, 1909–1912), 23:47.

11. The allusion is to Rudyard Kipling's "The Cat That Walked by Himself," in *Just-So Stories* (1902), frequently reprinted.

12. The reference is probably to the unconsummated passion that developed between the young Dorothy and her middle-aged and married employer, Wilbur Phillips. See Sanders, *Dorothy Thompson,* I. 6.

13. Doris Stevens (1893?–1963) was a mutual friend, well known for her militancy in the women's suffrage movement. See her *Jailed for Freedom* (New York, 1920). Jane Burr (pseudonym of Rosalind Mae Guggenheim) was also a mutual friend, well known in New York literary circles in the years just before and after the war. A minor writer, she also kept an inn in the literary colony of Croton-on-Hudson, N.Y. Rose Wilder Lane lived for a time in this village in 1919 and again in 1925.

14. Josef Bard was a young Hungarian Jew displaced by the war. Trained as a lawyer, he aspired vaguely to writing a treatise on the political state of Europe; in reality, he was an occasional journalist and sometime assistant to Marcel Fodor, through whom he met Dorothy. He would become her first lover and first husband; later his novel *Shipwreck in Europe* (New York, 1928) would present stinging portraits of both Dorothy and Rose.

Letter 2

Rechte Wienzeile 31
Wien IV
August 13, 1921

My Rose:-

The steady flow of our communication has been broken. I have been completely demoralized; here today and gone tomorrow. I went to Budapest in search of news, and found none, but the weather was too hot to be combatted. I sank down at the Ritz and didn't move for a week. Then I came home for a few days, but *mon ami*[1] lured me off to the Platensee, a lake in Hungary, promising me cool baths, long loafs on the shore, and sails on a windy water. I went, and found the hottest place this side of hell. A perfectly flat lake, lying in a treeless country, the sun on its agate colored water so strong that it seared your eyes to look. We went on a Robinson Crusoe adventure the first day and spent the rest of the time lying on our stomachs and gasping with heat and pain—from sunburn. By way of a change we went on a visit to the nearest village on market day, and a Hungarian village in summer is a thing to be visited once and avoided ever after. Not a tree. Not a scrap of shade. Just yellow and white adobe houses, with stark walls and gleaming windows, standing in dust. When I got back to my "hot" Vienna flat, with its drawn green blinds, and Frau Freudenberger, standing in the offing with cold beer and a patient smile, I gave one gasp of joy.

Be still my heart and take thy rest,
Home staying hearts are happiest . . .

It's Longfellow,[2] darling—shades of me childhood! I remember Lucy Price, the prize anti-suffrage speaker rolling it like a sweet morsel off her tongue.

(It's a complete diversion, but I find myself getting conservative. Lucy, as I remember her speeches—I had a debate with her once on the good old days—ten thousand farmers in Chautauqua county with the audience "packed" with suffragists in the fashion which we "pure" women, who were going to reform politics always used so blithely—Lucy, to resume, said many things, which in my maturer days I can applaud. One being that politics was not only no sphere for women but no sphere for anybody. And therefore why the fuss.[3] Here in Central Europe, for instance, one has a chance to observe daily the complete failure of the political remedy. I should say more accurately the failure of politics as a remedy. These countries are going to rack and ruin. The Entente, which is in measure responsible, does absolutely nothing, because it can't agree on a policy. On a political policy. England wants a Danube Federation, Italy a South Slav federation to guard her from Russia, France a Habsburg, pro-Catholic restoration to guard her from Germany. Meanwhile Central Europe wants Herbert Hoover, someone who sees realities and doesn't care a damn whether Karl is on the throne or Hungary is a Republic.[4] Here is where Germany comes in. Having her political hands completely tied by the Entente works to her advantage. In came her financiers. Reconstruct. Tighten economic lines. She'll have the whole bunch of Balkanized states in her pocket one of these days, mark my word.)

Now how did we get there—oh yes, speaking of Lucy Price . . . and the heat. And staying at home. Which is to say that at this moment I am waiting for a taxi to come and bear me off to the Westbahnhof[5] and thence to Lindau. Lindau, my dear, is on the Bodensee on the exact border between Germany and Switzerland, with Austria on the other hand. I'm off to meet Beatrice Sorchan,[6] beautiful, rich and young, from New York, an exotic orchid in the garden of my hardier friends. Beatrice, whom I chiefly love because she is so heart-warmingly good to look at.

Thou art so very sweet and fair
With such a heaven in thine eyes,
It almost seems an overcare
To ask thee to be good or wise. . . .[7]

Beatrice demands that I come to Paris to meet her. I say Vienna. We compromise. So I am off. She is batting around Europe for a few months—a yachting trip along the French coast, a walking tour through England. Damn her—I am sitting up all night tonight, riding second class, in my desire to see her. Why couldn't she come to Vienna *wagon lit*![8]

I have a new flame in Vienna, Col. Causey, the Technical Adviser to the Austrian government, age seventy or thereabouts. He's been in Vienna for two years and with the curiosity characteristic of Americans doesn't speak a word of German. The other night he took me to dinner at the Huburtushof, a fashionable open air restaurant near Schönbrunn, where they have excellent food and a sort of cabaret. He is well known here, and always gets many kiss die handes,[9] because he flings kronen around so liberally. Seeing us together, the male chorus who were performing in the cabaret came *en masse* to our table and in the presence of all guests carolled a charming little ditty called "Ich kenne auf der Wieden ein kleines Hotel". Literally translated, the chorus of this risky little song is as follows:

I know in Wieden (a section of Vienna) a little hotel
In one of the lonely side streets,
The night is so short, and the day breaks so soon,
Come with me to that little retreat.
Don't care what the morrow will probably bring
The world is but music and sun, dear.
And once you have kissed the whole night through
Thereafter you keep on forever.

And the verses—oh, the verses. All the assembled guests grinned appreciatively, and the Colonel leered with joy and pleasure not understanding a word. Oh, my dear, it was *funny*.

And now it is time to take my train, and I haven't thanked you for sending me the letter from "Austin"[10]—I'll send it back after I have passed it around to a few people—nor begun to talk about all the things on my heart. When I'm back from this mad trip to

Lindau we will talk together again. Meanwhile write . . . your letters

> . . . are all that to me love,
> For which my soul doth pine,
> A green isle in the sea, love . . . [11]
>
> Au 'voir..

Dorothy

---

1. Josef Bard.

2. Henry Wadsworth Longfellow, "Song: Stay, Stay at Home." Dorothy misquotes the opening lines slightly.

3. Following her graduation from Syracuse in 1914, Dorothy had worked for three years in the suffrage movement in and around Buffalo, N.Y. (Sanders, *Dorothy Thompson,* pp. 20–25). For a representative description of the circumstances, see the *New York Times,* Oct. 31, 1915, 2:6. The account mentions Lucy Price and her style of debate.

4. In the background here are the problems posed by the breakup of the Austro-Hungarian Empire after World War I, as the Allied Powers (the Entente) were meeting in Paris in an attempt to adjust national boundaries to complex political realities. Typically, Dorothy is impatient of ideology and international interests as she surveys immediate human problems that need pragmatic solutions. Herbert Hoover, already renowned as a businessman, had gained additional fame as head of the Commission for Relief in Belgium, which addressed the problems of Belgium and northern France. Karl (Charles) was the last monarch of the Austro-Hungarian Empire; in the spring of 1921 he had returned to Budapest to attempt to resume his throne.

5. Main railroad station to western Europe.

6. Beatrice Sorchan had been Dorothy's assistant during her days of work with a private social-service foundation. Dorothy is about to join her for a walking trip in the Bavarian Alps. See Sanders, *Dorothy Thompson,* pp. 32, 76.

7. I have been unable to identify these lines.

8. *Wagonlit:* sleeping car.

9. The Huburtushof no longer exists; the Schönbrunn Palace with its grounds is one of the landmarks of Vienna; "many kiss die handes" is garbled German and English, and any correction would make Dorothy's spontaneous German better than it was.

10. Rose's journal identifies a past lover only as "Austin." It might have been Austin Lewis, British socialist, labor lawyer, and friend of Jack London: Rose had moved in those circles in San Francisco in 1915–1918, and from such sources had composed a magazine-biography of London just after his death (*Sunset,* Oct. 1917–May 1918). Her correspondence with Lewis continued at least until 1934. See her journal for Oct. 17, 1927, and April 24, 1934.

11. She misquotes slightly the opening lines of Edgar Allan Poe's "To One in Paradise."

Letter 3

Rechte Wienzeile 31
WIEN IV
September 3 [1921]

My dear Rose:-

I am in a mood of singular depression. Whether it is the heat, which returned today with a vengeance and gave me a dull headache, or whether it is my conscience, which reminds me that I have spent the better part of the day reading Joseph Conrad's *Romance,* or whether it is missing Josef, who has been in Vienna for the past week, or whether it's just my age and state of mind, I don't know. Anyhow, I'm in no mood to write. Yet I am lonely, and need someone to talk to, and you are the only person within anything like talking distance who will perhaps be sympathetic.

By this time, no doubt, you will have seen Josef because I gave him a letter to you and very particular instructions to call. I hope you like him.[1] I suppose it's almost too much to hope for, not because he isn't the most likable person on earth but because one's friends never do like the men one loves. Such at least have been my very few experiences. He's shy, also, and not greatly at ease with strangers, unless he takes to 'em immediately, which he seldom does, but he's a thoroughly sweet and good soul, and I love him.

I didn't tell you before about my contemplated marriage . . . shall I confess why? Because it still seems to me, although we go ahead making plans galore, utterly and completely unreal. It is an "impossible" marriage, of course, from every point of view. Economically. Here we are, both poor as Job's turkey. Josef, who is a clever boy, is educated to be a lawyer. He won't practice law in Hungary, where he already has an excellent and enviable reputation because of his published works, because he hates the damned country and wants to get out of it, and a law practice would tie him there for good. On the other hand, law is the *hardest* profession to take to another country—to England or America. He's the correspondent now of the A.P. in Hungary, and perhaps eventually journalism will let him out,[2] but his citizenship is against him when it comes to getting ahead into anything real. And here's the damned law which says that when I marry a Hungarian I become a Hungarian, passport revoked and everything. In our present financial state I shall have to grind ahead at journalism, which is my only assurance of a living, and in that profession the loss of my citizenship may prove to be a really *serious* handicap. My paper can't send me anywhere, because my government won't protect me—I mean anywhere where there's the slightest element of doubt. So I go thinking around in a circle . . . getting nowhere . . . except when he's here, and then it all seems much simpler. I wonder why.

Rose, I wish you'd sit down and give me some honest-to-God advice.[3] I won't promise to take it, so you can afford to give it. But Rose, dear, I *do* need it. I never felt so strangely alone . . .

If I ask you for advice, I suppose I ought to tell you that I've tried the other way . . . but it satisfies nothing in my heart. If I were more courageous I suppose I would just live with Josef openly, but I'm frankly *not* courageous enough.

Vienna isn't big. All the American colony would know, because, with my unfortunate talent for making friends, I know most of them. And Vienna is bored . . . English speaking Vienna is, I mean. And when those dreadful peace women were here I got a little dose of what their everlasting tongues can do. Then, of course, they gossiped chiefly about me and Fodor.[4] Dirt dogs! They simply won't believe that a man and woman can be intimate friends, can collaborate together on work, can be seen rather often in one another's company, and not be lovers. And Fodor and I might be priest and nun as far as the utter sexlessness of our relation is concerned (although I am not sure the illustration is apt). To go to Budapest would be even worse, for Budapest is only a village, really. So it's either a clandestine and intermittent relationship or it's marriage, or it's—the end. And the first won't do . . . it isn't what I want or what he wants. Please help me Rose. Talk to me. I need you.

You see I believe in you, in the rightness of your instincts, and in the warmness of your heart, and, somehow, in the genuineness of your affection for me . . . because I know how genuine is mine for you. Help me to distinguish what are realities in our situation and what are just cobwebs.

I won't be disloyal to Josef, will I, in saying that I have all sorts of conflicts in my heart. I am so scared of marriage. Sometimes I want love, and protection—yes, *protection,* not of the practical kind, but the protection of love itself . . . the surrounding kindliness and sympathy of someone who loves you more than he loves anything or anybody in the world. And I desperately need to love someone who needs me. I feel this in my heart . . . I am getting to be a selfish pig, and I don't want to be. Too, I want a home . . . some course to my life . . . some stability in the compass. But then, at other times, my heart sits in me and bleeds like a thing in chains. I am half-inclined to throw my things into a suitcase, lock the door of my flat, take the only one hundred dollars I have in the world, and start away for another city, and a new environment . . . I want so to be free. I know if I marry I'll never take risks again in the same way. I'll never start off across the world with nothing in my pocket and be able to say, "Well, it's my *own* life, isn't it? And if I *do* starve??" And you say I am "swift and sure"—oh, *Rose*! See thou how murky-spirited I have become.

Josef, you see, wouldn't like to go off to China with a few dollars in his pocket. He looks in upon life, finding it in his own self and soul. Going off to China both appalls and bores him. And I, finding so little in my soul, go eagerly snatching at new experiences, new sights . . .

Enough of this . . . talk to me, Rose, do . . . I need you.

What are you writing? You said in one letter, "Enclosed is a short story . . ." and it wasn't enclosed! *Why* are you going to England? Was it a bait thrown out to draw this confession? But, no, you never draw confessions. That is why I trust you with this one. But tell me, tell me, about the venture you fear will be your third tragedy.[5] (There's a humorous acceptance of fate in your attitude, which must have its advantages! I am *not* prepared to accept even a first tragedy. I want to be happy. I want Josef to be happy. I WILL be happy.)

. . . But there's a little overstraining at that WILL. A freudian would arch a knowing eyebrow, and whisper "the compensatory striving . . ."

I wish like the devil you would come and see me.

Dorothy

---

1. Rose did not meet him at this time; but when she did she did not like him: see Letter 18.

2. Journalism would not be his escape; he had neither the talent nor the interest. See Sanders, *Dorothy Thompson,* p. 76.

3. Rose's diary for September 10, 1921, records a "letter from Dorothy asking advice. Wrote her eight pages of it!" Unfortunately, this letter has been lost.

4. Marcel Fodor, Dorothy's European mentor, friend, and partner in many of her enterprises. See Sanders, *Dorothy Thompson,* pp. 67–70, 79–80.

5. Rose was about to begin a romance with Guy Moyston, AP reporter and a friend from her San Francisco days. Her diary records a two-week visit to London with him, September 3–17, 1921. She and Moyston, incidentally, both appear as characters in book 4 of Sherwood Anderson's *Dark Laughter* (1925), as a result of their meeting him at a party in Paris in 1921. See Holtz, "Sherwood Anderson and Rose Wilder Lane."

Letter 4

[September 14, 1921]

Rose:-

I wonder whether Josef caught you in London or in Paris or whether you missed each other altogether.[1] I hope not. But I am glad that you wrote to me before you saw him, and grateful, very grateful, for the letter. Rose, you are a dear. For the interest and affection of that letter I shall be eternally and humbly indebted, as well as for a good deal of clear-thinking.

Wrestling with my soul during these last days I have come to a conclusion. I'm not very proud of it and it's not very characteristic, but it's the best I can do. It's just—to wait. Not to wait for love; I see no necessity for that, and have seen none. But to leave this marriage question on the knees of the gods. After all, they have been, for the most part, kind great gods to me, and I don't think they would wilfully hurt me. I rather trust 'em, and I don't at all trust myself just now. I'm going to drift a bit and let "the inexorable course of events" point my way out. As I say, I am ashamed of this attitude, but my mind runs around in a circle like a squirrel in a cage.

One thing I'm certain of—that is that it is a mistake not to heed the "nagging voice." The voice that is the essential "you," crying in the wilderness. I remember when I wanted to come abroad, and leave a good job, and a safe harbor, in a country full of friends, to come to a land where I had no friends and no connections and to embark without money upon a profession for which I was quite untrained, all my friends thought me mad, but the "inner voice" told me this was the thing to do, and I must do it, and always I was lighthearted and happy. When I was in London a year ago last summer, and for two months hardly knew where my next meal was coming from, and lived together with Varya[2] in a little furnished room in Brunswick square, I was happy and lighthearted, and never, for an instant, sorry. That was because I was doing what I did with my whole heart. Oh, this horror of being torn!

Why is it that we fight self-destruction, if by fighting it we can give life? I suppose it is something you can't generalize about. The old evangelical enthusiasts had it about right. You must follow your "call." Some people have a "call" to self-destruction. Something in them tells them they must have children, for instance. But nothing in me tells me I should have children. Indeed, I believe that if I had 'em they wouldn't be very nice. I have only one loud and neverceasing call, and that is to preserve the integrity of my own self. Why? What is there to preserve? Artists and poets and all the great have that. Remember Jean Christophe.[3] But I am not an artist, or a poet, or of the great. Why do I fight for this third-rate life of mine, as though it were of consequence? I feel it of consequence, and do nothing with it and it breaks my heart. (All this is very incoherent and senseless. I leave it hoping that it will say what I feel, because you are a clever person.)

No, I am sure marriage has nothing to do with happiness. But neither has love—not sexual love, to call a spade a spade. It's something you need, and long for, and it satisfies an essential you, but it doesn't bring you happiness. Beauty brings you happiness. Impersonal beauty, cool beauty. Your Albanian was right. Look back over the "illumined moments" in your own life and see which are associated with "love." That walk last January—do you remember, along the Loire[4]—that was an illumined moment, which I shall remember and be grateful for, forever. How cool it was, how spontaneous, and how, in its every essence, transitory, but caught at the moment, and therefore eternal.

Then there was this last trip to Landau. The first night, before I knew whether my friends were coming or not, and whether, therefore, I had any purpose in being there on the Lake of Constance; feeling at first a little lonesome and lost . . . and then, poking about through the queer sweet little streets suddenly having that exaltation of spirit, that present conviction of the beauty of the world, and how full of romance it is for those who have eyes and ears and sensibilities, and how glorious to be free to see and feel and go.

But what conflicts. Josef wants to marry me because he loves me. There was a time when he didn't want to marry me, and then I wanted him to!! Because I knew that if he really loved me he *would* want to. Contrariwise the more I love him the less I want to marry him . . . because I am so afraid our marriage won't be successful . . . But the social pressure. What damnable social pressure, applied in a moment when my powers were weak and my mind murky put me in this position of being, so to speak, "betrothed." Of all positions most absurd! You're right about social pressure being even worse when you're married. I am feeling it already. Josef, in his sweet naiveté, told a few people that he intended to marry me. Quickly I see a change in their attitude. Hitherto no one has thought much at seeing Fodor and me constantly together. Now they lift an eyebrow. Josef is annoyed. He is generous. He says he doesn't mind. But he does mind, and I know it, and I am so irritable with poor Fodor, and our relationship which was as sexless as that between two sixty-year old cronies, is suddenly darkened and made horrid. Attar[5] meets Josef and says, "I see Miss Thompson every day on the Karnterstrasse with Fodor." Josef is peeved. Doesn't mean to be but is. No good to say, "But I am lonely in Vienna, and Fodor is a good friend, and we are invaluable to each other in work; he as a news-collector, and I as a news-analyzer and presenter." There is no explanation which will mitigate in the mind of Josef's friends my impossible conduct with Fodor. Only Fodor, who *wanted* to marry me but got over it wonderfully, and relaxed into the friendliest and most humorous acceptance of his lot, understands perfectly how much I love Josef—though he's never been told. Only *he* understands how perfect is my fidelity. Isn't it funny?

But how I analyze myself. After all, my conflict is the universal one with anyone who has any brains—awful sentence—and I ought to be able to work out my problem on broad lines without picking out every detail in my psychology. I hate people who go probing around in their own minds, bringing the results of their excavations to be examined by their bored friends. Don't bother about me, Rose. I'll get through some way. Probably by letting the gods do it for me. Anyhow, I love Josef, and I am almost happy, particularly when he's 'round.

Did you see Varya? Did you see the baby? I had a letter from her—such a pitiful, sweet little letter, scared stiff, that came the very day that Mark's telegram announced that the child had arrived safely and that Varya was well. She will be glad that it's a girl; poor darling, she was sure that both she and the babe would die! I long to see it. Varya and I led a communal existence for so long, that once she remarked to me, "We have a headache this morning." Hence I feel a strange tie with all her life. She's a dear, headed by temperament toward self-annihilation from the very first. I only hope her baby is healthy, good-looking, and not too clever.

And you, my dear Rose, what do you do? I hope Bigelow[6] came bearing rosy prospects in train. Why doesn't he give you an editorship in London, a nice, secure, more or less interesting job with enough money attached to give you what you must have and enough leisure to permit you to turn out one novel a year. Of course you ought to be writing novels. You have the novelist's brain. Analytical, a little cynical, rather subjective. You are interested in realities—in deep-lying purposes, and motives, and emotions. Your people need space to move in. The short-story writer is a sublimated journalist. He must be interested primarily *not* in the afore-mentioned things, but in situations. It's better if he has fixed ideas, for then his doubts won't get in the way of speedy and conclusive action. I think *Diverging Roads*[7] is tremendously hopeful, and I am very anxious to see you do another novel. I find that I remember it very vividly . . . the opening chapter—a wonderful description of village atmosphere—like a lazy person who lies abed when he knows he should be up—inaction without ease, I think you said. No, it was better, but that was the idea. I see Helen—sea-gray eyes—I wish you had given us a few more sentences like that one to fix her in the vision completely. Do you remember the description of Linda in *Linda Condon*?[8] Just a few strokes, but she's there and lives forever. (Linda, Goddess of Beauty, in the Greek sense, before Titian created his sensuous temptresses. Linda, to whom Poe might have written "To Helen," whose only excuse for existence was her beauty, but who knew enough to shield it from all contamination as it were a sacred gift. Do you remember the final picture, "a slender, faded woman, in immaculate gloves and a perfect hat"?) Paul, too, was very real. But you knew Bert too well. Your own feelings about him got in the way. Subconsciously, you were pitiful and tried to spare him, and so spoiled for us the luxury of a really passionate indignation. We all wanted to hate him and couldn't quite. But, Rose, you can *write.* When I think of you piddling around on Red Cross newsletters and articles and short stories and translations, I should like to shake you. I have been reading Phyllis Bottome[9] lately. She can write too, but her gifts are hidden in a vapor of mawkishness. She doesn't know life, which you do, and her people don't live. She catches you with a few charming sentences, but she leaves you cold and unconvinced. Whereas you are consistent and convincing. But she's successful—heavens yes.

By the way, I have just finished reading Conrad's old novel, *Romance.* Marvelous thing, to me. I read it breathless and laid it down with cold hands and a fluttering heart. If I could write, that's what I'd try to write about. Youth. The time of life that fears nothing, believes everything, suffers everything, bears everything, is happy in everything, is ignorant of everything. Do you remember that marvelous court scene? How the boy fights for his life, telling his story, not with pathos but with hopeless rage . . . driving his hand down upon the spiked rail which surrounds the dock and impaling it—without noticing it . . . and yet all the time feeling in himself an exaltation. . . . "I had made them *see* things."[10]

It takes robustness to write a novel like that. Conrad must write at a pitch of feeling that would exhaust an ordinary person completely. And certainly you aren't going to do the work you should if (1) you are overrun with kindly friends; damn your hospitality—do they think you a college fraternity house having a perpetual "warming"? (2) you fritter your energy on senseless stuff (I speak far more harshly than I think, of course, it isn't senseless. It's damn good—but *relatively* senseless). I was going to list a third, but that's enough.

I wish you were here (Oh yes, I am another of the clinging friends, but I can afford to indulge myself. I'm *not* there). But I want to talk to you about books and marriage, and art, and what not.

I'm sorry about Riga.[11] Still, one can travel and ruminate. Don't think about the Russians while you're there. Think about your new novel.

This is a dreadful letter. My eagerness to talk with you runs away with my typewriter. Forgive me.

I send much love and appreciation,
Dorothy

---

1. Rose and Josef Bard probably did not meet until later in Berlin. Much of this letter seems to be a comment on Rose's advice.

2. Varya was Barbara Deporte, a young woman who had been Dorothy's companion on the trip to Europe and her partner during their first months abroad. She had married in late 1920 and had settled in England. See Sanders, *Dorothy Thompson,* pp. 24–25, 56–57.

3. The allusion is obscure, perhaps to the French general of that name who rejoined Napoleon during the Hundred Days.

4. The walking trip along the Loire (Dorothy, Rose, and another writer named Kate Horton) is recorded in Rose's diary for Jan. 1–3, 1921.

5. I have not been able to identify this person.

6. W. F. Bigelow, the editor of *Good Housekeeping,* was apparently in Paris scouting for manuscripts.

7. *Diverging Roads* (1919) was Rose's first novel, a version of the breakup of her marriage and her emerging independence.

8. *Linda Condon* (1919) by Joseph Hergesheimer examines the relationships of beauty, love, marriage, and money. Dorothy perhaps reflects on this book in paragraph five of this letter. The quotation is approximate but inaccurate.

9. Phyllis Bottome (1884–1963) was a prolific novelist and poet and a prominent member of the Anglo-American society in Vienna. She and Dorothy would publish a joint effort, *The Depths of Prosperity* (London, 1924), a melodramatic novel to which Dorothy perhaps contributed the American background.

10. Joseph Conrad's *Romance* (1903) is an extravagantly adventurous tale. Dorothy quotes from the climactic scene of part 5, chap. 4.

11. Rose was perhaps planning a trip to Riga, a major entry to Russia from the west at this time, but she did not go.

Letter 5

Sunday
September 24 [1921]

Dear Rose:

Your stories came this morning, with breakfast and Fodor. I opened the envelope, and waved Fodor firmly away, though he was anxious to discuss a pending political catastrophe. I've read both "Innocence" and "Desert Sands"[1] two or three times, and I want to tell you right away how I feel about them.

I found "Desert Sands" immensely interesting. I have some criticisms, which you can take for what they are worth. I'm not a critic or a writer, and when I tried to formulate my feeling about it into "constructive criticism," I found myself either vague or presumptuous. However, I will do my best.

It seems to me—to paraphrase a criticism which Wells made of Woodrow Wilson—that the form isn't equal to the texture.[2] The material is all wool and a yard wide. Absolutely genuine, all the way through; the persons; the situations; the milieu. There isn't a false note. If you are in Albania, one *feels* that you know Albania, and the same of Paris. You know your people through and through. The descriptive bits are quite right and perfect as your description always is. But your first picture of Blythe—a cameo white on black—isn't sustained throughout. That's what your story ought to be, a cameo. A whole novel, a portrait, a complete thing, in miniature. You have material here, of course, for a novel in two volumes. And to reduce it is a tremendously difficult and delicate thing. That's why I wonder why you make it hard for yourself by using the most difficult possible method.

Because the oblique method is *always* hard, and here you not only use it, but you complicate it by having half a dozen people tell the tale. And it seems to me that your material is too precious to be having so many people take a swipe at it. It must be put both delicately and austerely. You have got to make Blythe Williams stand out in perfectly sure outlines, all the more because she stands for an idea, rather than a personality in herself . . . because you are not so much interested in the particular *emotions* of Blythe as you are in the *significance* of Blythe. This makes it all the more necessary, it seems to me, for you to center your story very accurately. But as a matter of fact, after the first five pages, your story ceases to be focussed consistently and continuously. Leslie comes in, and she, like Blythe, is beauty run in desert sands. Why is Leslie, "the most brilliant Almost"? Blythe is that also. Blythe is the tragedy of eagerness, questfulness and gallantry wrecked on a careless, or cynical, world; the Sir Galahad setting out without his sword—because there are no longer swords for Galahad. That, I take it, is your theme, and it's a tremendously difficult one, and to illustrate it you need a picture in which every unnecessary detail has been eliminated. I don't understand at all why you introduce Leslie. She is *so* well done, and for that reason irritates me all the more, because she shifts the center of attention. As far as the action is concerned, you don't need her at all. You, as the story-teller, could just as well get the letter. I understand Kit and Harriet, but why have two of them, except as an indulgence of your delight in doing quick, illuminated sketches of people. But after all, this isn't the *Canterbury Tales*! I'd eliminate both—even Kit. I know you want her as the contrast, the "voice like a green thing trying to live in aridity" (hold on to that phrase whatever you do with Kit), but why can't you, the story-teller, supply the pitifulness, the unrelinquished hope, which you extort from Kit. It seems to me if you would clear the stage of these three delightful or interesting, but to me, unnecessary people, and make your scene with yourself (the story-teller), Blythe, and Arnold, your whole picture would come out in clearer outlines. I can say this all much more briefly. The richer your material, the simpler your dress.

As for "Innocence"—I found it an unalloyed delight. I think it's a perfect little gem. I don't know where in the world you will sell it, but I wouldn't change any of it, for anything. Have you tried it on the *Atlantic,* or on the *English Review*? I can't think of a possible other market.

Of course, neither story is any good as a pot-boiler, and when you talk of going back and writing American fiction (after the fashion of Gene Stratton Porter)[3] I grin like the masque on a theater program. Because you can't, Rose. You might as well face realities. You can no more write like Gene and her crowd than you can love like them, or feel like them. What makes 'em go, bless you, all of 'em from Gene to Harold Bell Wright,[4] is because they are so died-in-the-wool sincere. They believe what they write. Put their whole hearts into the mush and nonsense, and so are convincing. You could be ever so clever an imitator, but the simplest reader would glimpse the leer in the background.

I guess that the trouble with American fiction is that it's getting too good for American editors, so they have to turn to the followers of H. G. Wells and Mr. Galsworthy. I haven't read much American fiction, or much of anything lately, but what I have read seems to me head and shoulders above the contemporary English stuff. Our Americans really seem to be trying to do something new, and there are some remarkably clear voices. Willa Cather, Joseph Hergesheimer, James Branch Cabell, whoever wrote *Invincible Minnie,*[5] haven't, to my mind, any equals among the contemporary English, except Conrad, and he surely belongs more to the States than to England. Wells and Galsworthy drivel sentimentality; *profound* sentimentality. Not the home-and-mother-kiss-and-marry-nature's-wonders of Gene Stratton Porter, but the "splendid Destiny of Mankind" sentimentality of Mr. Wells' *Outline of History.*[6] It's all the same thing, really, underneath. For me, I adore old Professor Marcàly's remarks about the evolution of mankind. Prof. Marcàly—dare I explain—is Hungary's most distinguished historian; at present barred from the University of Budapest because he is a Jew and kept his chair during the Bolshevik regime, instead of resigning in indignation as the present powers think he should have done. Prof. Marcàly remarked to Josef the other day: "I have been reading Mr. Wells' history, and I see that he believes in evolution. But the first picture in his history is of our prehistoric ancestors, those of the tooth and claw, and the last is of Clemenceau, Lloyd George and Wilson at the Peace Conference, and I don't see how the first and the last pictures prove his thesis."[7]

That's a long digression from my point, which is that England seems to be offering nothing just now except the rather cheap cynicism of Rose MacCaulay—I read *Dangerous Ages*[8] and think it's clever but—, the sex-wallowings of Lawrence, and the school of Wells and Phyllis Bottome.

My dear, my dear, I am sorry that you are beaten and sore, and I wish I were there to let you indulge in an orgy of self-pity, which wouldn't do you a bit of harm. But I won't give you up so easily. I can't sit by and refuse to protest against your being consumed alive by the desire for the impossible lover. Fight, my dear, fight! Not because it is right to do so, but because it is essentially right for *you* to do so. I'd say something different if you were a real hedonist, but you are anything but. You will either have to fight and transmute your desires into art, or you will die. "Why *not* die?" you ask. And I haven't any clever intellectual answer—not even the obverse "why . . . ?" I, too, I suppose, am a sentimentalist. I'm not a bit sure of any splendid destiny for mankind. I'm not sure that we aren't all puppets for gods who shake the heavens with ironic laughter. But I do know that we are all in the same boat together, headed for an unknown destination, and that we aren't even able to sink the boat. Most of us have got to stick on board. And when one jumps overboard, it doesn't encourage any others to jump too, or it doesn't upset the boat entirely and so end the terrible journey, it just makes all the rest feel a little more unhappy and discouraged. Whereas gallantry, and courage, and humor, and the production of beauty, however transitory and even illusory that beauty may be, ease the way a bit for everyone. You have a very great gift for friendship. There may be some providence that keeps you from being immersed in a great and wholly successful love—which would almost certainly shut all the rest of us out of your heart.

You have also great resources for enjoyment closed to less sensitive or discriminating minds. You enjoyed, for example, your cockney attendant and his Hitalian primitives . . . a lovely tale, that. Your cockney had really found a solution, too, after all, wistful as he may have been for the blue skies of Italy and pictures where the painter put them himself. Hitalian primitives never let you down, do they?[9]

As for me, I am at this moment very happy. I am not quite sure why. I am in love, and I am loved . . . what shoals ahead I dimly guess, but "*Vivimus, vivamus*" was my class motto at prep school—let us live while we live. I still feel in my heart the inexhaustible, fascinating romance of life. I look ahead with interest at my own life, most of the time, feeling something of that detached yet engrossed interest which one feels at reading an exciting novel and anticipating the end. Already I half-guess the end, as one foresees the outcome of any story, a third way through. But, it may be an O. Henry tale, after all, with a funny quirk at the end. I always get a certain objective interest, almost enjoyment, out of all things that happen to me, good or bad. Something in me remains untouched, quite aloof, and critical, able even to derive a certain enjoyment out of my own tragedies, if they are well done. The only times when this sense forsakes me is when I do something I am really deeply ashamed of, and since I am a hardened sinner in most particulars, I seldom *am* deeply ashamed. I can lose my virginity outside of marriage with equanimity; I can lie roundly for the sake of effect[10] or because it is more convenient; I can shirk my job, cheat all corporations and bureaucracies, detest my relatives, neglect my acquaintances, drink, smoke, swear, and neglect my health; jibe unkindly at the respectable; be extravagant—positively, Rose, when I think of the major and minor sins which I can commit without a qualm—without ever bringing a wrinkle to the brow of this impersonal self who watches over my actions with detached interest—I am deeply gratified. I have a few weaknesses which I must guard against if I want to keep this self-possession, if you can call it that. I have a low love of admiration and a tendency to snobbery growing out of it . . . but why rehearse the things one *is* ashamed of!

And I love beauty, all kinds of beauty, and am renewed by it constantly. Woods, and walks, and rivers, and lakes, and hills; pictures, and cathedrals, and old villages, falling into ruin gracefully and sweetly; music; children; old who no longer struggle; all healthy creatures at work; beautiful characters; the gallant, the courageous, the unselfish. All these things bring me delight, very real, very vivid. And of these manifold forms of beauty I find much in this world. I don't suffer perhaps so much, from thinking about the industrial age, and the glory and loveliness that might be, because I feel tremendously, and in spite of everything, the glory and loveliness that are. This is something that isn't arguable, and perhaps is all illusory and will vanish ultimately. But I don't think so. Because will even the memory of feeling this way vanish?

I think it is hard, if you are unsentimental and honest, to find a *raison d'etre* for life. But my attitude toward it is like B.L.T.'s toward tobacco.

> "Tobacco is a filthy weed—
> I like it!
> It satisfies no earthly need—
> I like it!"[11]

I still am under the spell of the *intrinsic* value of life. I *like* it.

And so, my dear, do you. With some of us this which I have described is a more sustained feeling than with others. But we all like it. There may be chapters in the book that are boring, and we might like to skip them; or we might be irritated by the style, or puzzled by the plot, but every one of us hangs on in the hope of a satisfying quirk in the end. So there you are.

Just at present I am in the state of Blythe in Rome. I haven't gotten a permanent wave because I was terrified out of it by the description in *Linda Condon.*[12] But I go twice a week to the coiffeur, and am massaged, and vibrated, and curled. And I am letting myself go on some new clothes, which, unless the shears slip at the last moment, will be highly successful. I have a new fur coat, not at all elegant, but smart; of wild-cat; soft, yellowy-gray, with stripes in it; short and loose with a voluminous chinny collar, and an impertinent little turban with a green feather. Then I have a suit; olive green with a lovely silvery haze in it—duvetine. There's a frock, first, cut Russian style, with a high collar and a side fastening, its only trimming a narrow band of beaver down the side. It has a knee-length coat, straight-cut, with a loose back, and a high, rolling collar of beaver, and therewith a tiny, tight little muff. And the suit has also its own hat, likewise of the green-gray duvetine, with a tiny rim of beaver. It's all to be finished Wednesday, and then I think Josef and I are running away to the Semmering.[13] The summer population has quite deserted it, and there are tennis, and walks, and wonderful views, and . . .

I am enclosing a copy of a letter from Varya—there's a sweet person! Might try having a baby, Rose—it seemed to work with Varya![14] Or is she like the shop-girl in the theater? "Did you like the play?" Ans: "Gawd, I had to like it! Didn't I pay fifty cents!"

Much love,
Dorothy

---

1. "Innocence" was published in *Harpers* (April 1922), pp. 577–84, and as second-prize winner in the *O. Henry Memorial Award Prize Stories of 1922* (New York: Doubleday, 1923), pp. 23–35. "Desert Sands" was never published; a partial copy is in Dorothy Thompson's papers; a complete manuscript is in the Hoover Presidential Library.

2. The allusion to the remark by H. G. Wells is obscure, but its import probably has to do with Wells's perception of Wilson's incompetence at the Paris Peace Conference; see note 7.

3. Gene Stratton Porter (1868–1924) was an immensely popular writer of romantic fiction and nature lore. In 1921, the editor of *Good Housekeeping* reported to Rose that Porter had turned down his offer of $45,000 for her next serial sight unseen (Diary, Sept. 16, 1921).

4. Harold Bell Wright (1872–1944) wrote *The Shepherd of the Hills* (1907), a popular moralizing novel, and many others of the kind.

5. With these major writers of the 1920s, Dorothy includes the now-forgotten Elisabeth Saxnay Holding (1889–1955), who published *Invincible Minnie* in 1920. It is a study of the blighting effects of a woman's dogged determination to marry.

6. H. G. Wells had published his *Outline of History* in 1920; it offers an optimistic evolutionary theory of history. By this time, John Galsworthy had published the early volumes of *The Forsyte Saga,* the great study of the English propertied class.

7. I have not been able to identify Professor Marcàly; but his remark refers to the failure of Wilson's idealism in the face of the harsh demands of Clemenceau and Lloyd George at the Paris Peace Conference. In 1919 there had been a brief Communist government in Hungary.

8. Rose Macaulay (1881–1958) was an English novelist better appreciated for her deft style and wit than for her serious import. *Dangerous Ages* (1921) deals with the crisis points in women's lives through four generations of a family.

9. The anecdote has been lost with Rose's letter. Her diary entry of Sept. 9,

1921, notes the Italian primitives in the National Gallery in London and a guide for whom she ordered a copy of the *Autobiography of Benvenuto Cellini.*

10. Dorothy was prone to exaggerate the drama of her accomplishments; see Sanders, *Dorothy Thompson,* pp. 81–82, 93–94.

11. Dorothy quotes from a poem by Graham Heminger; probably she saw it in the popular column by "B.L.T." (Bert Leston Taylor) in the *Chicago Tribune.*

12. The incident is from chapter 9 of Joseph Hergesheimer's *Linda Condon* (1919).

13. The region around the Semmering Pass, southwest of Vienna, is noted for its climate, scenery, and resorts.

14. Dorothy apparently did not know that Rose had lost a baby in the first year of her marriage (Rose Wilder Lane to Charles and Joan Clark, Feb. 8, 1944).

Part II

Letters 6–17 (1927–1928)

Introduction to Part II

A gap of five years separates this second series of letters from the first. The period marks the duration of Dorothy's marriage to Josef Bard, during which her correspondence with Rose apparently fell off—although Rose seems to have tried to keep it alive from her side.

The marriage failed, according to Dorothy's biographer, because Dorothy's growing career left Bard in the uncomfortable position of an appendage to his wife. In 1925, after three years of marriage, Dorothy had been promoted to head the Berlin bureau of the *Philadelphia Public Ledger.* In this position, she began to move at the center of a set of international notables. Her income increased substantially; and although she saw herself as merely a hard-working wife whose income would permit her husband's greater talent to flourish, Bard felt himself neglected. The result was a series of infidelities and finally his demand, in November of 1926, for a divorce to marry another woman.[1]

In her grief, Dorothy again sought Rose's counsel. Rose had gone back to the United States for a time in 1925, but in 1926 she returned with her friend Helen "Troub" Boylston to live in Albania.[2] We hear Rose's voice for the first time in this exchange of letters and get some sense of her tough-minded tenderness in her ministrations to the friend who had plunged into an ill-sorted marriage despite her best advice. As a survivor of one failed marriage, Rose could offer both compassion and wisdom; she could also offer distraction and entertainment in her descriptions of life in Albania.

A brief interruption in the exchange is marked by Rose's anger at again being dropped by her friend. Dorothy's busy life and the uncertainties of European mails account for the hiatus; but so also does Dorothy's renewed interest in life after her meeting with Sinclair Lewis.

---

1. Sanders, *Dorothy Thompson,* III. 4–6.

2. Rose Wilder Lane and Helen Dore Boylston, *Travels with Zenobia: Paris to Albania by Model T Ford,* ed. William Holtz (Columbia: University of Missouri Press, 1983).

Letter 6

Haendelstrasse 8
Berlin
January 10, 1927

Rose!

Tonight it is late, but I have not slept for many nights. Nights now for me are terrors toward which I look through dully aching days. And so, to ease the terror, I looked through old letters and old manuscripts and found amongst them a letter from you—from the time when we wrote to each other, and this letter was on the subject of marriage. And fascinated, I read it through, wondering at how little impression it had made upon me in those heydays of love, wondering at how illuminated your analysis and how bitter the prediction. For here I stand, dear Rose, thirty-two years old, and alone. Josef has gone. Just like that . . . gone. He did not take even my photograph with him, nor any of the little things I gave him, nor even the manuscript of the book which was to be ours,[1] not anything, not anything . . . he is gone. He is gone, and something queer has happened to me . . . I think I've died. At first it hurt, but now it doesn't hurt anymore. I say yesterday he was here . . . and six weeks ago we were in Munich, and there are his shirts back from the laundry which I ought to pack up and send to London, and the bathrobe smelling of him, and the flat just furnished, small and intimate, with an office for me in town so I wouldn't disturb him. I see the picture of him with his clear forehead, the head I loved so, the clock on the wall we bought together in Vienna, sort out the rings he gave me, and wear the little pearls, and I do not even cry—and all the life I have built up has crumbled, and nothing has any center, because Josef is gone. He bought me *muguets*[2] and said he would go away to make a life for both of us—all the separations I could stand, because he was there, in me, loving me, me loving him, and then he wrote from Paris I should get a divorce, and he gone, and I have only the shirts, all starched stiff that I ought to send to London. Oh, Rose, because I could never do anything except with all of me, I loved Josef with all of me, and was so proud, so proud . . . friends didn't matter any more, nor that I should make beautiful things . . . he would make beautiful things for me, and I would make a beautiful life for him. He writes "You have such a splendid life . . . go on with it . . ." But I haven't any life, because he has gone. Rose, I am afraid. Afraid that people who say they like me don't like me, that the gods who always were kind to me will hurt me . . . turn upon me . . . I am afraid of being hurt, and I have never been afraid of anything in the world before.

I think, Rose, I am done for. I know it hasn't any sense, but I think I am done for. There was a hand inside me, pressing my heart, and now it does not press any more—he went away six weeks ago—only there is nothing there to press.

He didn't even leave me my love for him. He didn't even leave me standing up. He knocked me down and went away.

Brain goes automatically, reading newspapers, registering over a treaty here or a change of government there, fingers don't even fumble on the typewriter, but I am dead, Rose. People don't see I am dead. It's so funny. First, when I loved him, I was afraid, and afterward I was never afraid, and all the time he plotted to undo me, and now he has gone.

Rose, I shall never get over it.

Thank you for the Albanian stuff—much I didn't know—amazing, interesting . . . one spark it enkindled of indignation.

He says I should be his friend . . . funny, that anyone should want me for a friend, who doesn't even exist.

Dorothy misdated this letter as 1926.

1. This book was probably Bard's projected *The Mind of Europe.* See Sanders, *Dorothy Thompson,* p. 76.

2. French for lilies-of-the-valley.

Letter 7

[undated]

Dorothy, my dear,

Oh, Dorothy, you are really very dear to me. I should not write you now at all. I know I should wait. It doesn't seem to me that I have a thought in my head. I care so much because you are suffering so. There's nothing in me but a cry, Dorothy, my dear, *don't*!

And yet I could say something to you, if it were only possible to say it, because I know all about it, so well. You don't know how well I know it. Though I was not left in that swift, clean way. It is really much better to be killed quickly than little by little, you know. No, of course you don't know.

The only thought I can get hold of is one that will seem so brutal to you. But it is true. Sometime you will look back on all this, and be glad it happened. Someday you will know that you never loved him, that you only loved your image of him—something made out of yourself, maybe out of the best that was in you. I don't know. I've often wondered about that, myself. Whatever it is, it dies. And in a strange way, you will be glad of that, too. Because after all, always, every day of our living is a little bit of dying, and that's all right. It really is. There's something in you that's deeper than even this thing that's happened, and that will go on, my dear; it will go on, and come out of it all, and be glad. Because—I don't know how to say it—because if a thing like this hadn't happened, you wouldn't have had it to come out of.

And I know that all this doesn't help one bit, now . . .

Go on, for a while, on your brain, my dear. As you say, it works automatically. Let it go on working, and for the rest, bathe and eat and sleep. You needn't do anything about the days, you know. They will keep on going by. *You* need not do anything at all. Dead, you say. Yes, it is like that. There is a peace in being dead. That's why you have it now; because you need peace. Oh my dear, there's something in you, too deep down for even you to know it's there, that knows what you need, and gives it to you.

You say you are done for. Yes, dear Dorothy, you are. There was a person whom you knew and thought was yourself, and she's gone, quite. There was too much of her in that image that's been taken away. She couldn't survive losing it. Someday you will remember her, and feel that you are thinking of a character in a book you read once. You knew her so well . . . and it will be strange to think that she wore your name and your appearance; that other people still think that she was you a few years younger. And, dear Dorothy, not even this matters. Life in itself means so much more than all of these selves of ours who were living once, and now are dead.

But again, all these words will have no meaning to you at all, now.

And all I can say is do not try to care about it all—about your feeling so strangely like an automaton moving without any reason at all in a strange world that has no meaning at all, except possibly a dangerous one; about your knowing that you are done for, that you never will get over it. You will not care about these things, except when now and then you feel you should struggle to be alive. Don't care about them. They do not matter. They really, really, do not matter, darling. You need not struggle at all. You are only a brain and a body, for awhile. Your brain will go right on doing its work, and your body doesn't need anything but food and rest.

And someday you'll know that the gods who always were kind to you have been, in this, kind again. Don't think me brutal, my dear, and please don't put aside the few poor things I can say because it seems to you that I don't understand. I know it seems that I don't understand, it seems to you that no one else can. And words mean nothing. It is so blithe, so callous, the way in which your friends can handle all this with words, giving you these worthless things in place of what you've lost . . . We are all so clumsy, my dear, and words are all we have, poor signals like bonfires and flags trying to express what shipwreck is.

Write to me if you can and want to. Sometimes it's a rest to write . . . And do not hate me because I can not say the things I know no way of saying.

Dear Dorothy, it isn't the end; it's only the end of one of you, the close of a chapter. A character goes out, and doesn't come into the story again. But there's the story, going on—after a little pause, a rest. Wait, and don't care about anything, and there's a faith that will come back to you. I shan't try to say any more, because you may not want me to go on with these words.

Letter 8

Tirana, Albania
January 25, 1927

Dorothy dear,

I said I wouldn't write you any more words that keep on so hopelessly failing to help—and I'm not.

But I wondered if perhaps you mightn't like to come down here for a week or so, looking over the situation for the paper. We would love to have you come. Troub's busy writing, and we could have some walks; the mountains are lovely. And the situation is really interesting. I do think, unless other work ties you up there, that a trip down through Zagreb and Belgrad—Zagreb especially, if you could get hold of the leaders there—to Ragusa, and so on down here, would furnish some good stuff. We would meet you in Ragusa with the car, if the roads were passable at all, and if not, there are always the boats to Durazzo.

It really does look like a nice little war here, perhaps, along in June.[1] Though of course it may end in nothing but another bitter diplomatic explosion.

All my love to you, dear, dear Dorothy.

R.W.L.

---

1. Albania was a miniature of Balkan politics. The regime of Ahmet Zogu had only recently been restored after being displaced by a short-lived revolution; the country, moreover, was under pressure from both Yugoslav and Italian interests.

Letter 9

Tirana
February 16, 1927

Dear Dorothy,

What I'm wishing to send you is our Albanian spring. It comes so kindly here; not with the shy uncertainty of northern springs, nor with the sudden overpowering rush that—I suppose, having never seen it myself—the tropical springs have. One morning the wind from Italy is quietly pushed back to the stormy Adriatic by a wind from Montenegro. All the clouds go away, and the sky is very blue. The wind from Montenegro is cold and smells of snow on hundreds of miles of mountains. The sun is very hot. The two combine to make the most delicious spring you've ever tasted, and everything grows in a sort of glow of enjoyment. All our bulbs are coming up—or rather, growing up, for their cold little noses have been up in the chill for some time—with a confident eagerness. The cold-frames are all over busy with popping seeds; zinnias and cardinal climber and cosmos. Every morning Troub digs up a sweet-pea seed—always the same patient and unperturbed one—to see what it's doing, and every morning its yellow root is longer; nearly an inch now.

Springs are different, as one grows older. They used to be so hopeful. And then, for a while, they became Edna St. Vincent Millay's *Second April*—that's a hard, bitter little green fruit! "Life in itself is nothing—an empty cup, a flight of uncarpeted stairs—"[1] But now, with hair growing really quite white, one knows that life in itself is everything—that all we've ever wanted else has, really, been an intensification of our awareness of living. One outgrows the need for these external aids to that intensification. Spring is a pageant, another of the marvelous varieties of this inexhaustible spectacle of external things. Leaf and bud and flower are the same thing as a seed—no more hopeful, no more *living,* than it is. But it's good to feel the sun so warm and to have a garden beginning its first chapter again—like one of the old friendly books that have been filling the days by the fire.

You ask me to tell you how we're living—and how can that be done, when you've never seen Tirana? Well, in the first place, you must come over the hills from Durazzo and see in the distance at the foot of the mountains—with old Dajti[2] stretched like some lazy prehistoric monster against the sky above it—the long stretch of trees that's Tirana and the white minarets rising. And then, when you come into the town, you turn into the Rruga Kavajes, back toward the east, from the Durazzo road, instead of going on toward the painted mosque at the end of the street. Rruga Kavajes will very soon—by the time your imagination can get here—be white with summer dust and sun. Water buffalo go down it, with their fuzzy, lumbering, wide-eyed calves; and trudging donkeys bearing loads of wood, or dried lavender, or thornbushes, or filled jars of mountain water—pottery jars, made and baked in the kiln that's smoking a little off to your right. Peasants walk behind them, padding in rawhide *opangi*;[3] or veiled peasant women, stick in one hand, the other clutching the edge of a black cloak across the face, their bare feet leaving more prints over many in the dust. The sun is very hot on the back of your neck. Mallard-colored ducks are swimming in the little pond by the road. And sometimes a squawking Ford goes by, scattering the other traffic, and sometimes an English officer, riding, very haughty, very "Englishman among the natives."[4]

After you pass the Turkish Legation there is nothing but high walls on your left, and on your right there's a garden, very charming, with many little tables under the trees; that's a cafe. So you come to our street, which is a narrow little winding way, cobbled, between high walls on either side. Our door is the third on the right; a noncommittal door, of new, unpainted (but we intend to paint it) wood, under its own little oblong red-tiled roof. The walls are very thick, so that the door's always in shade. There's a black iron knocker—native work—on the door. You essay to knock with it and are stunned by the clamor of great brass cow bells. You don't know until this moment that we've fastened an iron rod to that knocker, run it through the door and attached to its hidden end a Salonika cow bell—that is to say, a large, hammered brass bell, very sweet but firm-toned, with a smaller, similar bell for a clapper. You have not recovered, when you hear running steps on a graveled walk. A key turns in the lock; the door opens; Teqi stands before you.

Teqi is the *kavass.*[5] He's twenty-four, tall, quite good-looking; wears a well-tailored livery of gray cloth—like an American army uniform without insignia—and a black fez. He's a Moslem from Permet, in southern Albania. He's a sweet thing, *very* intelligent, hard-working, and more than faithful; a perfect servant. When the first hard earthquake struck us—before we got used to them—Troub and I, convalescing from influenza, were lunching by the fire in the sitting-room. Yvonne sat by, to aid and abet and entertain with conversation. Teqi had just gone to the kitchen—separate building, outside the house—to get the dessert. Suddenly, the house began to behave like a maddened bronco. Yvonne, the cat, I, and Troub, were one long streak (in order named) out of the sitting-room, the living room, and the house. John, the cook, also fled from the kitchen. Teqi instantly rushed into the quaking building, up the unsteady stairs and into the sitting-room—to us—it being his job, as *kavass,* to take care of us in danger. He did it so quickly that he couldn't have had time to think about it; it was merely instinctive reaction. He has a wife and baby in Permet, and sends them every cent of his salary the day he receives it. He did not know a word of French when he came, in late November, he now understands everything that's said to him, and replies fluently, if not always perfectly grammatically. But I shouldn't leave you standing there in the gateway all this time.

Teqi, of course, has orders not to admit anyone, as we're working. He is, however, intelligent. He will not turn you from the gateway. He will escort you up the graveled walk. You're in the little front court; the gravelled walk divides it in the middle, and the house goes clean across it, making its fourth wall. It's a large, imposing house, but there's a twinkle in its eye. It's all cool and dignified in blue-gray whitewash, with cream-painted trim; a two-story house. The walk runs straight through an archway in the lower story—and through the archway and the halls you look into the back garden. There's a window on either side of the archway. But the front door is on a balcony above the archway; curving steps go up to it on either side, and there's a frivolous curley-cuey iron balustrade, hand-wrought iron, painted the gayest of blues, following the curving steps. Teqi will take you through the front door—which is just enough on the bias to give you a hint of this house's really frivolous nature—and you'll be in the living-room.

It's fifty feet long, and just not quite wide enough in proportion. The floor's painted green and waxed; Albanian rugs on it. Fireplace at one end. Six windows along the front wall, three on either side of the door. Cream plaster walls; wooden ceiling. Bookcases built in around the fireplace. From the windows you see the 50x50-foot court, cut in two by the walk. Its walls are white, with little red-tiled roofs all around; the court's sodded, very thriving green grass; raised flower-beds with sod retaining walls and edges run all around the walls and on both side of the walk—they're further ornamented with lines of white pebbles, and the narcissi and the tulips are coming up in them. There are two trees, varieties unknown to me. And over the top of the front wall you see the Dibra mountains.

Behind this living-room there is the sitting-room; almost square, with a fireplace on one side. It has two windows looking out at the back garden. The walls are half a meter thick. Then there's the dining-room, and my room beyond it; and a hall with a bathroom (only we have no tub as yet) and the stairs going down. The floor below has four large rooms, cement floors, cream-plaster walls, opening from the halls.

There was a little back court, like the front one. The well's at one end of it, with a raised stone terrace around it, and a little hood over. The kitchen door is at the end of this terrace. But we took down the back court wall, and threw it into one with the garden. About an acre and a half, walled all 'round, with many trees: walnuts, cherries, figs, hazelnut. Flower beds run all around the walls, and there's a terrace under the big walnut tree for having tea on. Old Ibraim, the gardener, putters around all day in this garden, lovingly adding little trim of pebbles to the beds, digging a weed here and there, or sitting in rapt contemplation of a little wild daisy that's just blooming; now and then he pats it very gently.

Ibraim was twenty-five years a gardener in Constantinople. He retired with a comfortable fortune, built himself a beautiful house in his native village in southern Albania, and settled down with his wife and four sons to a good old age. The Greeks came in, in 1912, burned his house, cut down his orchards, killed his stock. His four sons were killed fighting them. He came a refugee to Tirana with his old wife. Having no money at all, they starved. He could not get a job as a gardener. He bought four oranges, and with them on a handkerchief spread on the sidewalk, started a fruit shop. He made just enough to keep himself and his wife alive. When we came here last year, he was buying fruit a dozen at a time and had three handkerchiefs full on display. He was too happy to speak when we took him on as gardener. He *loves* gardens. He's about seventy years old. We pay him eight dollars a month and his food—allowing him to take home his supper to divide with his wife. He has gained at least twelve pounds since he has been here; there is now more to his face than wrinkles and bones. He's a gentle old soul with a lovely sense of humor, and every time he opens his mouth an Albanian proverb drops out.[6]

Teqi, Yvonne, Ibraim, and the house-boy, Haire, are now our whole household. John, our cook, has gone—did I write you?—from our *ménage* into the brick business. We hope to get an Austrian cook, but in the meantime Yvonne does splendidly.

As to how we live, I am working as always, darn it! Just at the moment, doing an Ozark serial[7]—or anyway, I ought to be. Troub writes a little, reads a little, spends a lot of time in the garden, goes riding. There's always tea from four o'clock on—usually in five languages. People drop in.

By the way, a *New York Times* correspondent is here now. The *Ledger* really *ought* to have someone, just to look over the situation. Everybody else is covering it. Not that there seems—always the Balkan reservation—to be anything new right at the instant; but something's certainly going to break this summer.

There's been a cabinet change; it isn't really the "fall of a government" here; Ahmet Bey's the government.[8] Djemil Bey Dino sidestepped the Foreign Minister appointment; he doesn't want it. No one does! His brother-in-law, one of the Yrionis, has been appointed, but is hanging back with all toes stuck in. Djemil Bey is still officially Minister to Rome, but he's in Geneva. My opinion is that Albania will try to have the League refuse to register the Treaty of Tirana. The only hope is now to lean again to the Serbs. God, *what* a game it is! A baby rabbit in a pack of hounds—and still alive, after fifteen years of it! They say Ahmet is very tired. I haven't seen him. He's under guard—soldiers a dozen thick—every minute of day and night, and never appears in public: a prisoner. And he a mountain Mati man![9] Foreigners here enjoy a lot of cheap sneers at him. Personally, I think if he walked down the street he would live about ten minutes, and when he's gone, Albania's gone. There are some seven hundred blood feuds against him, and heaven knows how much reward offered by both Italy and Serbia—"unofficially," of course. Just as the Great War was started unofficially. Golly, how I *love* the Balkans! There is no other place on earth like it. Rather ten years of the Balkans than a cycle of New York.

Only I'd like to have enough of an income to live on, and—as our second-hand furniture man in The Village used to say—"just enjoy." Troub has a weeny income, darn her! Every quarter I gaze on it with a mouth sinking for the third time. Have you read the *Panchatantra*?

> Money will get anything, get it in a flash.
> Therefore let the prudent get cash, cash, cash.[10]

I wish I had realized that immortal truth some fifteen years ago.

Otherwise, I've no regrets. (And that isn't a very gnawing one, though it would be heavenly not to have to do Ozark serials.) Do, Dorothy dear, when you're my age *not* have to do Ozark serials.

I'd love to tell you some of the amusing things that happen to me, but just lately little that's amusing has happened in the even tenor of my Balkan-suburban days. Only the other day I met an English major, purple and panting. Seems he'd sent a cable to somewhere in Sussex, England, naturally addressing it so. And a few hours later he was sent for to come to the post-office, and the clerk—not speaking either English or German, only most of the other European and Near Eastern languages—said to him that he must put the full address on. He must write, "England, United States of America." You may imagine the English apoplexy. It seems there *is* a town in the States named "England," and there it was in the book. If the Major could have kept his temper, it would have been all right. The clerk eventually comprehended that he meant "Angleterre," and was perfectly willing to send the cable so. But the Major said he would be, with qualifications, damned if he'd send a cable to his own country addressed in further qualified foreign lingo. So it ended by his throwing an inkbottle at the clerk and vowing that when he wanted to cable home, he'd write a letter. Whom the gods will destroy—and certainly the English in these parts, and further east, are mad as hornets!

Very much love, Dorothy my dear—I *must* get at that damn serial!

My dear, my dear, of course no advice does any good—only maybe, if you'll just not try to "see" anything—or do anything, or think anything. It isn't necessary. Everything goes by, dear Dorothy, *everything*. You needn't do anything at all about it, you needn't even just let it go.

---

1. Edna St. Vincent Millay, "Spring," in *Second April* (New York, 1921).

2. The mountain range of that name.

3. The native sandals.

4. Albania had a number of British military officers as advisers to its primitive army.

5. A *kavass* was a kind of combined porter and footman, but also the head of the household staff.

6. Albania had been a part of the Ottoman Empire until 1912, when a short-lived independence tempted neighboring Greece and Montenegro to occupy undefended parts of Albanian territory. Independence was reestablished in 1921. Thus Ibraim's career epitomized his country's.

7. The serial, *Cindy,* appeared in *Country Gentleman,* April–August 1928, and was later published in book form as *Cindy: A Romance of the Ozarks* (New York: Harpers, 1928).

8. Ahmet Bey Zogu (later King Zog) was the Albanian prime minister, trying

to balance his country between external Yugoslav and Italian pressures and internal threats of rebellion. In return for financial support from Italy, Albania signed the Treaty of Tirana (1926), which gave Italy rights of intervention; under the protocols of the League of Nations, registration of the treaty certified an international acceptance. See J. Swire, *Albania: The Rise of a Kingdom* (London, 1929), pp. 478–81, 509–11.

9. The mountain people of the Mati region were renowned for their fierce independence; Rose's admiration for them is apparent throughout her *The Peaks of Shala* (1923).

10. Rose quotes approximately from *The Panchatantra,* translated from the Sanskrit by Arthur W. Ryder (Chicago: University of Chicago Press, 1925), p. 435.

Letter 10 [Rose to Dorothy]

[March 11, 1927]

"When a man dies, he is cast into the earth, and his wife and child sorrow over him. If he has neither wife nor child, then his father and mother, I suppose; and if he is quite alone in the world, why, then, he is cast into the earth, and there is an end of the matter."

"And do you think that is the end of a man?"

"There's no end of him, brother; more's the pity."

"Why do you say so?"

"Life is sweet, brother."

"Do you think so?"

"Think so! There's night and day, brother, both sweet things; sun, moon and stars, brother, all sweet things; there's likewise the wind on the heath. Life is very sweet, brother; who would wish to die?"

"I would wish to die—"

"You talk like a Gorgio—which is the same as talking like a fool—were you a Rommany Chal you would talk wiser. A Rommany Chal would wish to live forever."

"In sickness, Jasper?"

"There's the sun and stars, brother."

"In blindness, Jasper?"

"There is the wind on the heath, brother."[1]

Oh no, my dear. My letter wasn't beautiful; I am not at all beautiful, and how do we know even that there is beauty abroad when it snows in the Tiergarten?[2]—Those lovely, lovely soft flakes drifting down across the lines of the bare trees! I remember it all so well. For once I went taxi-ing through it, with a man who was making love to me, and I remember too that I let him hold my hand to keep him quiet so that he wouldn't disturb me with his poor little humanness—so that I could really see the snow falling in the Tiergarten. I don't remember anything else about him, not even his name, not anything. But I do remember the Tiergarten and the snow. No, how do we know there is beauty in it? It's only that there is beauty in us—something incommunicable, unshare-able, something that's ours to us—mine to me, and yours to you—beauty's a response, a something evoked, evanescent, ethereal—a fleeting through nerves and spirit. Nothing *is* beautiful. . . .

Funny: just this morning, madly seeking an idea for a short story, because heaven knows I need money, I ran across a line in one of my notebooks: "The cult of beauty is as ugly as any other. Any creed is ugly, as a stone wall in front of a window is ugly, because it shuts off the view."

And I remember that that was really a comment of a woman I knew. On the next page she's quoted. "I find life beautiful even when I am in utter misery." And my own comment added—"In utter misery; that is, when you are most intensely occupied with your own sensations."[3]

Isn't that the reason that the wind on the heath makes living always worth while to us? Because *there's* an evocation, a response, that's as utterly impersonal as anything that we can know can possibly be. Beauty's so intensely personal that it isn't personal at all, in any ordinary sense. Beauty's so deeply *us* that it has nothing to do with years or experiences—whitening hair and friends and enemies, bills and income responsibilities, plans and hopes and tragedies and price of butter, they're all superficial. Their sum is what we think of as our lives. And then clouds blow into the sunset over the Mati mountains, or there's snow falling in the Tiergarten, and there's something in us that's deeper than all these other "own sensations." So for an instant we forget to be either miserable or happy.

But the instant can't be held. Friends and enemies, bills and responsibilities, human relationships, human beings, can't be beautiful; they have nothing to do with beauty. We can't make beautiful lives, or beautiful things—at least I don't think so. We only muddle along as best we can in a world of confusion and delusions; such an entertaining world, such an Alice-through-the-looking-glass world, with the ludicrous always in its tragedies and the tragic always in its comedy, a world in which any thing is every thing and no thing can really be grasped, until at last one feels that there *isn't* any reality there at all. But I don't know that there needs to be.

Why do we struggle so? Why do we *want* so desperately? There's an equilibrium in us, if we'll let it be. There's one eternal day, eternally going around our earth and sweeping away before it at every passing all the things it left behind it twenty-four hours ago. We are always fighting it, always trying to build solidly, always clutching the things we had, determined to keep them, to reform them into our own patterns, to make them enduring and beautiful. But the day that left us last night comes on from the west this morning, and brushes over us and brushes them away. We suffer because we fight so, because we *want* so passionately, and so passionately in opposition to life and death and time and eternity.

A garden's a joy. Ours grows like anything. There's such a satisfaction in the spectacle of so much life and death in tune, and not opposed to anything. One's imagination lives every day a little while in that strange untroubled vegetable world, watching how it changes and doesn't care. Every day comes by, and changes everything; not a seed nor leaf nor bud remains the same or tries to. There is no "intelligence" at all in a nasturtium or verbena, and that's why they have their patterns. Flowers crystallize on their stems as snowflakes crystallize in air, because they don't attempt to, because they're passive, both to their own qualities and to the external universe.

Yet this gets *us* nowhere, of course. We are not vegetables. And yet, there's lots of placidity just in watching them. Every morning, full of eagerness, I go out to see the baby nasturtiums and marigolds, and the narcissi and tulips, and to gloat over the cold frames. And old Ibraim putters about, brooding over every tiny promise of a new leaf. He is such a dear . . . It turns out that he is not really old. Or rather, that he really is, but that his years are not so many as the wrinkles on his face or the white hairs on his head. He appears to be seventy, at least; he is forty-seven. We were startled to hear it, and he said, with that wise, warm smile of his, "It is that I have suffered so much."

He was with the Turkish army in the Dardanelles. That was after he had been for twenty-five years a gardener in Constantinople; he made a small but sufficient fortune there, by industry and thrift, and then came home to Albania to live on it. He had his family, wife, four sons and a daughter. He built a good house for them, and had his gardens, and then the Greeks came in, burned and destroyed all his property and killed his four sons. After that, he was through all the wars, and at last he got back as a refugee to Tirana.[4] He had nothing at all; slept in the streets and starved. Finally, somehow, he got hold of enough money to buy two oranges, and with these on a handkerchief on the edge of the sidewalk, he started in business as a fruitstand man. In three years he had succeeded so well that he had three handkerchiefs spread, and bought his fruit by the dozen. And then he got this job with us, gardening again! And he is happy all day long. But he does look seventy.

Glory, but the world is lovely here now! All our great, green garden, with the trees in bud and the sunshine warm on them—the cat voluptuously stretched on the grass, and little Haire leisurely drawing water from the well, and Yvonne singing in the kitchen, and Ibraim fondly beaming upon the small wild daisies and the buttercups that we do not at all discourage from blooming in the lawns. It doesn't seem as though there could ever be any haste or trouble or vexation anywhere. Seems as though I had been specially created (by some incredible freak of the stars) for the Moslem woman's life. A paragraph ago I saw the landlord's mother at the gate in our wall, and heard the loom going behind her, so I went down to wish her a long life and to visit awhile. The landlord's family—they live next door—were all that's welcoming. There's the old, toothless, smiling mother, so old that she's free as a child, unveiled and gossipy with our workmen and servants—"mother" they call her, and she has a wicked tongue and a bright bird-like eye. There's the landlord's wife, a comely woman in her sheer white head-kerchief and neat tight basque; voluminous black trousers, flowered in white, caught up and tucked in a great bunch under her sash in front, and at the ankles neatly frilled around neat ankles. Her feet are bare, and very clean; pink and white as seashells. And there are four or five girl children and three little boys. The oldest girl is to be married next month. Already we hear from time to time snatches of hummed marriage-song over our garden walls, and pretty soon now the real songs will begin, and continue day and night for two weeks. She's sixteen, with a young round face, beautiful dark eyes and a charming smile; the giggly age, however, laughing all the time at everything and nothing. The landlord told us the other day about the marriage, when he was praying six months' rent in advance on account of the great expenses of the marriage feast; fraud that he is, for he has no more need of advanced rents than I have of a French centime; he is very rich. Learned, too, for he has a government post in the Department of the Sacred Law. He is marrying her to the son of Mustapha Mara, one of our most prosperous merchants; an intelligent and very business-like boy of nineteen whom his father often leaves in entire charge of the business. He is quite a desirable match even by American standards, except that he almost never shaves and apparently quite rarely washes. (The decay of Islam has that great disadvantage; were he truly devout, he would wash five times daily, of course.) We asked the landlord if the girl had ever seen her future husband, which was a most improper query, and Teqi-the-faithful-kavass was shocked white when he heard it. The landlord started in his chair and replied with emphasis, "Kam pa *une,*" which is to say, "*I, I* have seen him." Although they are so rich, they have the typical Albanian house; that is, the house of the exceedingly rich or the very poor Albanian who is neither Bey nor Pasha.[5] The high white walls enclose a large space of grassless, trodden earth on which the sun shines warm; the low house, rambling, whitewashed, has six or seven rooms, thick clay-brick walls and few windows. Inside there are wooden floors in the rooms but not in the halls, thin whitewashed claybrick partitions as high as the eaves, and over all the rafters of the roofs with the red tiles showing between them. In the living room there is a trace of foreign influence—proud modernism!—for the two beds, instead of being rolled up and laid away in their niches, remain all day made up on their cheap white iron bedsteads. For other furnishings, there is an enormous and very lovely old chip-carved Albanian chest—the dower chest—and a loom. The mother was working at the loom. It's amazing, the beautiful work they do, so intricate, so delicate. I am going to have a loom made and weave in our garden this summer. They brought us endless cups of coffee, of course, and we all laughed a great deal at our mistakes in Albanian. The bride brought out quantities of things from the chest; silks like cobwebs, so fine they clung to the fingers, and laces so delicate that really we could hardly see the stitches. I have never seen anywhere laces like the Albanian; they're always very fine little edgings, and the stitch is like the Armenian, but not exactly the same, and the designs lovely and yet rather prankish—a sense of humor in lace.[6] She showed us too the presents for the groom; shirts beautifully made, with bosoms of cheap European cloth, a figured shirting worth perhaps fifteen cents a yard; the sleeves and back and the long tail that does not show when the shirt is worn are made of the Albanian silk, fine as chiffon, with stripes like heavy ribbons in it, embroidered in gold. But of course, the European bosoms are the finest. Anything European is better than anything Albanian, and anything at all that's American is far, far the best. Also the bride had a number of pillow tops, bunches of flowers embroidered in colored silks on cheap cream-colored sateen; the designs are awful, but the coloring and the work perfect. The mother sat weaving at her loom; the bride had stopped her own task of winding threads from the skein to the shuttle, in the sunshine outside the window. It was all so busily idle, so in tune with the morning. Their lives go by like the days, without effort or struggle; just naturally passing . . . pigeons coo in their cotes all along the eaves, and the sunshine moves along the white walls. And the weaving goes on, and the bride sits on her heels, on a straw mat spread on the ground and lets the thread slide through her fingers from skein to shuttle. A thing that looks so easy to do, and for her is easy, since she has done it all her life. But we tried it, and the whole intricate mechanism of wooden wheels and spools and spokes was possessed by a madness, and the thread broke—and broke—and broke—There's much I must learn, before I can do Albanian weaving!

This rambling letter to you, Dorothy dear, was started days ago. Days of great excitement, tense and emotional. For the carpenters and the masons have arrived; floors are coming up, foundations going down, sacks of cement arrive and boards are being sawed, and studding and rafters mysteriously erect themselves in air. Houses are the abiding joys; they are the most emotion-stirring of all things. An automobile is regarded with fond affection, a typewriter becomes the inseparable companion, clothes can stir sentimentality, and the bit of bric-a-brac is a toy one would weep to see torn away—but houses are real, deep, emotional things. How much excitement in the cutting of a window, what enormous importance in the angle of a roof! Albanians are right in knowing that far worse than to kill the criminal or the enemy is to burn his house.

And it seems to me that I have written you all these pages saying nothing. But that there's no value in continuing to write, for I think only of nothing to say.

Never mind, my dear, whether you write to me or not. There will always be time, some other time, for writing letters; most surely they don't matter now.

All my love to you,
Rose

This letter is dated from a copy Rose kept in her papers.

1. The passage is from George Borrow's *Lavengro* (1851). The conversation is between a young Englishman (a Gorgio) and a gypsy (a Romany Chal) in chapter 6.

2. The Tiergarten is a famed zoological garden in Berlin. Rose had visited there on January 4, 1922.

3. Rose refers to her 1920 notebook, "Notes for a novel: *Freedom.*"

4. Apparently forgetting her last letter, Rose repeats the story of Ibraim—and tells it better.

5. Some Albanians had earned titles and honors in the service of the Ottoman Turks; the titles here imply an acceptance of Turkish modes of opulence.

6. Rose's interest in needlework was lifelong and detailed; see her *Woman's Day Book of American Needlework* (New York: Simon and Schuster, 1963).

Letter 11

April 16, 1927

Dear Dorothy,

For God's sake and mine, and if there's pity in your heart, S.O.S!

We are descended upon by an American woman with two children—American children. The house is hell.

Mrs. Danforth is an ancient San Francisco acquaintance of mine.[1] She has rented her house and tied her husband's nose to the grindstone and brought her two angel darlings to Europe for two years. She does not speak a word of any language but American. The children are twelve and seven. She has forty dollars a week.

The Italians swooped upon her and took $250 in return for a frantic flight from Naples to Bari. She should have made it, of course, for $50 or so. She is therefore broke and on our hands, and beyond words terrified by any prospect of stirring out into Europe again. But she has to stay in Europe two years, because she won't admit she'd made a mistake and go back.

And Dorothy, if we don't get her off our hands, we shall—we *can't* stand it!

Most of our furniture is wrecked and in the basement. We have covered our floors with old straw mattings and still hope to save them. The plaster is off our walls. Two windows have been broken. Our garden is being ruined. One fig tree has already been killed. The servants are run ragged, and I think the cook will either go mad and kill someone or leave us flat. They have been here three days. The mother hates us with a deep deadly hatred because we don't appreciate her sweet darlings. But she won't leave because she is literally scared white at the mere thought.

Also we are rapidly going broke. Our food bills are more than doubled, and it is necessary to hire donkeys and attendants to take the children out of the way a little of the time. And there is no hope whatever of getting any work done in order to get any money.

Therefore, Dorothy, for God's sake, help me if you can. Do you know any *pensions* in Austria where she and the children can live on $40 a week?

Do you know what it would cost, about, to live in Munich? Have you any Munich addresses of hotels or *pensions* where it could be done on $40 a week, in Munich or elsewhere in Germany?

Do you know the names of cheap hotels in Venice?

If we send her to Vienna, would Fodor meet her and take her to a *pension*? If so, what is his address?

Do you know any schools—combination day- and boarding-schools—that she can afford for the children anywhere in Austria, Switzerland, or Germany? Or Budapest?

She still has vague remnants of her original intentions, which are to go on to Venice, thence to Vienna, Switzerland, Germany. Somewhere she intended to find a school for the children this winter.

Our only hope seems to be to make connections for her, somehow, along the route, so that she won't be terrified to start out again. We are willing to do anything whatever, ourselves. We can take her personally to any place necessary and get her settled, if we have to. Only, we can't afford it. But we will do it anyhow, if we've got to. But we don't know where to take her.

If you know a hotel or *pension* in Vienna, where she can live on $40 a week; if Fodor would meet her at the station, put her in a taxi, and take her to it, then Troub or I could take her as far as Venice, and put her on the Vienna train.

Do whatever you can for me, won't you?

There is every indication here that our bearers of the white man's burden will pull off a neat doublecross in the next crisis. Look for it, and you will see it.[2]

General Percy,[3] sent out here to help with the gendarmerie, was the pup with a sore ear a couple of months ago. Wouldn't even buy furniture for his house because he didn't expect to stay. Now he is chief of both gendarmerie and army for the north and is expected any hour to be given charge of the whole army, both north and south.

There is a story printed in *The Telegram,* C. A. Chekrezi's Tirana newspaper, in the last issue, to the effect that England has asked Italy to explain Article One of the Tirana Pact,[4] and that Italy has refused to do so. Chekrezi's article is dated Durazzo and says vaguely that "Italian newspapers state—." Names of Italian newspapers not given. *The Telegram* was suppressed last October for reprinting an article from the *Near East,* which gave details of the Baron Aloisi interview with Ahmet last July—the first Italian attempt at getting the Pact of Tirana, the attempt that was defeated by Ahmet with England's help. The *Telegram* was allowed to resume publication last month; and it doesn't print anything not passed by the government. Therefore the publication of this story is interesting and significant.

My dear, Ahmet's correct name is Ahmet Bey Mati, or else,

Ahmet Zogu. Zogu is the family name. Bey Mati is the title. The original family name was Zogu. In the fourteenth century, after Scanderbeg[5] died, when the Mati became technically Moslem, the name was still Zogu. The next generation, however, became Zogoli—through the combination of the Turkish "ogli," meaning "son of"—with the original family name. In 1922, when Ahmet became the whole government, during the revolution and the absence of all other members of the government, he began to sign official proclamations as Ahmet Zogu. At that time he dropped the Turkish title of Bey Mati and also the Turkish form of his family name, and returned to the pure Albanian family name of before the 14th century.

Where do you get your information from Tirana? Some of it astonishes me. And also I don't believe it. My dear, there absolutely is *not* the smallest bit of truth in any reports of an uprising inside Albania. I don't know where you get the information, but wherever you get it, it's false. Albania is, as I write you, absolutely quiet. The only danger of trouble is outside the borders. You can absolutely depend upon that fact. When there are further reports of revolutions in Albania, don't believe them, and you will be right. The danger is among the Albanian refugees in Jugo-Slavia or in Italy. And you can know which by noting whether the news of revolutions in Albania comes from Rome or Belgrad. If Rome, it's the refugees in Jugo-Slavia, if Belgrad, those from Italy. These political refugees have all been offered amnesty, not once, but several times. From 1922 on, Ahmet made every effort to induce Fan Noli[6] to work with the Albanian government. He finally persuaded Fan Noli to come in, gave him every aid and honor possible, assisted him in all kinds of ways, as Bishop of the Orthodox church. And Fan Noli pulled off the 1924 revolution, before which Ahmet retreated without even an attempt to fight. Six months later, on Christmas Eve, 1924, Ahmet came back from Serbia, and Fan Noli's soldiers wouldn't even try to fight for him. John Clayton[7] was here; he knows, if you think my information is untrustworthy because of my personal bias. Fan Noli ran away with the entire contents of the Albanian treasury and has been raising hell outside ever since. Fan Noli is a brilliant man, but he's a fool in Balkan affairs. He went wrong, first, because he was friendly to Soviet Russia, and second, because he couldn't keep order even in the streets of Tirana. The whole country was falling to pieces under him; going back to war conditions; highwaymen and brigands everywhere; no lives or property safe. That's why the people didn't rise to his support when Ahmet returned. Fan Noli is typical of all the "outside" Albanians. And they themselves are not united. Each one of them is inspired by personal hatred of Ahmet, by envy of his success, and by ambition to overthrow him and be dictator of Albania. They will take help from either Italy or Serbia to that end. Inside Albania there is a great deal of discontent. But all Albanians inside the country know that Ahmet is the best leader; he keeps order, he does get some building done, and so far he has held the situation as steady as it can possibly be held. Thousands of people don't like him, hundreds hate him; but nobody wants to see him gone, simply because they know it would be out of the frying pan into the fire. His followers are *not* "deserting him in droves." He has no followers worth mentioning. He is holding the situation alone. Those who might be called his followers are figureheads who do what they are told and get what they can in graft. He has consistently tried to get followers, helpers among the best men of Albania, but they have all been Fan Noli's in one way or another. His strength is his personality, his intelligence, his incredible and exhaustless working energy; and he is supported by the army as long as the army is paid. The Mati men, with few exceptions, will follow him anyhow. So will a large part of the Dibra.[8] The rest are practically mercenaries. But Ahmet holds them because he is the only man who can keep the government going well enough to pay any salaries at all. You go wrong on this situation unless you remember all the time that this is a feudal psychology clear through, soaking, permeating the whole country. Think of it as a group of robber-baron castles of the middle ages, held together by one man who's trying to make a modern republic of them. Germany did the same thing, not so long ago. History ought to give you the picture. Ahmet is the King of Prussia a century or so ago. Call him a dictator if you like; but it doesn't convey the picture, not to American readers who think of the South American republics. All the little kings of all the other states—that is to say, all the other chiefs of other Albanian districts—wouldn't join the Mati, as the other states joined Prussia. They ran out of the country and keep getting aid from Italy and from Serbia for their attempts to get back again and overthrow the Mati. All except Fan Noli, who is apparently an idealistic adventurer with leanings toward Communism.[9] WHAT a spectacle! Fan Noli's the Connecticut Yankee in King Arthur's court. Only he can't quite pull it off. He would have, if he hadn't held out that friendly hand to Russia; both Italy and Serbia joined then, for the minute or two that was necessary to let Ahmet come back. Ahmet's not making any mistake about Russia; he told me five years ago that Albania needed a couple of centuries of capitalism before there was any use of even considering the undoubted merits of communism. But what I am getting at is this: DON'T BELIEVE THERE IS A REVOLUTION IN ALBANIA. Because there isn't, and there won't be. The trouble comes either from Italy or from Serbia. My own belief is that the Scutari scrap last fall was financed by Italy in order to get the Tirana Pact.[10] And the real root of the situation is in Downing Street. Watch it, because there's going to be a shift in the prevailing winds, and darn soon. By the way, if you have anyone in Macedonia who can give you the detail of the military dispositions there, you have a real story. I'm told on good, and unprejudiced, authority, that the positions of the army posts on the frontier, with their backing of local headquarters to general headquarters, shows Serbia's intentions beyond any doubt, to the practiced military eye. Albania can't hold her borders at all; of course, they were drawn to the sole end that she couldn't.[11] I'm told that the British Empire with all its land forces couldn't hold Albania against the present Serbian formation, given the handicaps of the topography.

Look, Dorothy my dear, for God's sake, help me out with the difficulty of these children! Send me even the hastiest of dictated notes. Answer my questions about *pensions,* prices, schools, as well as you can. Think about it a little, if you can possibly do so. The house is bedlam. I am a nervous wreck. I can't put it too strongly to you. Save me if you can.

Love,

Rose

---

1. Rose's obligation to Alice Danforth was significant: she had lived in her house while writing her first novel, *Diverging Roads,* in 1918 (letter to Guy Moyston, Oct. 31, 1925). The visitation lasted three weeks.

2. As European correspondent for a major U.S. newspaper, Dorothy would naturally be interested in the internal politics of Albania, which manifested all of the complexities of Balkan affairs. Rose's diary shows several inquiries from her.

Briefly, it can be said that the struggle of ethnic Albanians for self-determination following the collapse of the Ottoman Empire was threatened by attempts of Italy, Greece, and Yugoslavia to annex large portions of Albanian lands and to establish political domination and military control. Internally, the country was divided by a struggle for social and agrarian reform on the one hand and the conservative interests of the large landholders on the other. Following World War I, the victorious powers in their reorganization of Europe agreed on the principle of an independent Albania, but this principle did not prevent the larger surrounding states from intervening in Albania's internal politics. Albania was admitted to the League of Nations in 1920; by 1922, Ahmet Bey Zogu had emerged as prime minister, largely with the support of the landed interests. His shaky government was soon toppled, however; he fled to Yugoslavia during a reform government under Bishop Fan Noli, who established diplomatic relations with Soviet Russia. This connection alarmed the Yugoslavs, who intervened to restore Zogu in 1924. Later, however, Zogu turned to Italy for support, obtaining financial subsidies on terms that made Albania virtually an Italian protectorate. Rose admired Zogu immensely for his personal courage and decisive action. She had ducked bullets during a brief insurrection against Zogu in 1922 when she was gathering material for her *Peaks of Shala* (Diary, March 8–11, 1922; letter to Mama Bess, March 21, 1922; letter to Guy Moyston, March 15, 1922). She identified strongly with his efforts to keep Albania independent on the stage of world politics. Her reference to England's role apparently has to do with the shifting attitudes of England toward Italian and Yugoslav interests in Albania. Nominally committed to Albania's independence, England at first opposed the growing Italian influence. Somewhat later, however, alarmed by apparent Yugoslav intentions to foment insurrection along the border with Albania—which might have precipitated another Balkan crisis—England accepted the Italian influence, which Rose would interpret as a "neat doublecross." For a brief background to this period, see Rumadan Marmullaku, *Albania and the Albanians* (Hamden, Conn.: Anchor Books, 1975), chap. 4. A more detailed account is in Swire, *Albania,* chaps. 9–11.

3. General Jocelyn Percy was stationed in Albania with an international *gendarmerie* established by the League of Nations. Rose reads his new authority as a sign of England's influence. See ibid., pp. 489–90.

4. Article One of the Tirana Pact was a "mutual assistance" agreement; there was considerable international speculation that it would serve as a pretext for Italian intervention in Albania. Baron Aloisi was the Italian minister to Albania. See ibid., pp. 478–79 and chap. 11 passim.

5. Scanderbeg, the greatest Albanian national hero, led the battle against the Turks from 1442 until his death in 1468.

6. Fan Noli and Zogu had begun as members of the same reform party; Zogu later became prime minister by allying himself with the conservative landowners' party. Rose's admiration for Zogu's personal abilities makes her account a partial one; he did, however, bring peace to his divided country.

7. John Clayton was a journalist and mutual acquaintance; Rose refers to a letter from him, Dec. 24, 1924.

8. The Mati and Dibra were regional—essentially tribal—factions.

9. In June 1927, Fan Noli justified the fears first aroused by his establishment of diplomatic relations with Russia: he signed the Communist Manifesto and urged

a revolution and a Soviet-style government for Albania (*New York Times,* June 19, 1927, II, 6:3).

10. In November 1926 a brief tribal uprising at Scutari was put down by government troops. Swire (*Albania,* pp. 474–75) argues for Yugoslav influence rather than Italian.

11. The borders of Albania had first been drawn by an international commission in 1913 to the satisfaction of no one; a 1921 commission altered the line to Yugoslavia's advantage (ibid., pp. 366–68).

Letter 12

Tirana Albania
October 26, 1927

Dear Dorothy,

The last time you dropped me definitely as not worth bothering about, I held on for four years to the hope that there'd been some misunderstanding on your part or mine. And you may remember the many letters which I wrote you during those years. I don't mean that I'm going to repeat from asterisk, my dear. There's a certain clear ruthlessness in you which I've always admired; it keeps your life from having blurred edges. I can admire it even when I'm its victim. Only this time I think I shall see—which I couldn't believe before—that I *am* its victim. So this note will end, in that fashion current among our grandmothers, "And so no more from . . ."

And this time you haven't asked me for a prophecy, but I make one all the same. Don't bother about it now; let it wait another ten years. It's this: Every woman has love affairs. It's the rarely fortunate one who has a sincere friend—I mean a *friend.* The time comes, eventually, when one sees that a sterling silver friendship was really a rare thing, worth, perhaps, a little more than the other things one threw it away for.

This sounds fearfully didactic, and there's comedy in its solemn portentousness. Oh well, we're all comic more or less, and for the first time in all my life I see that there really is a comic element in the effects of cruelty. Never mind.

RWL

Letter 13

Handelstrasse 8
Berlin
December 25 [1927]

Dearest Rose:

Now *this* time you do me an injustice. Be it acknowledged, I am the worst correspondent in the world. I neglect my friends most of the time. I reach out an arm to grab them in moments when I need them—and then disappear back when the rescue is effected. It is the truth. But actually Rose, I wrote you twice. I was terribly disappointed not to see you in Vienna. I would surely have come, but was already on the way to England, and I telegraphed and wrote two letters to you, care of Fodor in Wien. Not until eight weeks ago, in October, when I was in Wien for two days, did I find that they had arrived too late, but I still believed that Fodor had forwarded to you the two letters. *Didn't* he? Because they had lots of news in 'em.

Roses, I have been in a hectic state. I am in love, thank God, again: I have been two months buried in Russia (alone)—which is the reason why your letter wasn't answered sooner—I have written in the fortnight since I got back (including Christmas) thirty thousand words of copy. Rose, please, love me still, even as I, worthless as I am, *do* love you.

The reciprocant of my passion at present is Red Lewis.[1] I am going to marry him. Don't spread it around. He's not divorced yet. He is adorable and I am happy. Rose, I want to write you naturally, and you've embarrassed me!

Rose!

Dorothy

---

1. Dorothy was just beginning her romance with Sinclair Lewis, who was known as "Red" by close friends (Sanders, *Dorothy Thompson,* part 4).

Letter 14

Tirana
January 10 [1928]

My dear,

I'm sorry. I don't want to embarrass you, ever. I don't want to do anything but love you. And I wish to God that I bore being hurt better than I do. It seems, at long last, to be making me a very horrid person, a suspicious person, an unjust one. I am really terribly sorry. Please try to forget it, remembering that sometimes one can't bear to leave the heart on the sleeve any longer, and that want of practice makes one clumsy in trying to protect it.

Of course, letters don't matter . . . No, I didn't get any, not a word.

As to the news, what can I say? Fodor led me to expect as much, through saying nothing at all. You know that I'm glad you are happy. I feel a thousand years older, since trying to recall a person I once used to be, who also cried whole-heartedly, "I am in love, thank God, again!" And you know so well what I think—and feel—about marriage. Darling, you're a brave and rash and wonderful person, and Heaven help you—which, of course, Heaven always will.

Can I say any fairer than that?

And Oh, my adorable Dorothy, what becomes of all the perfectly good point of view which you so well expressed, last summer a year ago?

It's the great joy of being in love, that logic flies out the window. Little by little, as I sit gazing upon the few inadequate words that my typewriter has stammered out, smoking and smoking and smoking meanwhile, and standing my hair on end with agitated fingers—little by little, I say, memories return to me. To find one curve of one cheek the loveliest line in the world, to see in the mirrors of two eyes the very best you are or ever hoped to be—and to believe that they are not mirrors at all, but clearest glass—to have a heart that will start, and stand still, and leap again, at the sound of just one step, just that one only step, of all the steps of all the feet in all the world . . . To know, to *know,* never to doubt, that this one thing that you have is good, is the best, is the one thing always to hold to, to keep, forever and forever, against all the winds of time and chance—By gosh, enthusiasm stirs once more in my old bones! Yes, you're right. Being in love is something to thank God for.

(There's also a great deal to be said for being out of love. But never mind . . .)

My own small bit of news, pale and limp, I offer under the

same seal of secrecy. (I don't know why, only that I *hate* discussion of me and my affairs and intentions.) I've subleased the house here and am going to the States pretty soon, in April, probably, for a dozen reasons, none of any value except in the aggregate. The weightiest, probably, is that you were right in a prophecy you once made; you've forgotten it. Albania, you said, would become Main Street.[1] No, not quite that, not Main Street—the *Via Mussolini.* My Albania's sunk, and so rapidly, for the third time.[2] I never wished to live in Italy. Not the blue of Capri nor the lagoons of Venice (at that, a much over-rated imitation Orient) can reconcile me to the population. Not even the lovely curves of sound in the singing language. And here, in submerged Tirana, we have *only* the population. Last week, while walking past the Holy Garden with my small Mr. Bunting, a terrier of Malta, on his leash, I chanced to pass an Italian creature who kicked him. This is really too much. Don't you think?

Besides, our "social season"! Our official balls! Our Tennis Club and its uncontested elections! *Tempora* and *Mores fugit.* No, what's the plural? *Fugavit,* or something. Anyway, that's what they do, and so shall I, at least temporarily.[3] I positively look forward to the lights of Broadway—stupendous, astounding, cosmically comic spectacle of the grandeur of humanity, taking the firmament in its two hands and eternally scrawling across it in letters of gigantic light "A slice of lemon peel and a bottle of Somebody's ginger ale make the best horse's neck you ever tasted· a slice of lemon peel and a bottle of . . ." The world has not seen its equal.

My dear, I chatter on so. I wish that you would write to me, but I shan't be disappointed. It doesn't matter, if you won't quite forget me. If sometimes you'll feel a little twinge of the regret that sometimes is an ache with me, regret that we've always been separated by time and space and events, even though the events have been those you've chosen. I shall always mourn the journeyings we've never had together, the places and people I've never had a glimpse of through your eyes. I shall always, I suspect, a little hate the husband for having that part of the world, of living, that's only yours. But then, I always have a bit of a growl in my throat for men, all men, for them in general. You know I can't help it. I know it's unreasonable.

They take up so much time, they divert so much attention.

The situation here straightens out: a virtual occupation. Our neighbors to the west are realists; they take the cash and let the credit wait till more convenient occasions.[4] The trouble now is in Macedonia, where submerged populations behave as submerged populations always do.[5] And the old *Via Egnatia* still leads, as it always has from—approximately—Durazzo, east to Constantinople.[6] But my interest in it all is waning. Constant repetition dulls receptivity, and it is all such an old, old story.

Blessings on you, my dear. It's marvelous to be young; I send you my envious love.

Rose

No, I won't be disappointed. I set my teeth and swear it. And it's true truth that I don't want you to miss one golden moment in writing to me. But if there should ever be a little time when the Idolized is out of town, and if you should use it in writing to me a real letter once more—it would be a great asset to you on Judgment Day, outweighing probably *all* your sins—a great charity to the perishing.

---

1. The reference is to *Main Street* (1920) by Sinclair Lewis. This best-selling novel gave Americans—and the world—a now-classic view of the banality of middle-class American life.

2. Rose puts the growing domination of Albania by Italy in a sequence with its partition by surrounding states in 1914 and its earlier subjugation by the Turks.

3. *Tempora . . .*: Times and customs change, Rose laments, momentarily forgetting her high school Latin, which would have provided *fugiunt* as the verb form. But she reaches for the root sense of *fugere,* to flee, to describe her saddened departure from Albania.

4. Treaties of 1926 and 1927 opened Albania to extreme Italian exploitation—in trade, banking, and military training—which made Albania little more than a client state.

5. A significant ethnic Albanian population in Greece suffered persecution under Greek rule.

6. The Via Egnatia was a road built by the Romans to connect Italy with the eastern reaches of the empire. Rose speculates on Mussolini's imperial designs in the twentieth century.

Letter 15

January 17 [1928]

Rose of Roses,

Here's your letter, and here's mine. I don't think I didn't write because I was happy and didn't need you; I don't think I am such a cad. I don't think I didn't write because I was unhappy—I have been confused—and when I am confused, I am silent. Now I am clear again—I know it is all subjective, this clarity and confusion: probably glands, but my glands, then, are working better.

I foresaw Albania. Never mind, you've had *your* Albania. By all means leave it before it becomes too completely and entirely Mussolini's. Leaving it, you can keep it.

So it is, of course, with love. There is comfort to me in the thought that we may be deceived in our present and absurdly wrong in all our speculations about the future, but our past belongs to us, completely, wholly, and we always have everything we have put into it. Now that the pain of my first loving and losing is over, I rejoice in the whole of my experience with Josef, having it completely for myself, knowing that Josef has nothing to do with it, whatsoever. Now I can look at him in a picture and know that that is no brow where beauty sat, no curve of cheek as thrilling as the newest moon, no limbs like pillars of marble, or whatever the singer of the song of songs may have sung, but that I had my day of creation, and created me my lover and have him forever. And having him, thus, I am glad, at last, for another.

It isn't quite the same. I approach life with more humor. This is a gain and a loss. I cannot ever again reach that transcendental state of feeling myself one, flesh of flesh and eyes of eyes of another individual. I am not nearly so much "in love"—whatever that may mean. I cannot stretch my imagination to believe that SL is the most beautiful person in the world. I know him to be compounded of bad habits, weaknesses, irritabilities, irritancies. But he pleases me. He is a superb comrade. He amuses me: the first requirement of a husband. He heightens my sense of life. He opens a future for me, so that for the first time in years, I dream of tomorrow, as well as enjoy today. Thus, he gives me back a gift of youth. I like him, enormously, amusedly. I admire him, immensely and impersonally. I am absurdly happy in a quite head-on-my-shoulders sort of way.

We are going to Sicily on the first of March. Is there anything in the world to stop your making a rendezvous with us somewhere there? If you are enroute for New York, surely you can sail around Sicily and get off at Palermo or Syracuse. We stay until certain matters are regulated—probably until the end of April, when we have the highly entertaining plan of hiring a motor caravan and touring England, Scotland, and Wales until autumn. My sense of propriety is entirely met by the idea that our first house together should be one on wheels! Few things in life are so fitting! We picture folding beds which are, by day, settees, electric stove and lights, a folding table, shelves of books, a sort of luxurious gypsy camp. And a guest bed. For we two are gregarious human beings, more or less, our relationship is not so intense that we do not welcome visitors to the camp fire. Altogether there is a wind in this love, which pleases me, a ripple of mocking laughter, a thumbing of the nose at the world.

I like this man, and I am going to keep him forever.

Yes, there is something to be said for being out of love. Once, in a great moment, I wrote a sonnet about it. I think I was in the worst and lowest state of mind that I have ever been in. I was coming back to Berlin from Geneva, where I had been reporting the world economic conference. The thought of the office and the job, the senseless circularness, of life and its emptiness; the feeling of eternal repetition, and the chains of the emotional state which I was in and could not break, were almost driving me mad. At midnight we reached Basel, and without knowing how or why, I threw my bags out of the window and got out, leaving the train, on which I had sleeper and ticket. In the morning I took a tiny train that went to the Bodensee, down along the Rhine. It was the jolliest, gayest morning, with the sun glinting on the stream, and all the tiny, ancient villages crowding to its waters, and suddenly, quite incomprehensibly, I felt happy. And I wrote this sonnet, which is not a good sonnet, but which I like, anyhow.

How grand it is this falling out of love—
This falling out of you into the world!
I had forgotten how the rivers move . . .
I had forgotten how a leaf is curled . . .
I think I had forgotten that the sun
Is warmer than the beaming of your eyes,
And that the inmost soul of anyone
Is not the sum of all the mysteries.
Now I can celebrate again the rites
Of the world's loving; share its ecstacies;
Melt to the phallic strength of Dolomites,
Warm to the manly tenderness of trees.

> Even for you my love may yet revive,
> Seeing you part of everything alive.

I believe I have fallen forever out of that love which grows into the flesh of another. The world is wide and beautiful, on Broadway and in Albania, despite Mussolini.

Rose, I would adore to see you . . . and talk . . . and talk . . . and talk . . .

Dorothy

Letter 16

January 21 [1928]

Dorothy,

You are a darling. It's sweet of you to write me so soon. It seemed to me, when I was writing to you, that I'd quite drown if you didn't. You know, that desperate going down for the last time. But aren't we amusing creatures? Apparently, the real trouble was only that I was tired. Three days ago I quit work, flat, just like that. Just like the taxi-chauffeur leaves the girl, in the imitation O. Henry stories. Next morning I awoke as usual, and said to myself, "No work!" "No work!" I cried, and the whole world turned a summer (or, somer) sault and came up rosy and beaming.

My head's stopped being in a vise.
My temper's stopped aching all along frazzled edges.
My griefs sort of curl away in the sun, like cigarette smoke.
I sleep—Oh, gorgeous, to *sleep.*
And the further catalogue of my felicities would be thicker than Sears Roebuck's, including dawns, and mountains and our Mediterranean weather and little Mr. Bunting's ridiculousness and many other delights.

Yes, I know. You are quite right about Albania. It is only another love affair ended.

Dorothy my dear, are we going to continue foretelling each other's future with such beautiful accuracy? Do, please, do tell me more of mine, someday when it occurs to you.

No darling, I shan't meet you—in the plural—in Sicily. Indeed no. Alas, I am grown old, and fond memory brings to view the days when I used to be simultaneously in love and hospitable. You are a sweet idiot. I—for the moment—amn't. No, no, it can't be done that way—being in love can't, I mean. All this reasonableness, this open-eyedness to faults, it's the same old thing, in reality, Dorothy: the same emotion, the same blindness, the same—oh, everything. Glorious. No one but you—in the plural—can possibly be gladder than I am that you're having it. But it isn't reasonable, not at all, not the tiniest bit. It isn't even humorous. (Humor, anyway, is only reasonableness, a-viewing-with-a-sense-of-proportion.) Are you sure that your attitude hasn't, in reality, just a little automatic self-protection in it? A little hedging of the bet? Perhaps I am wrong, only, as I look back, I see that mine had. And I used to put it to myself just as you are putting it now.

About Sicily, no, but wouldn't you, maybe, do this? Let me know when next you're in New York so that I can come in from the farm for one good long talk, not with a plural you, just with you? It isn't, you know, that I wouldn't love to know Sinclair Lewis, who is to me only a legendary figure. I would. I'm sure he's interesting, and amusing, and everything I'd love to go farther than Sicily to know. But not now. Later. It's so long since we talked, Dorothy; our vocabularies are changed a bit. We'll have to start with a little feeling around for definitions. After all, there are—do you realize it? My goodness!—something like eight years of varied living between us and the old talks, and you just beginning all the new talks with him. You can't do both, to any of our satisfactions, and then there's Sicily. No. But someday, when you know him well enough to forget him for a day—I mean, to let him go out of sight without taking the whole heart of your attention with him—then you and I can talk, and then I'd be happy with Mr. and Mrs. Sinclair Lewis. You see how greedy I am. It's Dorothy I want, though that doesn't say that I won't love Mrs. Lewis. Still, the two aren't identical, and no one in a group of three is the same person he (she, it) is in a group of two. No more than he is the same in a group of two as he is alone. There's a sort of chemistry in it, or something else equally magic.

The caravaning is perfect! It's my own, *own* dream—to go caravaning in England and Scotland and Wales. I got the idea ages ago from reading Elizabeth-in-the-German-Garden's *The Caravaners.*[1] Have you ever read that very best book for convalescents? It's almost worth being ill for. It really is delicious. And ever since, I have yearned to go caravaning in England. I added Scotland some years later, and I added Wales the last time I went with Lavengro to the border of Wales and didn't go in.[2] It struck me then. Wales! With my caravan, I *would* go in!

It's one of the dreams that will never come true for me. My caravan remains forever in the loveliest country of all. No, I don't mean that. I mean it only a little. I'm really not so pessimistic. Not when I'm working.

The heavenly release of not working!

We are going to Greece sometime in early March, principally for spring hats. Athens isn't so bad for shopping, and in a burst of I don't know what—not generosity—we gave away all last summer's hats when we left the Albanian House. So that we may find ourselves destined to arrive in New York May-hatless unless we do something about it. We are sailing on the 12th of April, on the Cosolich line.[3] Again, please don't mention this to *anyone at all.* I haven't said a word to anyone else. However, if you'll send me a line saying where you can be reached in Sicily? Because quite possibly the steamer stops somewhere near, and we might snatch a moment to wish each other well, in passing.

The Albanian House is really only leased. Maybe I will come back again, after all. I really do love Albania. You know how one hangs on—it isn't the same, it's horribly changed, and still—just to see the mountains, and the little quiet valleys, and the red-roofed towns with their white minarets. My heart's really nothing but a wail all these days. Yes, the world is always beautiful, but I can't quite hold that pitch at which one sees the beauty even in its treachery. Sometimes I do, but not consistently. The fault of course, is in us, in our arrogance. We shouldn't try to impose our own patterns on anything, not on anything; we should be more passive, more open-eyed to everything and accepting. Unless ye become as a little child . . .

It's our attempts to be adult, to be *directing*—impossibility!—that do us in.

Your sonnet—yes, I like it too. It is true, and it is almost *quite* beautiful. My own song is a tag of magazine verse which I read somewhere long ago, when I was married and expected always to be. Most of it I forget, and none of it is worth remembering, but I always have remembered it—remembered, I mean, these fragments:

Now that you are gone, loving lips, loving hands,
Now I can go back to love—
I can run and stand in the wind on the hill,
Now that I am lone and free,
Whistle through the dark and the cleansing chill,
All my red-winged dreams to me.[4]

As I said, not worth remembering. But it said something for me that I never could say better for myself.

About your sonnet. Most of it is too beautiful to be so selfishly kept only for yourself. Can't you rewrite it, just a bit? Can't you kill (1st line) "grand"; (6th line) "beaming"; (11th line) "melt"? All the other lines are quite, quite right. If you would do all of those over, and also the 12th. The 11th and the 12th lines convey the idea, the emotion, but with, somehow, a lack of the clean, clear, swift precision of the others. I think perhaps it's not only "melt," but also "strength" in the 11th line, that doesn't *quite*—the meaning of the word is right, but the *feeling* of the word—the *word,* itself—is somehow woolly, fuzzy. "Strength": it's a word that has the consistency, the color, the texture, of a light gray blanket. Like "melt," *il n'est pas assorti aux* "Dolomite" *et* "phallic". (How does one exactly express *assorti* in English? Isn't there any way, or have I only forgotten it? Anyway, to continue—)[5] Phallic and dolomite are excellent, and the idea is superb. But you can express the idea with much more clarity. Those are your great qualities: precision, delicacy, clarity, with a quite terrific *force* of emotion. In the 12th line you get a weakness with the repeated "a" in "warm" and "manly." Both those words are weak anyway. And you don't save the line with "tenderness," three-syllabled on "e" and ending in the double "s." The only word in the line that stands up is the final one, and it can't carry the sagging weight of all the rest. "Trees" with the "t" and the coming-down-hard stress on the long double "e" is strong. It can carry a lot. But not quite that much. Go out and *feel* trees again, until out of that emotion which isn't like any other, the right words come up into your mind. But not the olives—I've a notion they *are* olives—of Sicily. What you want is pines, pines or oaks.

Dorothy, my dear, I beg you, don't leave that sonnet as it is and keep it only for yourself. Clear away these little roughnesses, these bits of clay still clinging to it, make it the quite perfect thing it is in your thought, your feeling, and then publish it.

You should be a practicing poet, anyway. You always have been a poet, you know. Just because you excel all your contemporary journalists in seeing and getting and handling facts, you seem to think that you're pre-eminently a practical person. So you are, but that's only a by-product of the whole you. I'm not the only person who would thank God for a little more seeing of the world through your eyes—and not because you see economic tendencies in Russia, either.

There has never been anyone else like you, for clearing away this muddle in which I struggle to live, for somehow giving me fresh air, and light, and the freedom to be me. There may be a man who can love on a hill in the wind, one who won't clutch and cling and muddle—you see, I'm *really* not entirely pessimistic!—and if there is, I hope you've got him. As to keeping him forever, I can imagine nothing more wonderful than always *wanting* to keep a man; it really doesn't seem so important, whether one does it or not. It's this not wanting to keep them, and yet not quite being able to disentangle one's self, never quite having the ruthlessness to strike the hands on the gunwale with an oar till they let go—that's the horrible thing. That's always my ending, as, once, it was yours. Because that was really the fact, really your trouble for so long. There's a divine obstinacy in you, that won't let go of the dream.

Oh well—

You will be coming to The States? Of course, sometime. Do let me know when, let me meet you in New York, or in San Francisco. Oh, San Francisco is the city for you! San Francisco might have been made by the gods expressly for you. I can't—as you're perfectly aware!—help low growls in the throat whenever I even think of your embarking in love again—though irrationally at the same time, I'm glad you are—but I will forgive Sinclair Lewis, I will melt into grateful fondness for him, if he will take you to San Francisco and build you a house on a hill above the bay. San Francisco, or Sausalito, or Carmel-by-the-Sea. Well, perhaps not build, renting will do. It's the only part of The States that builds most of the qualities we love in Europe into the new civilization. It's the one place on the globe that's made for you—for, I should think, both of you. A combination of beauty and plumbing. And how much there is to be said for both!

Reams, as usual. This is a new typewriter, learning to be talkative.

God bless you,
Rose

---

1. Mary Annette Russell (1866–1941) was the author of *Elizabeth and Her German Garden* (1898) and *The Caravaners* (1909).

2. The reference again is to George Borrow's *Lavengro,* whose narrator travels England under gypsy inspiration. See Letter 10.

3. Rose's plans changed suddenly. From her diary for this period, we can infer that a cablegram from her mother announced some crisis which precipitated an immediate departure from Albania on January 26, 1928.

4. I have not been able to identify this poem.

5. Idiomatically, the French would translate to say that *melt* just doesn't go with *Dolomite* and *phallic.*

Letter 17

June 25 [1928]
Salisbury
Old George Inn

My dear Rose,

Hal is asleep, "next door," in this rambling old English inn where next door means around a corner and up a tiny flight of stairs, and there, where a small door looks as though it would have 00 on it[1]—that's one's husband's room. And its other door goes into a stately hall, but if you start from there you must make a Cook's tour to get to your room (which is neither here nor there, except that when one is rather much married the decision of one's husband to go to sleep at nine o'clock is an excellent stimulus to letter-writing).

Dear Rose: you write the delightfulest letters in the world; also you say the thing one wants to hear: that—for instance—one is not a journalist but a poet. I know, of course, that I am a most extraordinarily good journalist, and that I am a most extraordinarily bad poet, but because I do, probably, feel life poetically, I would rather hear those words than any others. But do not make the mistake that all who feel and perceive with artists' hearts are poets. "Die Wille zu Liebe ist Liebe noch nicht," as Werfel makes Maximilian, the king, say to himself, acknowledging defeat.[2]

I need a collaborator. I really think that's why I go around marrying. I am sure I saw in Josef Bard a creative talent to express my own creative instinct and will, and with quite glorious zeal devoted myself to making for him the atmosphere and mood to write my books for me; hence he used them to fornicate artistically with my friends, ran away with a beautiful English creature, and—then—wrote an extremely good novel, and I say it although I and all my friends merely furnish copy for gentle ridicule.[3] Now, for a change, I have married me a demon, who writes as never I could write, but seeing life from an angle ever so foreign: all his values topsy-turvy from mine. And—at present—I feel as though I should never write anything again, neither reports on Russia nor sonnets to record the soul's travail, the soul's ironic victories. I cook, my dear, in the caravan. But I cook well. "What's worth doing at all—" my father used to say.

This, Rose, is a strange country. England, I'll bet you it's stranger than Albania. I know a man who works all day in the *Daily Telegraph,* writing—sometimes brilliantly—of books and politics, and every night he comes back to a village whose chief distinction is that all the little girls can stand on their heads. And he doesn't think it's funny. He's proud of it. I don't know when the first little girl went into reverse and started the custom which has been practiced ever since on the village green, but it's a tradition. The British will go on doing *anything* once they've started. The funny thing is they can almost persuade the whole world to join them. But if only they'd discover that something else can be done with heads besides stand on them: nobody *thinks* in England except a few Irishmen, Scotsmen, and Jews, and once in a while some upstart from the lower classes who wasn't taught early enough that it isn't done. "Thank God the Prince of Wales isn't an intellectual," said someone writing in the *Express* last Sunday, thus paying Britain's hope and pride the ultimate compliment. Did you ever think that the whole moral of Wodehouse's stories and Lonsdale's plays is that the canny Britisher keeps a butler or valet to think for him? H. G. Wells' mother was a lady's maid and blood always tells.[4]

We have stopped caravaning for a week, while Hal writes and I darn his socks.

Did I say that one reason I'm glad I'm going home and that

we're going to buy a house-with-lawns-surrounding-it is that then—as I dream—you'll come and stay with me a *long time* and we'll talk.

and talk
and talk—Rose
and Dorothy

---

1. The oo allusion is not clear; perhaps she refers to the diminutive size of the door and room.

2. Franz Werfel (1890–1945), German novelist and playwright, is best known for his novel *The Song of Bernadette* (1942). He was the author of the play *Juarez und Maximilian* (1924), which Dorothy cites here. This line, which is from scene 12, may be translated as "The will to love still is not love."

3. Josef Bard married the "English creature," Eileen Agar; the marriage was long and satisfactory (Sanders, *Dorothy Thompson,* p. 106). In 1928 he published *Shipwreck in Europe,* which contains satiric portraits of both Dorothy and Rose.

4. P. G. Wodehouse (1881–1975) wrote many stories of Bertie Wooster and the incomparable butler, Jeeves. Frederick Lonsdale (1881–1954) was the author of a number of sprightly drawing-room comedies in the 1920s.

Part III

Letters 18–35 (1928–1932)

Introduction to Part III

This series of letters covers the period between Dorothy Thompson's marriage to Sinclair Lewis in 1928 and her next step on the ascent to fame, the renown that would reflect on her from the award of the Nobel Prize for literature to Lewis in 1930.

Both women had returned to the United States at this time. Rose had given up her Albanian venture and had come back to her parents' home in the Missouri Ozarks—an act of filial responsibility. Dorothy had given up her Berlin appointment with the *Philadelphia Public Ledger* to make a new life with her new husband.[1] Ahead lay an undetermined future as free-lance journalist and, again, an intention to subordinate her own career to the greater talents of her husband. It was an attitude that Rose found dangerous, and she said so.

The diverging lines of their separate careers had by this time become clear. Rose was intermittently and often profoundly unhappy with her apparently inescapable duty to remain with her aging parents. Dorothy, both wealthy and famous by virtue of her marriage to Lewis, had as her province all of the United States and Europe. Yet Rose continued to be generous in her support and friendly offices—not only in the matter of Dorothy's pregnancy, but also, where she could, in forwarding Dorothy's career. As the Lewises visited California, Rose wrote to introduce her to her old friend and editor, Fremont Older of the *San Francisco Bulletin:* "To me," Rose wrote to Older, ". . . she's one of the most beautiful of living creatures."[2]

Nonetheless, the gulf their friendship had to bridge was growing by any measure. Nothing marks the distance more clearly than the arrangements made when the Nobel Prize was awarded to Lewis: Dorothy was free to travel to Stockholm with her husband because Rose came to Connecticut to care for Dorothy's baby.

In October 1930, Rose had gone to New York City to visit friends and to confer with publishers. She was there when the Nobel Prize was announced in November, and she was on hand to aid as Dorothy prepared for the trip to Stockholm. A letter to her mother gives a picture of Dorothy's hectic days:

> I've just spent the afternoon and evening with Dorothy; she's had ten teeth out and is a wreck, not to mention having to buy a complete

> wardrobe for the trip to Sweden, and see editors, and wind up the affairs of three households before sailing on the 29th. And she has to go to Philadelphia tomorrow to see the Curtis people, after getting her new teeth in the morning, and the P.E.N. is giving an official dinner for Hal on Tuesday. And I don't know what else. I never saw a person so busy, in bed at her hotel with a nurse on one side changing dressings on her gums, and a telephone at her ear and messengers coming and going and packages being delivered and telegrams arriving. She is going from Sweden on into Russia, and then out to Germany where she will join Hal again. He's going to England while she goes into Russia.

Clearly Rose had already agreed to take charge of Dorothy's household and her five-month-old son, Michael. The Lewises had temporarily taken the house of columnist Franklin P. Adams. "I'm going up to Westport with Dorothy tonight," Rose continued, "to look over the house and the staff. I think it's going to be rather fun being there, for one thing because all the servants are French, which will keep up my French. And it's only an hour from New York so that I can come in often, and having two cars and a chauffeur is going to make getting about very easy."[3]

Thus began a three-month labor of love. As Dorothy extended her European trip to revisit Germany and Austria on the advent of Hitler's rise to power, Rose supervised a household that ran less smoothly than she was willing to report. Tension was high between her and the staff, according to her diary: "I'm a fool," she noted briefly at one point. Meanwhile, her ministrations included sending pictures of the infant Michael Lewis to Stockholm and reporting the child's weight gain since Christmas in a New Year's Eve cablegram to Dorothy in Berlin. She met the Lewises at the boat dock and shortly thereafter returned to Missouri.[4] She had been away from home for five months.

We begin this period with Rose's reply to Dorothy's letter recounting her honeymoon trip. Rose found Dorothy's self-abnegation in this second marriage a frightening reversion to her marriage to Josef Bard; and her analysis of Dorothy's situation was so frank and detailed that, upon reflection, she did not send the first version of the letter. It remained, however, in her files; and when read with the second version that Dorothy did receive, it affords a fascinating subtext to Rose's more diplomatic efforts to rescue her friend from a destructive delusion.

1. Sanders, *Dorothy Thompson,* part V.
2. Rose Wilder Lane to Fremont Older, Feb. 25, 1930 (Bancroft Library, University of California–Berkeley).
3. Rose Wilder Lane to Laura Ingalls Wilder, undated [Nov., 1930].
4. Diary entries, Oct. 16, 1930, to March 20, 1931. The cablegram is in the Syracuse University Library.

Letter 18

July 11, 1928

Dear Dorothy,

Your letter has come, and I am happy to have a word from you. I got it at the village post office, stopping there on my way home after driving Genevieve Parkhurst[1] to the next town to catch an express going to California. Strangely enough (though these things happen so often that I don't know why we call them strange) we had talked of you all the way to her train.

She's been here a week, with a novel of hers that's half done, and—as usual—a score of ideas for special articles. She'll stop in Reno for a month or so, her younger daughter being occupied in getting a divorce there, and then she'll go on to the Coast for the remainder of a three months' trip. Meantime I am supposed to be working at full pressure ahead. Of course, it is not *impossible* that I might.

Otherwise for news there is only the item that Troub[2] has just lately had an impacted wisdom tooth out, and has suffered more agonies than the damned for longer than a week, part of that time with the assistance of morphine. She's better now, though, and also contemplates an attack of industrious literary production.

If anything could make me work, it should be the suggestion with which your letter ends, of a long talk with you. Genevieve also wants me to come East sometime this fall or early winter. I should, but so many thousands of words lie between me and such liberty.

There is a horrible little doubt in my mind, dear Dorothy. Shall I be able to talk to you? Your letter has truly made me unhappy, for it isn't a letter from you. Did you know that, I wonder? You go farther away, for in all the years that you did not write to me, at least you were there. Your silence hurt, but it hurt only me—a hurt that was in comparison, only a little thing and superficial. Now you write, and *you* are gone. This is more than a personal matter, a thing between you and me or any of your other friends. It's a break between you and the world that was yours, the world you created—I say it so badly. Where does the light of the candle go when it is blown out? I am afraid to meet the person who wrote me this letter, not because I doubt that Dorothy is still there, but because I know my own inadequacies, my clumsiness and shyness in personal contacts, I know that I won't be able to speak to you, extinguished. And I so desperately feel that you *should* be reached, set burning again. Your light means too much, is too rare, precious, to be lost. I know it won't be, it can't be. It will revive, someday. But the years go past—time is the real enemy—and time has stolen from you so many years already.

I have no right to write such things to you; resent them if you must. Whatever there has been between us, as persons, as friends, is less important to me than the resurrection of the precious and rare person that you are. And I must write. For if you meet me as you have written this last letter to me, I shall be able to say nothing to you, nothing worth saying.

I am not making the mistake of thinking that all who feel and perceive with artists' hearts are poets. You are a poet because you perceive and feel and express. Perhaps not in sonnets; it may be that the metrical forms are not your medium. I've seen only one sonnet of yours, and it had flaws, though it was beautiful. When I say a poet, I mean the word in the French sense, more general and more precise than ours. You have not written one paragraph in a letter to me (until this last letter) that was not the essence of poetry beautifully expressed. You have a feeling for form that appears spontaneously in everything you touch. But even if you hadn't, even if expression were, with you, awkward and ungainly, your spirit would transform it.

You don't need a collaborator. Collaboration of any kind in the expressing of yourself would be a hindrance to you. My God, Dorothy, you're not a police reporter with an idea for a dramatic detective story that you can't write. You're a sensitive person, with an infinite delicacy and precision of perception, and exquisite grace in expression. You have all the gifts, and are you going to be wrecked and ruined by a humility which in your blindness you sincerely feel—a humility absolutely false, a damnable lie? A thousand times I have said in my soul that if I could kill Josef Bard I would do it. The harm he did to you was, from the first, immeasurable; it was a devastation. There was nothing we could do about it in all those years. But now that he's gone out of your personal life, are you going to let the harm he did to you continue?

It was your very fineness that made you his victim; a cruder person with nothing to save would have resisted him on his own ground and never been, essentially, touched by him at all. He captured you by a reflection of values, partly your own and partly a heritage of old European cultures. He was (perhaps not altogether consciously) shrewd enough to utilize the advantage that an apparent superiority gave him. Because he knew things that you didn't know, because, as a European, he had a background that you didn't have, he was able to impress upon you your own inferiority. It was never in any respect a real inferiority. As human beings, there was no comparison possible between you. In tradition, the only difference between you was that he was a few centuries behind you. As a European, he was nearer the sources of a common culture and therefore knew them better; as a European, he knew languages and histories and variations of culture. It was an accident of environment that equipped him with these things that, to us as Americans, seem valuable. To him as the European, they appeared to be exactly what, today, they are: a heritage from a great past to a weakling present, of no value whatever except as last weapons against an inevitably conquering civilization-of-tomorrow that has nothing whatever to do with them. He used them against you. Didn't he? I know nothing at all about it, as you will realize. But did he ever overlook an opportunity to impress upon you, directly or subtly by implication, your American inferiority to him? Didn't he keep clearly in your mind your own essentially inferior position—the American, clever money-maker; the American, well enough as a mere journalist; the American, from crude, mercenary, ill-bred America? While all the time, in reality, which of you was mercenary, money-seeking, crude, ill-bred?

Of course, he hated you. He hated you from the first; it was obvious even in Budapest,[3] before you married him. He hated you because you were superior, and he knew it. I don't mean that he didn't love you. I know nothing about that, he probably did.

But even then he was revenging himself upon you because of his own sense of inferiority, and because there was something in you too fine for him to reach. Anyone could have foretold then—anyone undazzled by emotions—that he would use every weapon he had to frustrate any real expression of yourself in any artistic work. His only hope of maintaining any ascendancy over you was in continuing to convince you of your inferiority to him. You saw in him everything that was not there, including that creative spirit. The creative spirit is *yours.* And he succeeded in maintaining that ascendancy over you to the point where the struggle became too much for him and he collapsed, gave it up, got away. Even with your own will consenting, you couldn't so submerge and deny your own qualities that he could ever in his soul feel anything but immeasurably your inferior. That was the trouble between you and Josef Bard.

And even now you aren't free of him. There's trace of the harm he did you in everything you say about him in this paragraph under my eyes. "With quite glorious zeal devoted myself to making for him the atmosphere and means to write my books for me; hence he used them to fornicate artistically with my friends, ran away with a beautiful English creature and—then—wrote an extremely good novel—" That is not your voice. What trace of European slime combines in your mind fornication and art? You do not mean the phrase; it is an echo on your lips. And so far as that goes, his methods were those of the barnyard fowl. He exaggerated vulgarity and crudity, and he did that because his real motive was to revenge himself on *you,* to insult *you,* to have momentarily the sensation of dragging you down to his own level, debasing his wife in debasing himself and all women. He was a very unhappy man, and had he done to me what he did to you, I would have no more resentment in my heart than you have. But he did it to you, and that I shall never forgive. His novel is not extremely good. It is a fair enough novel as novels go, and it is amusing. It does not compare to any novel you would write. It has no feeling of beauty in it, it has no truth. It is a superficially clever and sophisticated thing, it is marred here and there—as most novels of the sort are—by a conscious smart-alecky-ness. And its motive is still revenge on you and on your friends. He wrote it to show you that he can write, that it was only your mediocrity that stifled him, and to say that your sexual morals are not better than his. And, incidentally in passing, to indicate that my easy virtue was also complaisant—he has not forgotten that I ordered him out of my room in the Duna Palota[4] in the middle of one of his dirty stories. He would, however, have forgotten it if he hadn't connected me in his mind with you as one of your friends of those days. This, my dear, is *not* "gentle ridicule." It is the struggle of an inferior person's love for another that he knows to be infinitely his superior. It is the old desire-for-power motif in psychology. He will not write another novel; or, if he does, it will be completely a poor thing.[5]

This is a terrible letter to write to you. Hate me for it if you must. I can not be silent and let the person you are and may be get lost completely. All these years I have said nothing. It is your life, your emotions, and I said to myself that I should not interfere. Also, I always knew that your marriage with Josef Bard could not last, that it would end someday, that you would come out of it stronger and clearer for having had the experience. I trusted your sense of values, your perception of beauty, everything that is the essential Dorothy. I still trust them. Good God, has Josef Bard succeeded in shaking your own trust in them? I will not believe it. I insist that this letter from you is an accident. I say that you are momentarily bewildered—excited and a little shaken in collision with stimulating "foreign values"—and that it is inevitable that the swiftness, precision, passion and delicacy of your perceptions lead you to take your color, momentarily, temporarily, from new places and persons near you. But I am terrified. It is this swift admission of inferiority that terrifies me. This "I am a most extraordinary good journalist, and . . . a most extraordinarily bad poet, but because I do, *probably,* feel life poetically—" This, "I need a collaborator—" And, my dear, three pages about England that are interesting and amusing enough, and only half true—not at all *true,* that is to say, as your letters have always been true—with no beauty in them. This is the first time I had ever had so much as a scrap of a note from you that denies *you.* I swear that it is an accident, that it must be an accident.

I do very much want you to be happy. But what does it profit a man if he gain the whole world and lose his own soul? So many souls aren't worth the trouble of saving, at that. But I knew you when you were young and proud and gay, and true to yourself as easily and instinctively as the compass is true to the north. And everything that is essentially you is a thousand times worth saving. Everything you have to say is worth saying, and you can say it. Don't tell me that you cannot say it; that is a lie. It doesn't matter how much you lie to me, but are you going to turn that lie upon yourself? Have those years with Josef Bard so shaken that instinctive truth to yourself that you no longer know your own value? Who are you measuring yourself by, what alien scale of measurement finds you so inadequate? There was a time when you did not stop at the shores of the Atlantic to think of Will Irwin[6] and say that you could never be a European correspondent for an American newspaper. Why are you stopping now to look at Shakespeare and Goethe and Dante and say that you are an extraordinarily bad poet? Can you ever write a novel like the novels of Thomas Mann or Virginia Woolf? Of course you can't. The only novels you can ever write are the novels by Dorothy Thompson. The world is full of artists of whom you can say, they "write as never I could write." And every one of them can say the same of you.

Of course, it isn't really the books that matter so much. Perhaps it isn't. I don't know. There was a time when beauty meant so much to you that the book you can write if you will would have meant more to you than anything else. There is always beauty—all the lost beauty that is never seen because the one person who saw it didn't make it visible to the rest of us. But, perhaps—I don't know—this is a matter for the conscience, which may not judge that it is a sin for the artist to be silent. Be silent if you like. It wouldn't be your silence that would so hurt and terrify me. There are as many ways of expression as there are moments in a day. You know what it is that frightens me for you, in this letter of yours. And I wouldn't be frightened, if it weren't for that echo of Josef Bard, that self-deprecation. It becomes too dangerously, too deeply, sincere; it goes so much more deeply than I ever feared it would. it makes you speak in a strange voice, no longer Dorothy.

Forgive me if you can.

The original of this letter is in the Hoover Presidential Library.

1. Genevieve Parkhurst was editor of *Pictorial Review.* Her novel, *Headlong* (New York, Holt & Co.), was published in 1931.

2. Helen ("Troub") Boylston, who had been Rose's companion in Albania, was also living with Rose at Rocky Ridge Farm at this time.

3. Rose had visited Dorothy in Budapest in early February 1922, according to her diary for that period.

4. The Duna Palota was a hotel in Budapest.

5. Josef Bard did not publish another novel.

6. Will Irwin (1873–1948) was a well-known journalist and free-lance writer; most notable in this reference was his renown as war correspondent (1916–1918) for the *Saturday Evening Post*.

Letter 19

Rocky Ridge Farm
Mansfield, Missouri
July 13, 1928

Dear Dorothy,

Your letter arrived day before yesterday. I got it from the post office on my return from driving Genevieve Parkhurst to the next village to catch her train westward. She has been here a week, full of ideas for special articles, as usual, and bearing with her a novel of her own which is half-finished and most promising. She's now on her way to Reno, where her daughter is getting a divorce, and then will spend the remainder of a three month's trip on the Coast. As it happened, all the way to Cedar Gap we were talking of you.

My dear, your letter was a bombshell to me. I am convinced that you are terribly mistaken about many important things. All day yesterday I wrote to you, but this morning I do not venture to send the letter. I am very much troubled; years ago in Budapest I was silent, and I still do not know whether I should have spoken, brutally and impertinently, or not. Whether it would have made any difference, whether you would have—or should have—forgiven an intrusion of this particularly uncalled-for kind. It isn't, of course, your forgiveness that is most important. If unforgivable things said would make any difference, would perhaps have altered the direction of your life somewhat—and again, if such an alteration would have been better for you—? In any case, I do not send the letter which is my real answer to yours. You once asked for my advice, and I gave it, and it made no difference.[1] At least, now I may as well refrain from thrusting upon you a counsel not asked for. Is this, my dear, the right attitude in one who sees the blindfolded on the chasm's edge—yet may herself be walking among hallucinations?

There is no news of us to tell you. It is hay-making time on the farm—a time and a place which would have charmed three persons walking long ago in the valley of the Loire.[2] Troub has recently had out an impacted wisdom tooth, and for a week suffered more than the damned, part of the time eased a bit by morphine. She is recovered now, however, and contemplates a period of intensive literary production—in a green tent on a hillside, in which we create a momentary illusion of Albania with the ritual of coffee-making. I also should be working, Genevieve having gone away under the happy impression that masterpieces for *Pictorial* will flow abundantly from my typewriter. But Carl Brandt and the Curtis people[3] have also these anticipations—of which it is so true to say that anticipation is better than realization. At least, it is Pollyanna to think so, since anticipation is mostly all that any of us have, in regard to my future works. I ask myself, "why am I so lazy?" and am too lazy to reply. It is, perhaps, enough to be happy, and it's true that the only crumpled rose-leaf is this laziness. And a letter from you, and a reply not sent—two briary bed-fellows.

Be happy, my dear. I, too, am a good cook. Be happy, and come home to a country which may not quite be God's own (since we have abolished God) but is most certainly the greatest country on His footstool. Come home to your house in green lawns. And perhaps we shall talk there—if I am not too shy.

Much love, as always,
Rose

---

1. This allusion presumably is to the letter, now missing, that Rose wrote in 1921. See Letter 3, n. 3.

2. This memory persists at the center of their friendship. The walking trip was Jan. 1–3, 1921, with writer Kate Horton as the third. See Letters 43 and 44.

3. Carl Brandt was Rose's agent at this time; the Curtis Publishing Company published *The Saturday Evening Post* and *The Ladies' Home Journal*.

Letter 20

In a field, again next to
Hugh Walpole (and, thank
God, sharing the
amenities of his house).
Keswick, Cumberland
July 23 [1928]

Oh, Rose,

Oh, Rose, because of that letter that you did *not* send. In answer to mine, which to quote the one you *did* send, "was like a bombshell," uttering, as it did, matters in which you think me "terribly mistaken." You can imagine the mental suffering I am going through because I cannot remember, to save my life, what I *said* in the bombshell letter. Your letters, dear Rose, I can always remember—even those you wrote very long ago, but I never can remember my own. I take it that I uttered views on life and perhaps on marriage, because you recall wanting to tell me once, in Budapest, where I was going off.

But what *were* those views, one month ago, when I wrote that letter? Because I have so many views on both, and like one of the brothers Karamazov (I forget which) I "find myself constantly capable of holding two diametrically opposite ideas at the same time."[1] So, if the opposite one of the one uttered will save me, take it that I am holding it at this time. "Curiosity," says E. M. Forster in *Aspects of the Novel* (an admirable book; a beautiful book): "Curiosity," he says, in one of those asides which have ostensibly nothing to do with the novel, "is . . ." just here I have been looking for the book, to get the quotation right, but that louse of a husband has eaten it up. The metaphor is mixed. *Mouse* of a husband would have been more *apropos* to the crime (but not of the husband). Anyhow, Mr. Forster thinks curiosity an attribute of a fourth-rate mind;[2] this confirms me in my opinion of my own. I am wonderfully curious about that last letter of mine and your true reaction.

Everyone, I think, is always terribly mistaken about marriage. I myself can never make my theories harmonize with my practice. In *this* marriage I am—most of the time—vastly entertained. This can be put down as a *constant.*

Dear Rose—this letter is a handclasp. I want to keep on having you. You *do* answer letters; you keep alive one of the almost lost arts: my end is not more than an encouragement. And nearly three months of a bucolic life has quenched whatever wit may have abode in me, one time or another. If I search the horizon for inspiration it reveals a baahing sheep and a neighing cow, or whatever cows do. Wordsworth, Southey, Coleridge celebrate the mountains which face us beyond the musical kine, but this fact cannot make them appear to me other than rather wooly hills; not like the rosy Dolomites nor the mysterious, forested mountains of the Tirol[3] that I love.

Our plans are—for us—quite clear. They are to sail on August 18th; go immediately to Connecticut to Harcourt,[4] and stay in the cot he has offered us until October. Then we move into New York into a flat and stay there for the winter. By spring we hope to have found the perfect house in the perfect place. The thought of America terrifies me, and your letter was a comfort. It came along with one from dear old Junius Wood, the *Chicago Daily News* correspondent from Moscow, who has been covering the conventions[5] at home and whose picture of America is, to say the least, horrifying. The next six months confront me with problems too complex for words: to find a place in N.Y., to find a permanent home. Hal—he is in *such* good shape, and I am *so* afraid of New York—America *überhaupt*[6]—and *drink.* And *my* work. What? How? Where? I wish you were to be within calling distance.

Hugh Walpole, by the way, is quite the nicest of Hal's friends whom I have met over here. He lives in a very sweet little house, just up the road, and is a gentle and humane soul; we've had many charming days together.

Yes, we must meet and *talk.* What do you mean shy? Neither of us will ever be more shy with each other than such nice people as we are normally are.

Dorothy

[Letter includes drawings by Sinclair Lewis and Dorothy Thompson of themselves. Lewis annotates his "Me: I'm thinner 'n' hell." Dorothy's reads, "Me: I'm fatter 'n' hell." There follows Dorothy's postscript.]

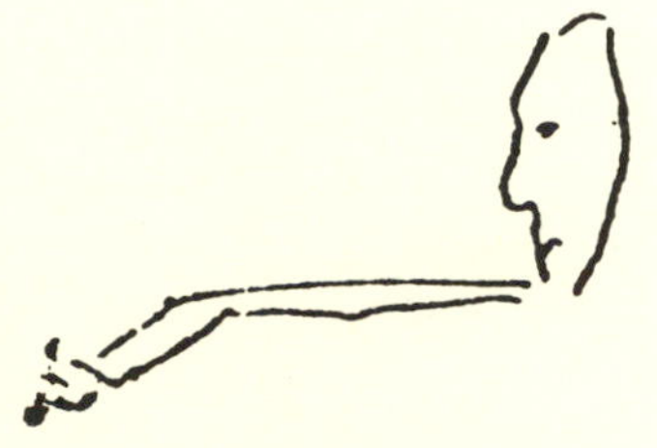

Only Hal's nose goes the other way. I've discovered that I'm really in love with Hal. I *like* his looks. Objective critics consider this a sure sign. Seriously, Rose, I probably wrote you three-fourths nonsense. I have sometimes horrible throwbacks—they're less and less often. Life *was* a nightmare.

—D.

---

1. Dorothy apparently is thinking of the remarks concerning Dmitri's character during his trial; see Fyodor Dostoyevsky, *The Brothers Karamazov,* trans. Constance Garnett (New York: Modern Library, n.d), part 4, book XII, chap. 6 (p. 741) and chap. 11 (p. 775).
2. "Curiosity is one of the lowest of the human faculties." E. M. Forster, *Aspects of the Novel* (New York: Harcourt Brace, 1927), p. 131.
3. The mountains Dorothy views in the Lake District are the Pennine Chain. The Dolomite Alps are in northern Italy; the Tirol is in western Austria.
4. Alfred Harcourt of Harcourt, Brace & Company, Lewis's publishers.
5. The 1928 conventions nominated Herbert Hoover and Alfred E. Smith.
6. America generally.

Letter 21

Rocky Ridge Farm
Mansfield, Missouri
August 9, 1928

Dorothy darling,

I'm in the middle of the most hellish story that ever refused to be written, and this is the end of a perfect imperfection of a day—except for your letter.

It's the lost art I love most and most regret in its passing. (Ref. to letter writing.) But caught in these cog- wheels. . . .

Only, I hasten to say that my dark direfulness had nothing whatever to do with marriage. Who am I—whose memories of experiencing it are so dim that I hardly remember I have them—to send opinions about it to you? Indeed, I haven't any opinions about marriage, any more. Is it a thing to have opinions about? All I've ever had, I suspect, were a few personal prejudices. (Not the word; shouldn't I say postjudices? Never mind; no mind, that is to say, after a day like this one that's going away in the smothering gloom of thunderclouds at the moment.)

And anyway, even I wouldn't be so impertinent as to shed my gray locks by hand, over a marriage I know nothing about, and trust to be all for the best in the best of all known worlds. His nose *does* appear charming, and mutual acquaintances tell me he has red hair. The only alarm in this letter is fatness. *Bant,* Dorothy dear, *bant.*[1] Live upon pickles and chalk—Byron did. Wasn't it Byron?[2] This I can say about your marriage: better that it end in tragedies that will restore your girlish figure than continue in the laughter that makes fatness. Now, *here's* something I've got real convictions about!

An answer to your letter will appear when this seventy-times-seven accursed story is gone to its destined place.[3] Send me your address. Please, SEND ME YOUR ADDRESS. Welcome home. America's all it's said to be, but there's no other place like it on this amazing earth. Be happy. AND SEND ME YOUR ADDRESS.

RWL

P.S. I have the letter I didn't send you.

---

1. The obscure term *bant,* meaning to diet by avoiding sweets and carbohydrates, derives from William Banting, the nineteenth-century English writer and undertaker who was identified with the regimen.

2. Byron's dieting was notorious for its oddities; see Leslie A. Marchand, *Byron: A Biography* (3 vols.; New York: Knopf, 1957), 1:254–60, 3:1095.

3. Rose's journal for this period identifies the story as "Gypsy Trail," published in *Ladies' Home Journal* in February 1929.

Letter 22

August 14, 1928

Darling,

I emerge from the dark deep curseful depths of a struggle with that story (now, Mashallah![1] on its way to New York) with a roar in my mouth. A roar about Forster, whose book on the novel I haven't yet seen, though I've ordered it, and whose exact words I don't know, owing to your omnivorous husband. But what, I ask, rearing, does he mean by saying that curiosity is an attribute of a fourth rate mind? *Mya gaosh,* as Yvonne[2] used to say in moments of such profanity that French wouldn't satisfy her. Curiosity's our only salvation. Wrench curiosity from us, and we'll be as happy as the animals. Curiosity's the source of science, it's the source (because it creates imagination) of art, it's the force behind almost all of our essentially human activities. Prehistoric peoples didn't migrate to find another food supply (in spite of that general explanation given now); they migrated to find out what was on the other side of the horizon. That's evident enough, when we consider what's today the source of all such migrations. Marco Polo went to Tartary to see what it was like. The barbarians sacked Rome because they couldn't stand any longer their curiosity to see it—curiosity merely exasperated by rumor—and when they saw it, they didn't know what else to do with it but sack it. America was settled largely because people were mad with curiosity to see a new world. All this, you say, doesn't apply to Forster's statement that curiosity's the attribute of a fourth-rate mind.

My protest is really against this habit of the intellectuals, of discarding the essentially *human* attributes as beneath their own high level of intelligence. It isn't a high level, when it does that. He might as well say that hunger's an attribute of a fourth-rate body. Curiosity's the hunger of the human mind. This attitude of disdain toward "merely vulgar curiosity" is the gourmet's disdain of a middle-western breakfast. It's the cushioned comfort of withdrawal from human realities. Let the gourmet work in a Kansas harvest field for a week or two. The end of most of our "intellectuals" is sterility because of this narrowing, this withdrawal. Because of this snobbish refusal to admit common origins, common meanings, the essential identity beneath the whole sordid magnificent comedy-tragedy of humanity. When Kipling says, "How shall I turn from any man where'er his hearth-fires shine, when"—I forget—"when all that comes to him at his, will come to me, at mine?",[3] the intellectual sneers at Kipling, who, Heaven knows, gives us enough reason for sneering. But it's exactly that lack in the intellectual that makes him, after all, negligible. Unimportant. The wholly complete mind, if it could exist, would recognize that the fourth-rate mind is merely one-fourth of the first-rate mind, which itself is no greater than the sum of its parts.

I write to you on a summer morning just a little mellowing to autumn. It is now exactly twenty-nine minutes past eight o'clock, Central Standard Time. I am so informed by the voice of The Banker's Trust, Des Moines, Iowa, speaking with authority through the radio. This is our Victor Record Programme, which has just given us a selection from *Rigoletto,* and now proceeds to render something truly astonishing by a jew's harp, a banjo, and a quartet in combination. This preoccupation with time is astounding. When the jew's harp ceases, we shall be informed that it is now exactly twenty-one and one-half minutes to nine, Central Standard Time. Dorothy dear, don't listen to what anyone tells you about The States. (No, not even what I may from time to time tell you!) Listen to this country. There was never anything like it. It's a complete break with everything that's gone before. It's a real pioneering into the future. The whole quarrel with it—Oh, these little, querulous, complaining voices, these futile protests, wings of gnats disliking the cyclone!—the whole quarrel with it is precisely that it pioneers, that it doesn't remain quietly and properly at home in the past. The truth is, that we can have no standards by which to judge it. It can only be judged by its own standards, and it hasn't yet sufficiently *become* to be able to state its principles. That sentence itself reveals our inadequacy; in spite of all efforts, I can't speak of America in terms of America; I assume a direction toward a state of having become, a condition of stability, of form. Whereas, very possibly it's exactly stability which America discards. The old Greek ideology is still so much of our minds that even in an attempt to get away from it we restate it. That's precisely what America doesn't do. The break with the past is complete. Is it possible for a civilization to *be* wholly dynamic? Wholly a vibration, a becoming, a force existing in itself, without direction, without an object for its verb? A civilization always *becoming,* never *being,* never never having the stability, the *form,* which is the beginning of death? If that is possible, at least it isn't possible for us—whose break with the past isn't complete—to think it, to comprehend it in our minds.

We don't like America—*I* don't like it—because of its lack of form. I want stability, with all the accompanying personal (to me) satisfactions and pleasures—leisure; quiet; time for thought; established standards that give one a foot-rule by which to measure thought, emotion, conduct, character; the sensation of permanence; the sensation of continuity with past and future—traditions in the past, definite purpose for the future. But what have my personal tastes to do with America? Nothing whatever.

(The radio is sending a photograph by air; astounding to hear.)

I do feel, here, that the falling-short is mine, not America's. The Lilliputian looks at Gulliver. It's true that human dignity disappears. Somehow, we've let the universe in. All societies have been snug little houses, with wall-board walls painted with pictures of infinity—neat, logical, hand-made pictures on walls erected to keep out the unbearable chaos of reality.

(Good morning, folks! says the radio. This is WOS, the Voice of Missouri. The weather for Missouri, generally fair tonight and Wednesday, slightly unsettled in northeast portions Wednesday. The time is exactly six and one-quarter minutes past nine o'clock, Central Standard Time. The estimated receipts of live-stock today: Chicago, sheep, 23,000,—hold-over hogs—)

But America hasn't any walls.

(In Chicago the weather is clear . . . temperature 80. For Omaha, the weather is clear; temperature 72.)

That, it seems to me, is the first thing to try to understand about this country; that there aren't any walls anymore. It's one explanation of the passion of the Fundamentalists, in every field of thought, not only religious. A desperate attempt to keep hold of sanity by maintaining the walls. No good: they come down on every side. Chaos is in. Can human beings live in reality? We've always thought not. We've never been able to bear it. All our attempt has been to get away from it. We couldn't bear the not-knowing, the having nothing solid, stable, to measure by, the vibration of an eternal *becoming* without beginning or end, without cause and inevitable effect, without tradition and purpose. Consider, that America has abolished God, has abolished all the gods. The Methodists and Baptists are no refutation of this; they haven't any God, they have only a moral code and an emotional attachment to it intensified by terror. The root of their feeling is identical with the root of our attachment to the crumbling island of Europe.

Oh well . . . this can go on forever. I spare you.

Cows, darling, don't neigh; that's horses. Cows moo. Donkeys bray. Roosters crow. Dogs bark. Tree-toads tear the night to tatters. Cicadas screech the day to shreds. All of 'em do all of it constantly, upon this peaceful farm. All of 'em but the tree-toads are doing it now.

(This is station WHB, Kansas City, Missouri. Stand by for market quotations from the United States Department of Agriculture . . .)

I am building a house.[4] Houses are my vice; without houses, who knows? I might have been a writer. I am my own worst enemy. I can't take houses, or leave 'em alone. This house is a five-room English cottage (anyway, rather English) which shall—Inshallah![5]—be all that both my father and my mother have wanted in houses. It's building on another part of this farm, and when, if ever, it's done, they shall live in it. I then inherit this house, which will no doubt be remodeled from foundation to ridge, and as soon as that's done, Allah be merciful, I'll depart for Cashmere, Samarkand, California and the mountains of the Meddite.[6]

Have you read Hilaire Belloc's *The Contrast*?[7] It's immensely amusing, saying many things we already know, and many that are so English we don't believe 'em and some that are stimulating (to me). It's worth the reading, anyway, if you haven't. Your reference to Wordsworth, Southey, and Coleridge reminded me of it; for I, as an American, was much disappointed in the celebrated English countryside. As Belloc says, words like "road, river, mountain, forest" mean entirely different things to the American and to the European. I don't know the Dolomites—do I? Anyway, if I do, I never knew their name when gazing on 'em, being the most superlatively uninformed of all travelers—but the Tyrol is recognizable, being the Rockies on their western slopes, with castles added by Hollywood working "on location." It's the English hill, which we'd describe as rolling prairie, and English mountain which to us is a hill, that are disconcerting.

You will be in America when you get this, if you ever do. (Aha! You did put your address on your letter! I was just deciding to try Harcourt, Brace, on a chance.) And letter-writing is one of my discords with America. You won't be able to write to me; no one ever is. As to apartments in New York, I, who read the *New Yorker* (including both sides of both covers every week) can imagine nothing more delightful than finding a New York apartment nowadays, being given the money to pay the rent. In fancy, I move into a couple every week. Nice little things, like a view embracing Brooklyn and Jersey City, two Babylonish hanging gardens on different levels, chromium fittings in all baths (baths for every room, and some for extra dressing-rooms) living-rooms 18 by 30, and seven wood-burning fireplaces, wrought-iron balustrades, and kitchens equipped with Frigidaires, electric ranges, tiled floors and, if desired, cooks and maids supplied. As to the perfect house in the Greatest City? Troub tells ravishing tales of most beautiful old houses almost as cheap as a song on the radio. Magnificent estates, seven bedrooms, tiled baths, separate servants' quarters, oil-burning automatic heating systems, in Newcastle, New Hampshire; taxed at $6,000, and purchaseable for $10,000. Newcastle is an island reached by bridge from Portsmouth. The prices make me weep, considering the terrific cost of building here, and that the family ties me in the arid middle, half way between the seas. Also, the advertising columns of *Country Life* tempt with offers of (apparently) the perfect place in Vermont, at prices running from $2,300 very slightly upward.[8] And when one has the perfect mouse-trap (a much better epithet, I consider, than "louse") one needn't think that the path to one's door will ever be over-grown with underbrush. In Vermont, defending a writer's privacy, one could always shoot by mistake, supposing the visitor to be a deer. Juries would acquit.

(You have, of course, forgotten that in your letter to me you called your husband a louse. But you did. Your entomological education is as deficient as your biological. The louse does not eat *books;* I always told you that you should have traveled *in* the Balkans, instead of skirmishing about their edges.)

RWL

---

1. Allah be praised! After her stay in Moslem Albania, Rose frequently dotted her letters with Islamic phrases.

2. Yvonne was Rose's French maid who accompanied her from Paris to Albania.

3. "How can I doubt man's joy or woe / Where'er his house-fires shine / Since all that man must undergo / Will visit me at mine?" From "The Fires," in *Rudyard Kipling's Verse* (definitive ed.; Garden City, N.Y.: Doubleday, Doran, 1945), p. 82.

4. The new house and the remodeling of the old one went forward as projected. The old house was Rose's home until 1935.

5. Allah willing!

6. By Meddite, Rose perhaps refers to the ancient region of Media, now northwestern Iran.

7. Hilaire Belloc (1870–1953), *The Contrast* (New York: McBride, 1924). "My thesis is that the New World is wholly alien to the Old" (p. 15).

8. Dorothy Thompson and Sinclair Lewis very shortly after this letter bought a Vermont estate (300 acres with two houses) for $10,000 (Sanders, *Dorothy Thompson,* p. 142).

Letter 23

[undated; late Feb. 1929]

My very dear Dorothy,

This isn't quite as silent silence as used to prevail in Europe—I see your name here and there, with scrappy bits of news of you. But my dear, what horrid news! And here I sit, really at intervals quite ill with helpless rage. Dumb with it, too. For there's simply no way to say what I think about your being met over here by a rotten experience like the Dreiser one. I know nothing about it except the references here and there in the public prints, but in sleepless midnight hours I am really furious at me for not being an "important" person; "importance" would have some value, used as a club now.

It's a rotten country, my dear; it really is. There's not a moral anywhere in it. We are far too progressive and advanced to have such an old-fashioned thing. We are "realists," God pity us. The spectacle of Dreiser's calmly swiping your Russian book[1] and being hailed with amused applause for the feat revives in me all the old emotions of the days when Freddie O'Brien swiped the $25,000 he owed me for writing *White Shadows in the South Seas,*[2] and all my loyal friends ran after his celebrity with cries of "our dear old friend Freddie!"

There's something absurd in this situation of mine, I know. Can you imagine me sitting here, immured in the snowbound Ozarks, fretting and fuming and cursing and ravaged by concern for you? And you're probably quite busily and happily engaged in many affairs, surrounded by any number of good friends, and taking this Dreiser affair as comfortably as the duck takes the rain. Nevertheless, it does make me so mad!

Vogue makes some reference to a suit filed, or pending, or something like that—very clever and humorous and thoroughly *comme il faut* in the modern intelligentsia style, *Vogue*[3]—and I feel like wrenching from 'em the $3.19 or thereabouts of my paid-up subscription! I hope you win it, my dear. Do, do, stick to it and drive it through and win it. I became so wearied by years of delay in the New York courts, and so sickened morally by the whole mess, that I let mine go. It was a mistake. There's no value anywhere to be gained, that I know of, in sticking to a thing like that. But anyway, do it. The few of us who represent, after all, an old-fashioned and modishly ridiculed attitude toward little things like decency and common honesty really should go down *fighting*.

Didn't I predict that you would not write letters? Certainly it was in my mind that you wouldn't. America is quite unconsciously wholly Bergsonian; time is real here. Therefore there isn't any. I never read Einstein, but I suppose he knows how it is possible for a day in Albania to be twice as long as the same day is while passing across these states. Yet I am eager for a word from you; why not send a telegram?

There's no news of importance about me. The new house being finished and the parents installed, I sat me down amidst the year's debris and discovered that no money remained for a trip to New York. (The house was planned, being so small, to cost about $6,000, and of course it did cost $12,000.) So I thought, "Well, let the typewriter see to it." And the typewriter balked. I haven't written a word since last July, and when shall I? There is no echo. Meanwhile I read Mme. David-Neel's adventures in Thibet,[4] and wonder what I really think of Proust—don't you find it surprising that he writes French in an *English* style?—and listen to Biltmore orchestras on the radio. The horses are well, though getting far too fat in the barns; the dogs are well. I am well, Troub is well. All, in fact, is no doubt well in the best of all possible worlds. We have a cook—by the way, do you happen to want an Austrian cook so good that she's really a chef? Rosa, our cook in Albania, has just written me from Holland that she thinks she can get a visa there, and do we still want her here? We do; we certainly do; for such cooks as Rosa exist only in dreams and in the servants' quarters of gilded halls. But we have no place to put her, in this old farmhouse. Besides, I doubt if we would keep her long here, so far from everything that she thinks America is and with no other servant within fifty miles. I can recommend her most heartily; she is neat, clean, honest, pretty as the maiden on the calendar, twenty-five or six years old, speaks German and Italian, is trained within an inch of her life as European servants are, and I am not exaggerating when I say that as a cook she is a genius.

We have, as I was saying, a cook and a hired man. Though I don't know why I began to say it. These short and simple annals—

Dorothy my dear, don't quite forget that I love you,

RWL

---

1. Both Dorothy Thompson and Theodore Dreiser had visited Russia in 1927. Dorothy's newspaper articles formed the basis of her *The New Russia* (New York: H. Holt, 1928). Shortly after, Dreiser's *Dreiser Looks at Russia* (New York: Liveright, 1928) appeared, bearing many passages similar to Thompson's. It was a situation in which friends took sides and which led, finally, to an ugly scene—blows were struck—between Dreiser and Sinclair Lewis. See Sanders, *Dorothy Thompson,* pp. 122–23, 146; Schorer, *Sinclair Lewis,* pp. 562–63; and Robert Elias, *Theodore Dreiser: Apostle of Nature* (New York: Knopf, 1949), pp. 250–51.

2. Frederick O'Brien (1869–1932) was the author of *White Shadows on the South Seas* (New York: Century, 1919), an exotic account based on his experiences in the South Pacific. It became a best-seller and was made into a movie. The preface acknowledges the editorial help of Rose Wilder Lane, whom he had known in San Francisco. Her account, pieced together from many of her letters, is that she undertook a complete rewrite of a hopeless manuscript, even creating new episodes, for which she was to receive a nominal initial fee and a share of profits if the book did well. The agreement was apparently an informal contract; her copy was either lost or appropriated by O'Brien; and although he made considerable money, she received only her initial fee. She sued but settled out of court, O'Brien having spent the money by that time. She puts the outlines of the matter succinctly in a letter to Heywood Hale Broun, July 28, 1929.

3. *Comme il faut:* as required. See *Vogue,* Feb. 16, 1929, pp. 126, 128.

4. Alexandra David-Neel (b. 1868), *My Journey to Lhasa* (New York: Harper, 1927).

Letter 24

37 West 10th Street
New York City
and for the time being:
Homosassa, Florida
February 24, 1929

Dearest Rose:

I don't write for many reasons—because I care too much for you, and therefore cannot write just for the sake of writing, or gossip, or write a "charming letter"; acquaintances get those—just that I may keep my hand in on that almost lost art. I have had too confused a six months—too many swirls of emotion, too many inner difficulties. Na-nu; what can one do?

I have been disgustingly ill with the 'flu and am not yet on my legs, really. I have got a wretched throat. But this climate, which is so damned fine that I loathe it—these countries of eternal sunshine seem, in our western world, to breed a Pollyanna mediocrity which is infuriating—but, be that as it may, this climate is doing me worlds of good. I want to talk with you. Won't you spend part of or all of next summer with me in Vermont? We have two houses, much land, hills, horses (probably), tennis, swimming, and I imagine will have good companionship—an excellent place to work in; the place is comfortable and simple. Lots of room. We shall be there from the middle of May.

Until then I don't know exactly where; we have a flat in New York but manage not to be in it. I go to Pittsburgh to speak on March 16th and then am coming back to Florida, probably, to join Hal. I had a lecture tour which the 'flu knocked to hell. This typewriter is awful, but I love you as ever—please write to me. The New York address will reach me only a day or so belated.

And think about Vermont. Think about it *seriously*.

Hal is swell; I am crazy about him, but this is the first time I have ever been married to a genius, and it has its good and bad side, as my dear father would have said. To *marry* geniuses, one must have an awfully reckless streak in one's nature. God grant only that it does not expire as age comes creeping on.

Dear Rose—
Dorothy

Letter 25

Homosassa, Fla.
Feb. 28, 1929

Rose,

About Dreiser: (because I realize that I did not answer your letter at all) really, it is too irritating. The old beast simply lifted paragraph after paragraph from my articles; I'm not speaking of material—we all got that where we could—but pure literary expressions. And, of course, ideas as well, because it never occurred to anyone else, for instance, to write about the social life in Moscow, and he lifted all that part of his book word for word from me.

Well, that is bad enough. But when I came out and accused him of it, he started a whispering campaign to the effect that I was on intimate terms with him to justify the thought that I may have gone into his room and purloined his *notes*!! And people are such stupids. Anna Louise Strong[1] gets off the ship and someone asks her about the affair, and she says she gave us *both* quantities of stuff. Why will people talk about things they don't know about? If she'd followed the controversy at all she would have known that "stuff" wasn't the question. The issue was literary expression. And anyhow I said in the introduction of my book that material had been furnished me by all my colleagues; God knows I gave 'em credit.

I am not going to sue—I know too much about literary suits. It would simply be furnishing wisecrackers with something to wisecrack about, and it is clear that Dreiser will stoop to anything. He really did create the impression with some people that I was his mistress. *That* swine! People always want to believe the worst, and nothing you can prove changes their opinion anyhow. Dreiser never has explained the twelve typewritten pages of parallel columns—stuff of mine which was published weeks and weeks before his came out—but no one really knows about it. They just say comfortably, "Ain't writers funny—here they were stealing from each other, I forget which was which, and now it seems they both stole from someone else." Morons!

But, no, Rose, I am not quite as excited as this seems. The moronity of the world, its base ingratitude, its insincerity, and its puerility, I long have known.

And *still,* it is a nice world.

I am trying to write fiction and failing utterly. If only I really believed that it was important to express myself. But I am so sick, sick, SICK, of people expressing themselves.

I am reading again the *Autobiography of Benvenuto Cellini*[2] and thanking whatever gods there be that there was once an age when men existed upon this earth. MEN.

Oh, to have been anything—a prostitute—in the days of Benvenuto. Proud days when a goldsmith spoke his mind to the Pope. "I thank God that I have learned and now I can report what the faith of Popes is made of," he says contemptuously to the Pope's own emissary. So can I say, I thank God I have learned what the faith of Great Novelists is made of. Although I do the old man an injury, for he is *not* a Great Novelist.

I myself think we haven't any. Thomas Mann is perhaps a great novelist. Perhaps this man Arnold Zweig; I think Ford Madox Ford almost is—the most underrated writer living. Hal—my Hal—has the talent and the spirit to be, only he does not know enough.[3]

I will not write fiction. (Of course, it is probable that I will. I must save some measure of economic independence, for if ever I felt that I could not go away from anyone, then I would hate that person. And if I am to follow him, thus, here and there, to Europe and to Florida, I must earn my living with something which I can always carry with me.) But there is too much writing; the world is unbearable from the terrible articulateness of the mediocre.

I embrace you—and expect
you in Vermont.
Dorothy

---

1. Anna Louise Strong (1885–1970), a prolific writer on Russia and China, was in Moscow as a newspaper correspondent when Dorothy visited there.

2. *The Autobiography of Benvenuto Cellini* was translated by J. A. Symonds in 1888 and subsequently became very popular. The passage quoted is from chapter 62.

3. Thomas Mann (1875–1955) was awarded the Nobel Prize in 1929. Arnold Zweig (1887–1968) was a German playwright and novelist; *The Case of Sergeant Grischa* (1927) was widely admired as one of the best novels of World War I. Ford Madox Ford (1873–1939), the prolific and widely renowned author, collaborator with Joseph Conrad, is best remembered for *The Good Soldier* (1914). The reference to "Hal" (Sinclair Lewis) is doubly ironic: in 1930, he would win the Nobel Prize, but his reputation would decline substantially in the years following.

Letter 26

March 12, 1929

Dear Dorothy,

I'm quite desperately sorry about the bad fortune. Influenza, Florida, and Dreiser all together are too much. Three of them, though! So that surely, unless—as I did—you broke a mirror on your wedding day, there'll be a change to fair weather now.

Ah, my dear, but why stipulate "these countries of eternal sunshine", or for that matter, our western world? All places breed a mediocrity that is infuriating. Myself, I look upon the Pollyanna quality in mediocrity as a mitigation. An idiotic grin is bad enough—but how far worse the idiotic scowl! We ask too much, anyway. We are eternally comparing things as they are with our own version of as they might be. What an absurd stupidity in us. Things as they are have the one saving quality that none of our preferable worlds could have—they're interesting. The "slight inexplicable inaccuracy" which the Devil introduces—and WHY isn't the man who wrote that[1] really the writer we all thought he was when we were young and passionately uncritical?—is something that none of us could put in. I *like* the world as it is, I really do. The only thing I hate about it is the steadily approaching moment when I'll have to leave—all the three-ringed circuses still going on, and I having had but the briefest glimpse of this and that, always having missed so much every second, and yet being compelled to rush away, as though I had another appointment which wouldn't wait. I'm so unaware of having any other appointment, and even if I had, how gladly would I let it wait, forever and forever! I really can't imagine a heaven which could recompense me for missing all the future thousands of years, of centuries, in which this circus will still be going on. The myth of the Wandering Jew[2] is really the expression of the human heart's desire. Immortality is a poor compromise between that desire and the observed fact.

I, too, want very much to talk with you. It pleases me that you are still there, dear Dorothy. But I don't know. There is so much that must be done, and all the months rushing down upon one like roaring locomotives, and passing with a roar before I've really seen them. And, as usual, I'm in no affluence that'll let me leave the typewriter. I've just spent $12,000 in building a new house for my parents, and what a blow it was to my bank account you can't imagine. Especially as I also lost most of last summer and fall, in bossing the job. (I love building houses. They are the vice that's always ruining me.) So I really can't promise myself Vermont this summer. You don't know how much I wish I might. Perhaps next fall. And I do so want to go to Samarkand, just once before I die! And Afghanistan, and Cashmere. But probably I'll be in New York next fall, either on my way to one of these places, or simply with a grim determination to persuade editors that I'm much more of a writer than I ever shall be. And therefore that they should give me prices that *will* take me to Samarkand. Not to mention my own Albania, which I haven't seen for a year and a month, now. Dorothy, I'm so sorry that you never saw Albania. And now it's dead. As you said it would be, and as I always knew it would be, and as I can't bear to realize that it is. But there are still the mountains. And if I am in New York, surely we may see each other then?

You know I can't like your husband ever—except by forgetting that he is. You would have gone to Albania with me, long ago, if you had thought of marriage as I think of it. You know—as one thinks of the sugar in the tea, that one doesn't take, preferring a simpler, more direct relation with tea. And when I met Fodor in Vienna and heard that you were happy, slim, and gay again, I thought that you'd come to the same, "No, thank you; Lemon please," point of view. We might have gone to Samarkand. We might have had a houseboat on the Shalimar.[3] We might—but no. I don't doubt that he is all you say he is, and I am glad that he is, and there are all kinds of half-regretful "sinces" and "buts" sprinkled through my gladness. Yes, yes—but why need he be a husband? Ah well, that's the way it is. And all for the best, no doubt, since—but—

How right you are about books! The world is made horrible by our articulateness. Yes, but that is because you are an artist, a poet. If one could quite lose the old—really quite outmoded—point of view; if one could think of books as this multitude of writers thinks of them, as our successful publishers think of them—after all, why not? Books, spearmint, radios, magazines, Chevrolets and O. Henry—O. Henry, either author or candy—the entertainment of the masses. Quite wholesome, in the main, harmless and amusing. If one could do that, one could make a fortune and buy a desert island. Myself, I sit here dumb before the spectacle of the words that appear on paper in my typewriter, clods of words, stupid, ungainly and meaningless. That makes me tear up the paper. And that's absurd.

What we really need most is quite simple. We need to know what we want. Then we would quite simply get it, and live blithely ever after. I want too many things. And so do you.

I have too many selves to know the one.
In too complex a schooling was I bred,
Child of too many cities, who have gone
Down all bright cross-roads of the world's desires,
And at too many altars bowed my head,
To light too many fires.[4]

I wish, though, that you'd recover from this mistaken notion, this "I am an extraordinarily good journalist and an extraordinarily bad poet." You were always the poet—that was, essentially, what made you such a good journalist. Though why you should wish to combine being a poet and a wife—do you think even Edna St. Vincent Millay's doing that?[5] Knowing what you are as a companion, I am sure that you are a genius as a wife. But as a wife *and* a poet . . . There are impossibilities it seems to me, before which any genius fails. Be happy, sweet maid, and let who will be poets.[6] Don't you think, maybe? After all, a life, I suppose, is the sum total of its moments—not of its, so to speak, its output. Not that I think it's so especially important to be happy. Certainly it would be deadly to be exclusively happy. But that's a purely academic idea, anyhow. There's really one sure thing, that you don't seem to have realized; that you couldn't ever, under any circumstances, be held anywhere "unable to get away," except by your own volition. I would drop you, my dear Dorothy, penniless, ignorant of Persian, Turkish, Russian, Armenian, or any of the Tartar dialects, into the depths of the Sultan's harem in Cabool, as the Sultan's favorite wife, and quite placidly wait in Cairo, paying the cost of Shepheard's best suite,[7] until your emergence at the end of an A.P. wire with a really fascinating tale of court life in Afghanistan, an acute analysis of the situation in Central Asia from every aspect, and a volume of unwritten poetry. You are not so helpless, my dear. And you know it perfectly well, when the situation arises. So it's strange to me, that even in the gloomy doldrums of influenza you should be viewing with horror a prospect of financial dependence. Financial dependence is really very pleasant. Also, it would be a new experience for you, really an adventure. Don't grow too old to love adventure, Dorothy; please don't.

With love,
Rose

---

1. The allusion is to H. G. Wells, *The Undying Fire* (1919). In chapter 1, the course of the universe is described as a chess game played by God and the Devil, in which the Devil can introduce a "slight inexplicable inaccuracy" into any move God makes—thereby requiring further adjustments in whatever plan his opponent intends.

2. The legendary Wandering Jew was doomed to live until the end of the world because he taunted Christ on the road to the crucifixion.

3. The Gardens of Shalimar in Kashmir were built by the Mogul emperors in the seventeenth century. The capital city, Srinigar, is on the Jhelum River and is laced with canals; the seventeenth-century British colonials often lived on house-boats, according to the *Encyclopedia of World Travel* (3d ed.; Garden City, N.Y.: Doubleday, 1979), 2:458–61.

4. I have not been able to identify these lines; they are perhaps Rose's own.

5. Edna St. Vincent Millay was notorious for her many casual liaisons, one of whom had been Dorothy's husband Josef Bard. See Sanders, *Dorothy Thompson,* pp. 86–87.

6. "Be good, sweet maid, and let who can be clever"—from Charles Kingsley (1819–1875), *A Farewell.*

7. Rose had stayed at Shepheard's Hotel in Cairo during her Middle East trip of 1923.

Letter 27

Rocky Ridge Farm
Mansfield, Missouri
December 29, 1929

Dorothy dear,

It was so good to see you again—and sad to see so little of you. But there's a contentment in my heart about you, which I've never had before. Darling, you are going to affront all the literature of the ages by triumphantly combining great beauty with the happy ending.

Your husband's unintentional conquest was complete. I will now confess that I was prepared to dislike him intensely—how intensely even I didn't fully know, until recovering my balance from the impulse. A deeper mind than Freud's must explain why I resented your being married again to anyone—it was probably part of my rebellion against . . . *je ne sais quoi*[1] . . . the pull of time, the principle, whatever it is, (and *if* it is), that's the universe. (I damn well better accept it. But I don't.) I remain the child who wants the moon. I wanted you to be forevermore the Dorothy of

1920—a song, a poem, a flame in the sunlight—Idiotic! But there it was. And there was also perhaps an unconscious conviction that true beauty and the happy ending aren't compatible; I was ready with wolfish ferocity for anyone who would rob you of either to give you the other. Besides, more prosaically, it isn't so usual for admirable women to love, or to be loved by, men who are worth the trouble. You know it isn't. Imagine, therefore, the furies battling beneath my—I trust—outward composure, when the doorbell rang.

I really like him enormously. There are so few men who have minds that run under their own power. Goodness knows no one's mind was engaged during those last few moments that evening, but I am convinced that your Hal and I would disagree endlessly upon every conceivable subject, with great mutual enjoyment. I resent the fate that took me away too soon. Every five years or so, I'm able to have some *talk.* You and I talk—how often?—and there's also Floyd Dell.[2] You're always snatched away. By the blessing of psycho-analysis, Floyd's glued to his own hearth, and when I can get there we talk through solid days and nights. The traveler upon the desert sees cool water recede across the blistering waste, and I had no chance to talk to your husband. Anyhow, I like him awfully. He's decent—a quality I value more than you might suppose, from my history—and he's thoroughly well-bred, and he's humorous, and sincere, and charming.

My objections to this marriage are hereby withdrawn *in toto;* I'm *for* it! Darling, you were quite right, and I—though you didn't suspect it till now—entirely wrong.

Genevieve, somewhat troubled by these articles of ours[3] which she sold, sight unseen, urged me to take the matter up with you by letter, and arrive at a *modus scribendi,* if that's how it's spelled. This shouldn't be so difficult. The real idea is—isn't it?—something like *Is Sex Necessary?*[4] (I refer to the title only; not the book, which I haven't read.) From your angle, it's really hardly more than an elaboration of the point made in your half of the controversy as to America being a woman's paradise—that women in America miss complete sex experience. You argue, as I see it, that we need a fuller implicit recognition of sex in all encounters between men and women, and you point up this contention by a comparison between European society—where this recognition exists—and American, where it doesn't. It seems to me that this placing of emphasis removes your perfectly valid objection to writing the article as Genevieve saw it because this isn't the article that Genevieve saw. It seems to me that your personal position can very easily be taken care of, for the small proportion of readers who could see any personal reference in it, by a phrase or two noting exceptions. You are not discussing individuals, but an entire social attitude. Our conversation that night in your house began with personalities, goodness knows, yet it was obvious enough that you were not speaking of yourself, not comparing two men, but two continents. The European point of view, you said, was realistic, and I well remember your hurling at me, like an accusation, the words "But you *are* a woman!"

Indubitably. But I see no reason why that should lead to my having my hand kissed continually, either verbally or actually. I am a woman, granted. But I am also a person. I am, for example, a writer. When I meet an editor—whether Genevieve or Mr. Vance[5]—I wish that relationship to be the relationship between an editor and a writer, not one between woman and woman, or between woman and man. When I am driving a car, I am a motorist, and I wish my relationship to strangers encountered by chance to be the relationship between motorist and stranger, not that between *madame* and *monsieur*, or *la senora* and *el senor*. Furthermore, carrying the banner into the enemy's ranks, I think this country needs less consideration of sex, not more. I would like to see a community of human beings which would accept and deal with sex as realistically and healthily as animals do. (I prefer the American attitude because it does, in fact, approach this ideal more nearly than the European.) Most of the time it is much more important to a cat to recognize that another animal is a cat, not a dog, than it is to recognize that the other animal is a male cat or a female cat. I think it is more important to recognize that another human being is a human being, than to recognize male and female. Most of our activities have no more to do with sex than they have to do with ancestors. From one point of view, you can truthfully say that my grandfathers have everything to do with all my thoughts, emotions, and actions. But I do not see that it follows that everyone I meet should fix his attention upon my family tree. I contend that it is *not* "realistic" to emphasize sex as Europeans do; it is instead an attempt to force an arbitrary and in many aspects artificial classification upon human beings. There is, in fact, much more difference between me and some women than there is between me and some men. The sex classification is socially not so important as many other classifications, for instance, race, character, religion, social experience, education. Dr. Sabin[6] is—if there must be a choice—more properly classified as a biologist than as a woman. As a biologist, she'll find it a nuisance to be treated as a woman. And good God, what a dearth of free, sincere relationships between women the European attitude creates! Awareness of sex inevitably becomes, in social affairs, a rivalry. This is biological; witness the behavior of birds in the mating season. At all other seasons of the year, birds of the same species, of either or both sexes, consort amiably. The European attitude is an artificial insistence upon prolonging the mating season through the whole year and the whole life. A bird is, first of all, a bird, and secondly a female bird, and I insist that I am first of all a human being, and secondly a woman. I do not wish to be confined in a perpetual mating season. I have other things to do.

And so on . . .

Dorothy my dear, if you feel you can do your half of this controversy, do let's? I think it would be fun. Also, I would like that check, because these controversy articles bring in the easiest checks I know, being hardly more difficult to write than a letter, and my fiction-mechanism is flagging lamentably just now.

You may be on your way to California before this reaches New York. I am happy thinking of you in Carmel—that lovely, lovely spot! Think of me sometimes when you watch the sunsets over the Pacific. Now *that's* an *ocean*! None of this dull, gray, unimaginative water such as fills the Atlantic. The Pacific's a sea that at heart is akin to the Aegean—inhabited by the unknown, and aware of mysteries, a sea that breeds myths with its fogs. Have the happiest of winters by it, Dorothy darling. And if you see Fremont Older,[7] give him my love. There's an old oak, embittered by storms, that nevertheless dwarfs all these younger growths.

Very much love, and all my hopes for your new year.

Rose

---

1. "I don't know what."

2. Floyd Dell (1887–1968), novelist, poet, socialist, one of the editors of *The Masses* tried and acquitted on treason charges for advocating resistance to the

military draft in 1917, was a life-long friend of Rose's. See his *Homecoming: An Autobiography* (New York: Holt, Rinehart & Winston, 1933), pp. 334–35.

3. The reference here is to Genevieve Parkhurst, an editor at *Pictorial Review*. The articles, solicited but never written, would have been an extension of a joint article by Dorothy and Sinclair Lewis on either side of the question, "Is America a Paradise for Women?," *Pictorial Review* 30 (June 1929): 15, 56–61.

4. *Modus scribendi:* means of writing. James Thurber and E. B. White, *Is Sex Necessary?* (New York: Harper, 1929).

5. Vance was also an editor at *Pictorial Review*.

6. Dr. Florence Rena Sabin was awarded the *Pictorial Review* prize for outstanding achievement by an American woman in 1928. She was honored for her research on tuberculosis. *New York Times*, Nov. 16, 1929, 19:1.

7. Fremont Older (1856–1935) had been Rose's employer as editor of the *San Francisco Bulletin*, 1915–1918.

Letter 28

Monterey, California
February 19 [1930]

Rose, my dear,

I enclose the story; sell it, by all means, with my blessing! It's an admirable variation-on-the-theme. My telegram was not meant to be so cryptic as it seemed. You, my child, are the third writer who has informed me that she is using the Copenhagen monkeys![1] The spectacle of the women's magazines of the country swarming with Copenhagen monkeys at Christmas next moved me to gargantuan mirth. This, I think, is the best part of the story. My own interest in it is merely in the telling. I have never written it because it has saved too many dull dinner parties, and once written, I shall never again be able to tell it. But diakoku's, or whatever you call 'em, ain't monkeys, and a Park Avenue gent-about-town is no substitute for my Bidermaeyer major. Bless you, and may the sale of the tale net you neatly.

Long ago, you told me to go west, young woman. You may not recall that Sinclair Lewis, if I had to marry him, was to compensate by buying me a house in Carmel. You wrote me thus[2]—do you remember? And at last here we are, by this amethyst sea, in the only country I have yet seen in these United States which inspires the faintest breath of patriotism in my bosom. Only, it is different than I imagined it, wilder, more heroic, more dramatic, not without terror—Robinson Jeffers' country, not George Sterling's.[3]

We went to see Jeffers. We sat at his fireside and drank his homemade wine, a cross between a sherry and a Tokay, with a musky flavor to it. Una, his wife, talked about Shropshire, a country which Hal and I know and love, having walked clear across it once, and about Ernest Hemingway, not a word of whom Jeffers has ever read, but Una thought him lacking in poetry, thought the love story in *A Farewell to Arms*[4] too physical and unrevealing of deeper emotions, thought he does the whole thing too easily, and since I think exactly the opposite, finding this book almost pure poetry—whole passages sing in my brain—I was astounded. Anyway, Una chattered friendlily, Jeffers smoked at his pipe, and as far as I recall, said not one single word, except that his silences are warm and kindly; his twin boys, as silent as he is, moved in and out of the room, and we looked at the sea through the window, and I was happy to know him. He is a great writer, I really think.

In San Francisco I met friends of yours—Fremont Older, who delighted me. And I walked up and down Telegraph Hill[5] and found the place you told me about on the road from Blois to Amboise half a lifetime ago.[6] Why did you leave this town, Rose, which alone of American cities has enchantment? We lunched on the waterfront, from the most delicious of crabs and dined in Chinatown and in superb French restaurants, and although I was not well in San Francisco—pregnant ladies should not undertake four day train journies—I was happy.

Here we have a famous old house—the Sherman Rose cottage—Gen'l Tecumseh is supposed to have kissed a pretty Spaniard in its doorway and planted there a rose with whose blooming he was to return.[7] He never did, but the house is covered with roses, not red for passion, but a faded-out pink. Do you think they changed their color with the years of waiting? I find this horticultural miracle as probable, anyhow, as the legend. And on a divine site up the hill lies the ranch of Olga Fish, who is very rich, and pretty and charming besides, and who never would have existed—in her Anglo-Saxon blondness, certainly—if Sherman *had* married the Spaniard. Anyhow, the most important part of the legend is that it has served to enforce the conservation of this house and these rose bushes, in and under which we live so happily and shall until beginning April.

Rose, were we together we might write a controversy, along slightly different lines than those projected by Genevieve. Could I not drag you out here from your Ozark spring? Would you not like to look upon the face of this lovely country again? We have a guest room. Or failing that, might I not come to you for a few days on my way eastward? I shall be immense with child by then—these mountains will recognize their image—but I trust my faculties, such as they are, will remain unimpaired.

I am glad you liked my husband. I love him tenderly and admire him greatly, and am grateful to him for many things, among them, for this child.

My love to you always and unchangingly,
Dorothy

---

1. From Rose's diary entries we can surmise something of the meaning of this allusion to the Copenhagen monkeys. Apparently Dorothy had told Rose a tale about a figurine—perhaps a monkey—given as a Christmas gift, sold to raise cash, then desperately retrieved by the seller. Rose then made this tale the basis of a short story, changing the monkey to a "DiaKoku," a Japanese god of wealth. See "It's the Sentiment," *Ladies' Home Journal* 50 (Dec. 1933): 6, 44, 46; Rose's diary entries, Feb. 5, 6, 8, 10, 24, 1930.

2. See Letter 16.

3. George Sterling (1869–1926) was a California writer who was among the earliest settlers in a literary colony at Carmel. Sinclair Lewis knew him there in 1909–1910 (Schorer, *Sinclair Lewis,* pp. 146 ff.). Robinson Jeffers (1887–1962), known for his striking poetry formed on Greek models, lived at Carmel in a stone house he had built himself; for portraits of Sterling and Jeffers, see Kunitz, *Twentieth Century Authors.*

4. Hemingway had published *A Farewell to Arms* in 1929.

5. In 1917 Rose had lived on Telegraph Hill while working for editor Fremont Older of the *San Francisco Bulletin.*

6. In January 1921, on the walking trip they so often refer to.

7. The legend of Gen. William Tecumseh Sherman and the Spanish woman is recounted by Gertrude Atherton, *Adventures of a Novelist* (New York: Atherton Co., 1932), pp. 189–90. Its factual basis is described by Nellie Van de Grift Sanchez, "Grafting Romance on a Rose Tree," *Sunset Magazine* 36 (April 1916): 40. I have not been able to identify the reference to Olga Fish, presumably a member of the Lewises' circle in Carmel.

Letter 29

Monterey, California
March 1, 1930

Rose dear,

Yes, I will come to you, in case nothing untoward happens.

You see, I am going back to New York in any event. I have a doctor there the very sight of whom gives me confidence and peace of mind, and here there is no one for whom I have the same feeling. Then we must spend the summer in Vermont, on the farm, and although it may be difficult to travel across the continent with a baby inside one, I am quite sure that it would be even more difficult to travel, convalescent, with a baby in a basket. Therefore, I shall get home by the first of May and have six weeks to rest up in before I go to the hospital.

I am feeling low today. I've been perfectly well up to now, and all of a sudden I'm losing red corpuscles and having adverse laboratory tests, and having to go on a rigid and boring diet—no starches, no sugars, and buckets full of spinach—and sometimes I worry, remembering that, after all, I am thirty-six years old.

And my head is full of ideas, seething around all the time, but no strength is in me to realize them. They are only day-dreams.

This Rose, is a strange country. For all its sunshine, and for all its beneficent climate, it is a curiously tragic country, in fact it is the only part of the United States where I have ever felt that there was a tragic landscape. I mean tragic in the loftiest sense of the word. It has a terrifying beauty. The distorted, wind-swept trees; the great seas; the breeding sunshine and the mysticizing fogs; the rocks beneath the soil—archaic Greece must have been something like this. Only the breed inhabiting the land is not tragic, not grandiose, not strong enough for the land or the landscape. They are somehow ridiculous.

You must read Jeffers. He lives with his wife and twin sons in a house of rock he built, every stone of it, with his own hands. It stands on a cliff over the sea, and around it he has planted two thousand trees. He reads Greek, and aloud, to his twelve-year old boys, Dostoevsky. He writes terribly and beautifully, and his words ring like metal on stone. I shall send you *Roan Stallion,* and I beg you to read aloud to yourself the little poem called "Shine Perishing Republic." It is, if I remember well, on page 95. And his "Ode to Woodrow Wilson," where he has said all anyone can ever say.[1] He is one of the most beautiful men I have ever seen. He goes nowhere, ever. He was educated, as a child and young man, in Europe; he is a member of a cultivated well-to-do family, and has just a little money—just enough. He loves only this one spot in the whole world and draws all the inspiration of his poetry from it.

Of course you are right about Hemingway. One does not need to have read Aristotle to know when someone gives you a distinguished emotion. I read your analysis of his method vis-a-vis the stream-of-consciousness method aloud to Hal, who delighted in what you said. (Why do you not write criticism? Why do you not? You have a superb sense of values.) Hemingway is a realist with a difference. I know of no writer whom I feel to be more painstaking. I am sure he works like a dog. He is a prodigious observer. There are other prodigious observers, but I know of no one who can observe so much and out of it select so truly. Out of all these gestures, he seems to say, this single one implies the others. And of course you are right about the love story. I thought of a poem of Whitman's—I cannot quote it—something like this:

"I do not envy the President in his White House, nor the rich, nor prominent . . .
But when I see two old lovers . . . how it is with them . . . how all their lives long they stand by each other and help each other,
Then I walk away, sad, filled with the bitterest envy."

This is a travesty on the lines,[2] but their sense, I am sure. And reading *A Farewell to Arms,* I, too, was filled with envy. In the gestures between these two, Catherine and the Tenente, everything possible in a relationship between a man and a woman is implied. Some God-damn fool wrote that Catherine's last words were fantastic and amazing. I could only think they are more nearly precisely what I could imagine myself saying, under similar circumstances, than any death-bed lines I have ever read. And J. B. Priestly wrote that Hemingway ought to go back to Chicago and write about his home town.[3] Oh, God, critics!

San Francisco is, I think, a city for youth. I felt its enchantment, but I do not think I would capture it for myself, living there now. And California is far from the world—from my world, for better or worse. There isn't a newspaper in the state that one can read, for one thing.

Your letter, Rose, is a joy. I have already read it three times.

D-

---

1. See Robinson Jeffers, *Roan Stallion, Tamar, and Other Poems* (New York: Boni and Liveright, 1925), pp. 95, 99.

2. Dorothy paraphrases Whitman's "When I Peruse the Conquered Fame." See *Leaves of Grass,* ed. Sculley Bradley et al. (3 vols.; New York: New York University Press, 1962), 2:396–97.

3. For the reference to J. B. Priestley, see his review of *A Farewell to Arms* in *Now and Then,* no. 34 (Winter 1929), pp. 11–12. The earlier allusion to some "fool" is obscure; Dorothy might have had in mind Agnes W. Smith, "Mr. Hemingway Does It Again," *The New Yorker* 5 (Oct. 12, 1929): 120.

Letter 30

Rocky Ridge Farm
Mansfield, Missouri
March 8, 1930

Dorothy dear,

Conscience, speaking with a dreadful voice in the hours of the night that are farthest from the sun, convinced me that I must tell you that you'd best not come. This morning I don't know what I think about it. But at least you should know that this is one of the parts of our country which supplies all the arguments to those who are trying to get Congress to continue the appropriations for the Children's Bureau.[1] There isn't a really *good* doctor within 250 miles. The nearest next-best one is in Springfield, 50 miles away. The one resorted-to-in-emergencies is some miles in the country beyond Norwood, which is ten miles from here, and getting him on the country-line is no joke. I read in my diary that just a year ago I spent most of a thunderstormy night at the telephone, trying to get him for our hired man's wife, who was having a baby, and when at last I did get his number, he'd gone twenty miles down into Douglas County on an emergency call. He arrived, not having slept in the meantime, at nine next morning. The baby had arrived all right, and is now the pink of infantile perfection. But still . . .

I'm sure there's no need to worry, my dear; thousands of women have thousands of babies at thirty-six, and if one is thinking of danger, what else do all of us live in every moment all of our lives? Nevertheless, I do worry, because you are so precious to me, and even forgetting me, so precious, so valuable, as a person, as an end-in-itself. You have always trusted fate, and nettles have been soft to your grasp; and I truly believe they always will be. At the same time, I don't have any trust whatever in fate. So I worry, and that's quite ridiculous. You will remember that I'd never have let you dare anything at all, if I could have prevented it. I fear I'm one of these cowardly persons who'd lock the pearls in the safe-deposit vault and never, never take them out. So I wish that you would go back to the doctor in whom you have confidence, and stay there with him until the baby arrives. I don't like your going on diets, far away from him. And I don't like your traveling about in tiring trains with a seven-months baby who's not in a basket.

There's no need, after all, for you to be adventuring through layers of many centuries with that baby, before he's safely here. I don't think so much even of twentieth-century medicine, but certainly it's better than the medieval varieties. If he's born in Mansfield, you mustn't cut his nails till he is a year old, or he will be a thief. Whereas in New York—that is, in your part of New York, with your doctor—no such dangers await him. I'm sure he could grow up an honest man there, if you cut his nails every fortnight. My dear, I do want the pearl in safe-deposit; I want you with your doctor right *now.*

Come, come; you're not being fair to my Californians! Where is this archaic Greek to whom you would compare them? He's a Greek who never was on sea or land, Dorothy. My own belief is that the Californians are far nearer that concept than any other people have been—unless perhaps they lived in Sicily in the days of Frederick the Second.[2] They're a gay and open-air people; they're healthy, they're sun-burned, they're tall and beautiful, and they swim in their seas and climb their mountains. And they love beauty in nature, and they're hospitable to art. (And if they're a little *too* hospitable—well, that's only generosity stronger than discrimination. Isn't friendliness—a receptive and a rewarding attitude—all one can expect—surely far more than one usually finds—in the mass populace?) Aren't Californians suffering in your eyes less by comparison with other peoples, or even less by comparison with their own landscapes and sea, than by comparison with a concept existing only in your own mind? I am no authority on archaic Greece, heaven knows, having progressed no further toward a knowledge of Greek than the purchase of a grammar and dictionary and a New Testament in the original. But take a little item like the fact that there never was a villa built in Greece in a place which had a view of mountains or of the sea. Look at the temples at Delphi, with the most stupendous panorama in the world at their feet, and all of them turning blank walls to it, huddling in their hollow on the mountain side. The Acropolis is not on a hill for any other reason than the wholly sensible one of military defence. And the whole of Greek art, from the Doric to the most glorious blaze of the Byzantine, is almost wholly unaware of nature. One might say that the deepest profound difference between you (or the Californians) and the Greeks, is that you *see* California's beauty. It occurs to me that Giotto—now this is really amusing!—was really the great iconoclast, since it was he who first broke the mold of Greek form.[3]

It may be that the Greeks were truly the only great men, in one sense. But it was in a sense which you would be the first to repudiate, I think. For they were great by virtue of their ability to shut from their consciousness everything outside mankind. Anything is great, until it is compared with something else. Even the Greek gods were not gods. But that isn't arrogance of a superb pride; it's the arrogance of ignorance. That is why there is always a grating discord between any monument of Greek art and its natural setting; the Greeks were unaware of the natural setting. They were unaware, with the most astounding egotism, of anything whatever outside their own skulls. In a landscape as profoundly moving and disturbing to you or me as California's, they lived entirely inside their own mud walls—or marble. It was quite natural to them to produce, for example, an atrocity like the caryatids,[4] because they were completely blind to even the natural forms which in their nature are nearest to a purely human concept of beauty—I mean the logical, geometric beauty of mass in relation to power. To anyone but a Greek it is evident that the human body is not a pillar designed to support weight.

The truth is that the Greeks, as a people, were simple barbarians as alien to you or me as any hill-man in the Pamirs[5] today. The Greeks, as aristocrats and artists, were great in a sense quite as alien to any true concept of ours. I am convinced that if the breed now inhabiting the landscapes around you could be removed, and replaced by the Greeks of the brief Golden Age, or even by the Greeks at the height of the world empire, you'd be appalled. Of course it goes without saying that you could not endure life in the midst of their abominable cruelties. But quite apart from that, you would suffer excruciatingly from their art. You would see them blithely cutting down the trees, all the trees, those distorted, wind-swept cypresses, and the thousands planted by Robinson Jeffers. You would see them setting up large white marble lions here and there, with no relation to anything around them. It is true that you would see them naked, which would be a great improvement to the scene, but you would not see them bathing by thousands in their blue bays, as you see the Russians bathing today, for instance, all along the sapphire edges of the Black Sea. You'd be the only person left who would see the ocean and the mountains and the sunsets, and that would be frightfully lonely for you. And I can hear you now, raging about those small, tight, gratingly inharmonious Greek temples, glaring white, which would arise on every hand, with a perfectly oblivious disregard of the appropriate. They don't even have any harmonious relation to each other, those temples. And as you struggled against the devastation, you'd discover that Greek art was not a striving, through repeated experiment, toward an integral harmony, but that its root was a blindly obstinate refusal to admit—how shall I put this?—"natural law." That's evident all the way from the monstrously disproportionate Doric column to the splendor of Byzantine mosaic. The Greeks, with a kind of ferocity, were *human,* nothing but human. The Arabs looked at the stars, and the Romans looked at the earth, but the Greeks looked at nothing whatever but their own thoughts. They lived in a kind of vacuum.

I keep mulling around and around the thing I'm trying to express.

You say that the Californians are "not tragic, not grandiose, not strong enough for the land or the landscape. They are somehow ridiculous." But all that is true, from the same point of view, of the Greeks. It is even more true of the Greeks. For the Californians, however inadequately, do live *in* the landscape; they are aware of it, and so far as they are able, they are a part of it. In their very inadequacy there is an effort toward harmony, toward taking their proper place in a whole. All along the beach at Carmel, for example, there are houses which express humanity in relation to the universe; houses whose colors and forms express an awareness of the landscape. I find more human dignity in them than in the Parthenon. The tortoise builds a beautiful, hard shell, which has no relation to anything but the tortoise, and he tucks his legs and tail and head inside it—and that's what seems to me ridiculous. But the oriole hangs a raggedy nest to the limb of a tree and sits on it, swaying when the tree sways. Neither of them are strong enough or large enough to matter much to the landscape, and the oriole admits the fact precisely because it is aware that there *is* a landscape. By that admission and that awareness, to me it's a larger creature than the tortoise—and less ridiculous.

Darling, you flatter me enormously, but your suggestion is absurd. I can't write criticism. (Dear me, I can't even untangle the sentences of critics; I sit bewildered for minutes together trying to fit subject to predicate in one of Canby's[6] sentences, and making absolutely no sense whatever to it!) A critic must have a point of view, and I haven't any at all. Or rather, I have dozens, all mutually antagonistic.

Do you suppose we'll ever throw away the attempt at logic? I'm sure I have somewhere argued at length that man is essentially logical, and therefore forever essentially antagonistic to the universe. (This seems to be the Greek idea, which I've just been attacking!) It occurs to me that that's a narrowly western point of view, and that perhaps our two millenniums of being obsessed by our own demand for logic have been merely a legacy from the Greeks. Science, whose tool has been logic, now seems to be—what an anomaly!—discarding it. Logically perceiving the uselessness of logic seems to be the kitten pursuing its tail—the result is dizziness. Anyway for me. But what a relief! What a burden dropped, if we could ever cease to feel a compulsion to be logical.

I don't think you should bother about trying to realize ideas. Maybe they *are* nothing but day-dreams, all of 'em, always. Anyway, while all of you is busy doing something else, why trouble about ideas? It's far better just to be content to be a matrix for the baby. Creation is first of all a breaking-down process; the caterpillar becomes a jelly before it becomes a butterfly, and the nebulae produce the planets. I think you don't know that I once had a baby;[7] no one I know now does know that because I don't speak about it. But what I want to say is that I think you become something less than one whole person before you become two. No one ever seems to mention that—perhaps because most women aren't really whole persons, anyway, at any time. Only don't rebel against the day-dreaming, my dear. Your body's the only thing that's important now, and the only thing your body cares about is the baby. If it doesn't squander any energy on unessential things like ideas, it's quite right.

Tonight we are going on a fox-hunt. There's nothing in the world like an Ozark fox-hunt, and it crisps the hair of the English to hear about it. We call it "hearing a race," as well as "going fox-hunting." When I was a girl it was a brave sight to see the hunters setting forth, twenty or thirty men on horses, and often as many as sixty dogs, to the sound of the hunting horns. But now we mostly go in automobiles, carrying the hounds behind in trailers. The man we're going with tonight has just had a special custom-built trailer made, at considerable expense, for transporting his fox-hounds in comfort and style, and his hunting horn is an object of art and beauty as well as a musical instrument. He is the town blacksmith, and well experienced in that craft, having shod horses all through the war, in France.

We set out a little before twilight, taking with us potatoes and bacon and coffee-pots and frying-pans, and we choose a night when the weather's warm and the moon rises early. There are several fox-hunting regions, all within a radius of ten miles or so, and they're selected for natural beauty of the landscape as well as for the quality of the foxes inhabiting them. The first requisite is a high mountain-top, not too thickly wooded, from which there is an excellent view of many miles of hill-ranges. One wise old hound is picked out as the starter, and when we arrive on the mountain-top he is at once released. The other dogs remain with us, while we build the campfire and place the automobile cushions comfortably around it. Very soon the "starter" dog gives tongue, announcing that he has started the fox, and then all the other dogs are set free on the trail. Fox hunters who have any claim whatever to being practitioners of the art "know the mouths" of every good dog in the hills. A good fox hound with an exceptionally musical voice is worth hundreds of dollars, and many are priceless. They all have lovely names—Silver Bell, Mountain Maid, Robin Hood, Brown Lady—an' I'm a-tellin' you thar's nary pleasure to surpass a-settin' thar in the hills of a fair moonlight night, a-listenin' to them thar hounds a-givin' tongue from hill an' hollow, far an' near.

The excitement is tremendous. Bets are freely offered and taken, and the fluctuating fortunes of the race—reported freshly every moment by the voices of the hounds—are followed with such passionate interest that at any moment life-long friends may leap at each other's throats, and many a good fox-hunt ends in a shooting. That's regrettable, but after all, men are hardly themselves at fox-hunts. Meanwhile, the hounds pursue the quarry, miles to the north, miles to the south, over the moon-lit hills, and all the time giving tongue. Silver Bell for a long time is but one leap behind Robin Hood, then down the holler she gains, she hangs on his flank, she passes him! But she's not the stayer that Robin is. Give Robin time—thar on the up-hill way he'll be a-shootin' past her yet. "Listen thar—that's a strange dawg in the runnin'. Anybody yere know that thar dawg's mouth?" "Shorely; he's that yaller hound of Ural Dennises—an' he a-tryin' to sell me that dawg, yesterday was but a week ago, for a tree dawg! I says to him at the time, I says, 'Ural, that thar's a trail dawg,' I says; but Ural, he would maintain he was a tree dawg borned an' bred." "No; 'tis never Ural's dawg, 'tis a strange dawg I never hearn before. Ural's dawg, he has more tenor to his tone than what this yere one has." Passionate argument as to exactly how much tenor Ural's dawg has to his tone. Meanwhile, the faithful pack has succeded in turning the fox; the hunt is coming nearer. And now, if we'll all be perfectly quiet, motionless, it may be that we'll see the fox himself. The wise hounds try to bring him to the very mountain-top where we sit, with care not to drive him to windward. Parties on fox-hunts have seen the fox stand listening, with lifted paw and pricked ears, full in the clearing's moonlight, nigh enough that with a long reach they could've teched him. Then off again, and all the hounds sweeping past in hot pursuit.

All night long, till daybreak, this can go on, if the fox is a really good one. Sometimes the hounds overtake the fox running him in full sight, and then the hunters know by the change in their cries that the fox is in danger. The excitement grows far more intense, and there are passionate differences of opinion about blowing the horns. Some hunters will contend that the fox is a-makin' for cover just 'tother side of the branch, and will distance the dawgs again if left to have his way. Others protest that he can't do it, he's shorely nigh to winded, and far better to end this yere hunt now than to leave a good fox be ruint. The dogs really settle it, for when there's no mellowness left in their tones, then shorely 'tis a time for quick action. The horns are blown, the dogs called off. In but one more minute, 'twould've been too late. Only two years ago this comin' June, thar was a huntin' party down in Douglas County had no better sense than to leave their dawgs tear plumb to pieces as good a fox as ever was started.

Just about six miles south of town there is a fox known for fifty miles around. He is so fond of the hunt that it's never necessary to loose the starter. All you need do is blow the automobile horns, and that fox will come out and bark till you set the pack after him. That fox is good for an all-night hunt, any time.

As I say, it crisps the hair of the English to hear about Ozark fox-hunting. But we enjoy it, and so do the dogs, and the foxes. In our crude barbarian way, we don't any of us give a hoot in Hades what a visiting English major thinks of our fox hunts. After the dogs are called in, or just before the sun rises, we roast our potatoes and fry the bacon and pour the coffee and sorghum into our tin cups, and while we eat we tell tales of famous fox-hunts past and present, and speak lovingly of dawgs with singin' voices 'twas pure music to hear, now dead and gone. And then we put the hounds back into the trailers and come home.[8]

Which I'll be doing, sometime between this midnight and tomorrow morning.

RWL

I promise not to say one more word about it; only this—I do wish you'd take the baby back to your trusted doctor, *now.*

---

1. The Children's Bureau of the U.S. Department of Labor offered cooperative support of maternity and child-care programs to the states. The bureau's authorization expired in 1922; its renewal was subject to some controversy. See *New York Times,* March 4, 1930, 22:6.

2. Frederick II (1194–1250), king of Sicily and emperor of the Holy Roman Empire 1215–1250.

3. Giotto (1266–1337) was a Florentine painter and sculptor; he is generally regarded as the great innovator in the transition from medieval to Renaissance art. Notably, his characters have an air of passionate life.

4. Caryatids are supporting columns carved in the form of a female figure.

5. The Pamirs are an elevated region of central Asia.

6. Henry Seidel Canby, editor of *The Saturday Review of Literature.*

7. Rose's baby died at birth in 1909 or 1910, according to her only other letter to mention this fact (Letter to Charles and Joan Clarke, Feb. 8, 1944).

8. For another account of the fox hunt, see Rose Wilder Lane, "Reynard Runs," *North American Review,* no. 330 (Sept. 1930), 354–60.

Letter 31

Rocky Ridge Farm
Mansfield, Missouri
July 6, 1930

Dorothy dear,

Of course I knew you had no time to write. And just a little while after you left here someone wrote something about having seen you, so I knew you'd safely arrived. Then the radio announced Michael's safe arrival, even before Hal's telegram came, and everything was for the best in the best of all possible worlds. I hadn't quite realized how very dreadfully I was worried, till then.

Isn't it idiotic, but actually I didn't know where to reach you. You said you were giving up the apartment; to save my soul I couldn't recall the name of that neighboring hotel of yours, nor that of the hospital. Genevieve[1] was in St. Louis, and everyone else I know somewhere else, not in New York. Well, you should have guessed all I could have said, anyway, and did guess, I'm sure.

And how supremely considerate of your son to arrive so simply. Tell him that I like him enormously, already, just for that. What a bad augury for his future, though. He really must learn to be more ruthlessly roughshod in his dealings. Good manners are all very well, indeed quite essential, but there's something really American in the sincere kindliness of his action. I shall pray for him that he learn to be more European. Really, darling, I'm afraid it will require the intercession of Santa Rita[2] to prevent his being a writer. After all, why not? He would undoubtedly be a good one.

Many calamities have occurred to me since you were here, and nothing but further calamities appear in all the tea-cups. Not that I mean to bore anyone else with them. But since they include a sudden brief illness that leaves me wobbly, they must explain why I'm not writing anything that could be called a letter. You will send me your address, won't you? Because I do not know where the beautiful house and garden are. Though I suppose that in an emergency "Mrs. Sinclair Lewis, Vermont", would reach you. Send me your address, and Allah willing, I shall write you, really.

Indeed you are a beast, my dear, but you are so very much else that no one will ever really mind. I love you very much, as always. That's just a simple fact.

Rose

---

1. Genevieve Parkhurst of *Pictorial Review.*

2. The allusion to Santa Rita occurs several times in Rose's letters, apparently as a private joke regarding a patron saint for lost causes.

Letter 32

Westport
December 24, 1930

Dear Dorothy,

Your son has gazed upon snow. It began falling day before yesterday; that is, when I woke it had been falling and was still doing so, and the entire landscape was precisely like the most banal of old-fashioned Christmas cards which we never see anymore, even to the tinsel, as soon as the sun came out. Michael was entranced. Taken out for his usual 'most-all-day sleep in his carriage, he exclaimed with wonder at the dazzle, and listened attentively when it was explained to him that the phenomenon is snow.

We took a couple of snapshots, but how good they will be I don't know, as I know next to nothing about cameras and the light was, of course, tricky.

The telephone rang an hour or so ago, and the usual professional voice explained that it had a cablegram for Michael. "Yes?" I said receptively.

"Are you Michael?"

"No, but Michael is a baby and can't come to the telephone."

"When he can come to the telephone, will you please ask him to call 663 South Norwalk?"

"But he is a baby; he can't."

"Then when he can, will you please ask him to call—"

"Is the cablegram from Mrs. Lewis?"

"Are you Mrs. Lewis?"

"No. I want to know the signature of the cablegram." (With firm authority) "I am Mrs. Lane."

"OH. The cablegram is for Michael. It's signed 'Mother'."

"Very well. Please mail it to him at this address."

Because I thought, maybe he might not be here when he could go to the telephone and call 663 South Norwalk. But if he has it, he can always read it as soon as he is old enough to read.

There is absolutely nothing to write you. I have had a frightful cold and so have rather stayed away from the rosy- cheeked one. He is in abounding health and spirits, and his hair has grown quite long and is pure red-gold; I mean, not the pale anemic gold, but a very determined and forceful gold. He does not like his cereal, and the doctor is sending a new formula. The scream of sheer venomous rage with which he greets the appearance of cereal forecasts that he will be a young man of decision with a mind of his own. (I do not know why I put that in the future tense.)

Mrs. Waldron[1] came in a few evenings ago. I called her up the other morning to comment on the snow, and the upshot of the conversation was that I asked her and her husband to dinner here tonight. Feeling that really something should be done about Christmas, I had ordered a turkey, and the smallest was ten pounds. So I thought guests would shorten the subsequent period of hash. I don't know what else there will be; Renée[2] manages very well without instruction, and so I haven't bothered. The house just runs along quite smoothly and happily.

André[3] is now putting the base on Michael's Christmas tree, which he will have just before his bedtime hour of six o'clock. Tinsel in quantities and the gay glass fruits and dozens of candles will be on it. It is a little tree, just large enough to set nicely on the small coffee table before the fire. Miss Haemmerli[4] has a small cloth animal for him and a package addressed to him has come from Pittsburgh, marked "Fragile"; I have not opened it yet.

I have bought chains for the Ford, since when we went to town (Westport) this morning, we could not get up the hill again. So I told André to turn about and return to Westport for chains. (The Hupmobile's chains do not fit a Ford.) On the way we ran head-on into another Ford and smashed both bumpers. (I mean the front bumpers of both cars.) Jammed 'em right back against the wheels.

I really don't know how it happened, as I noticed nothing until I suddenly went headlong. A woman was driving the other car; it developed that she lives in the house just across the road from here, the For Sale one. She said that she saw André charging down upon her and was afraid to try to turn too quickly because of the slippery road, and that she has been driving nine years and never had an accident. André said that she had started to turn out to the left, that he thought she was going into a house nearby, and so turned to the left himself to pass her. From this I deduce that when she saw André coming rather fast, she did swerve a little to the left—one of these flickers of the front wheels that give the other driver an impression.

We were equally damaged, so I asked her if she were insured. She said she was, and I suggested that we both report to our insurance companies and have them mutually pay each other's damages, and by taking the matter lightly and being entirely good humored about it, we finally arrived at a decision to say nothing about it to anyone. André, after a great deal of effort, managed to remove both bumpers so the front wheels could move, and we parted amiably. She suggested that we not report the matter to the police. To my amazement, I discover that incidents of this kind, in Connecticut, *should* be reported to the police. In the Ozarks we never bother to bring in legalities unless someone is killed, in which case, a doctor makes out a certificate of death by accident. André says he himself can fix the bumper. I do not think it will be particularly safe, because a straightened bumper never has the strength of a new one. But it will be safe enough for all my purposes, and Michael does not use the car.

My own feeling is that the accident was just one of those things that happen, and I do not blame André, who is a good driver and no doubt acted properly with things as he saw them. Nevertheless, at that point there was no side road going to the house that he thought she was going to, and he was on the wrong side when we crashed. So any investigation would put him absolutely in the wrong. On the evidence of the tracks, it would appear that he deliberately swerved to the left to hit her. Therefore it seems best to forget the whole thing, from every point of view.

Nevertheless, it isn't my car nor do I pay the insurance on it—which I explained—so if you people want something done . . .

Nothing about the car is hurt in any way, except the bumper.

This is a stupid letter, but I am stupid because of the cold, I mean my cold. The house has been adequately warm; however, the weather has been very mild. Mrs. Wallace Irwin[5] called up to ask about Michael, worried because it was so cold on Long Island. I'm sorry to report that the oilburner drinks oil as a camel from the desert swallows the springs.

CHRISTMAS MORNING

Merry Christmas! Though by now it is tonight where you are.

Michael was an angel about the Christmas tree. That child is an intellectual prodigy. Miss Haemmerli and I sat him up in his carriage while we trimmed the tree, and he watched every motion with the greatest concentration—all the while, from first to last, at times uttering a gurgle and wriggle of approval.

When we lighted the candles he was entranced. He would have clapped his hands if only he could have managed to make them meet. Miss Haemmerli says it was your sister[6] who sent the package from Pittsburgh; if her address had been on it I would write her, for Michael was overjoyed by the little pale blue shiny wooden man at the end of a pale blue string, who came out of it. He bounced with delight, and holding out both arms seized upon it and at once conveyed the marvelously round sleek wooden head to his mouth. Darling, HOW I wanted a picture for you! Without a flashlight it wasn't possible. We immediately distracted his attention by a pale golden wooly dog, warranted sanitary by Miss Haemmerli, and he seized upon that too and held it in his other arm, and all his toes wriggled with passionate pleasure.

The Waldrons came for dinner, bringing him a large, bright yellow, wooden elephant. It was then six-ten, and Michael had retired but was not yet asleep, so as a Christmas treat he was allowed to receive his guests AND the elephant. He was then in his little crib, in a corner of your room by the hall door. Mr. Waldron will probably tell you how he received the elephant; he *shouted* gurgles at the sight, and kicked with all his legs and seized upon the elephant. Miss Haemmerli held it so that he could not put it in his mouth, and over it he regarded the Waldrons with large, round, beaming eyes and laughed like anything.

Papers report you and Hal on your way to England.??? God be with you till we meet again, and may it be soon. We have taken some more snapshots of Michael which shall be mailed you—if any of them are any good—as soon as they are printed. But you should not be so pampered, and if the absence of snapshots really would make you take the next boat, as Hal cabled, then WHY do we send snapshots?

Inshallah,[7] we shall see you soon. Much love, and may you live long and go on a smooth trail through 1931.

Rose

---

1. The Waldrons were Westport neighbors.
2. Renée was the household cook.
3. André was the chauffeur and handyman.
4. Rosa Haemmerli was the nurse in charge of Michael Lewis; see Sanders, *Dorothy Thompson,* pp. 170–72.
5. Mr. and Mrs. Wallace Irwin, both writers, were close friends of Dorothy's; see Sanders, *Dorothy Thompson,* p. 151.
6. Margaret (Peggy) Wilson, Dorothy's sister.
7. *Inshalah:* Allah willing.

Letter 33

Twin Farms
Barnard, Vermont
June 8, 1932

My darling Rose,

Hal says of course he will read C. Brody's book.[1] What he does will depend, of course, on what he thinks of it. He's prepared to think well.

My life, Rose, leaves too few moments for meditation, correspondence or old friends. You think "out of sight, out of mind," but it's not so. I love you always, Rose. But I'm inarticulate in letters. My life is all up and down. When it's down I can't write. When it's up I'm so busy holding on to its upness. Just now—and for weeks—it's been up.

I went to Europe in the fall and again at the end of April, both times for *The Post.*[2] I think my stuff is getting somewhat better. If you did, I should be happy. The news is: Hal and I are staying here until August 24th and are then sailing to Europe (with Micky) for six or seven months. We've taken a house in the Semmering—you know it, two hours from Vienna—and shall stay there for the winter. It's a nice house; it has lots of room and I wish you might decide to come and stay with us for a while. Somehow this doesn't seem impossible to me so I'm giving you the address: Sauerbrunn Villa, Semmering, Austria. It will be our home from Sept. 1 to May 1st 1932–33.

Your Micky is a big boy now. Stuttering words. He's as blond as ever and (I think) utterly adorable. I'm sending you a picture, though the one in the *Redbook*[3] is really much better, only I haven't a copy and only saw it yesterday.

Red is awfully well and happier than I've seen him in years.

Roses, *won't* you be coming east some time before August 24th, and won't you come here? I know country doesn't offer you much, but I'd like to have you with me once in our own real home.

I kiss you,
Dorothy

---

1. Novelist Catherine Brody was a friend of Rose's and stayed with her in Mansfield for several extended visits. The reference here is to her novel *Nobody Starves* (London: Longmans, Green & Co., 1932).

2. Dorothy had written a number of articles for *The Saturday Evening Post* in the preceding year.

3. I have been unable to trace this reference to *Redbook* magazine.

Letter 34

Twin Farms
Barnard, Vermont
July 28, 1932

My darling Rose,

Hal has probably written you about Catherine Brody's book. At any rate he liked it and said so. He said he wished that she had done certain things a little differently. Once in a while she did a little fancy writing in a modernistic manner, and it didn't quite fit. But this is all *nebenbei.*[1] The book is extraordinarily vivid, convincing, and sincere, and as Hal said (to the publishers) one of the rarest of things: a genuine proletarian novel. Swell title, too. Hal wrote the publishers, and they were pleased with what he wrote.

I tell you this because Hal himself is in New York having two ulcerated teeth treated, poor darling. And I don't know whether he wrote or not.

My summer's stint is about done: five articles for *The Post,* one for the *Red Book,* and one for *Pictorial.* If von Ziekursch takes the latter, I shall be surprised, because I said several things I really believe.[2] Anyhow, it has a certain radioactivity which most of my writing (how well I know it) lacks.

Thank you, darling, for your letter. But, oh, dear Roses, I honestly write as well as I can. Two souls, as you guess, dwell in this bosom. But as a poet, I was a hell of a bad one. For me, the closely reasoned argument has become the nearest thing to art which I can achieve. I have definitely forsaken the divine urge for the more seasoned thought (there never was much urge) and the thought isn't very seasoned. Yet I know that pure, logical, clear-cut thinking and simple writing on even politics can approach art. Keynes did it in *The Economic Consequences of Peace.*[3] But I don't think it ever has been or ever will be done for the *Saturday Evening Post.* As Hal once said, "I am a good trained hack, and I know almost instinctively how to write for George Lorimer."[4]

I want to do a book this winter, with no thought of magazine publication, to be called *The End of Bourgeois Morality.*[5] I want to analyze the revolution in the world in terms of a revolution in ethics. I am extremely ill-equipped to do it. To succeed I should have to read, and read, and read, even before I began to think. But mine, such as it is, is a deductive mind, that goes for the essential first and then has little difficulty with the associations, and I think I see certain things.

Anyhow, I should learn something doing it.

We sail on August 24th, and I wish to God I could see you first. What chance your coming over in the next six months? We shall have a house in Austria, in the Semmering, which is open to you for whenever and as long as you care to use it. And, probably, some sort of *pied à terre*[6] in Vienna. We go definitely until the middle of May—perhaps for longer. Hal's novel is done,[7] and he is more carefree and happy than I have seen him ever.

Micky is divine. Tonight as I left the house, walking across the lawn to the car, I heard him call down, perfectly clearly, "Good-night, Mummy, are you going in the car?" He's still in the state when such clear sentences simply bowl me over. His hair, darling, is paler and paler. Just now without a trace of pink, just tow. It has no smell even of curl. And he has six freckles, and big, wide, white teeth. He does not, in the least, resemble Little Lord Fauntleroy. But he still has a smile to take the heart out of you.

Stella Bowen, who is simply a swell gal—a wife once of Ford Madox Ford,[8] who took it hard, and an extremely fine painter, was up and did a portrait of me and Micks. If I can ever get it photographed, I will send you one.

Rose, are you ever coming to see us here, in the one home we have in the world? You know I love you always. . . .

d.

---

1. *Nebenbei:* incidental.

2. Dorothy published nine articles in *The Saturday Evening Post* between this date and the end of 1933; the five alluded to doubtless are among them. The *Pictorial Review* article was probably "Election! What For?," published in November 1932. I cannot trace the *Redbook* article.

3. John Maynard Keynes (1883–1946), *The Economic Consequences of the Peace* (London: Macmillan, 1919).

4. George Horace Lorimer was president of the Curtis Publishing Company, publishers of *The Saturday Evening Post,* and also editor of the *Post.*

5. This book was never written.

6. *Pied-à-terre:* a small occasional apartment.

7. The novel was *Ann Vickers* (New York: Doubleday & Co., 1933).

8. Stella Bowen was English novelist Ford Madox Ford's companion in the 1920s. For a summary account, see Douglas Goldring, *The Last Pre-Raphaelite* (London: MacDonald, 1948), pp. 203–39.

Letter 35

Rocky Ridge Farm
Mansfield, Missouri
August 3, 1932

Dorothy dear,

Forgive me for writing you at the end of a long twelve hours of work which has come to nothing—so that a wilting of spirit is added to our occupational ache in the back and knot in the nape of the neck. But I am so excited by your letter. Dorothy, life *is* a miracle. When I think of Micky, speaking. All this time he has been lying in the baby buggy at four in the afternoon, when I might see him wake up, and gazing at an inexplicable, somewhat perplexing but always amusing universe, with those blue eyes of his, and he has sometimes gurgled in surprise at the sight of his own feet kicking, and he has sometimes baa-aa'd in protest at cream-of-wheat. And now, suddenly, he speaks from a window and says, "Good night, Mummy, are you going in the car?" I can't tell you how I feel about it. It is simply incredible that such things can happen. You know—how can they? How can Micky become what he is, and what he is going to be? Somehow it seems to me more miraculous than his ever being, in the first place. I suppose that's because we can't imagine not-being; we feel that somehow Micky always *was,* that he arrived. But what has become of the baby? How did this youngster come here?

And then about your book. There is no imaginable book I would rather read. This was the book I wanted when I read *A Preface to Morals.*[1] I can think of no one better equipped than you in quality of mind, to write it. One thing at least is sure, that you will say something. You will speak clearly. And since you see this chaotic scene in terms of a revolution in ethics, you must see not only a debacle, but a purpose, that is to say a direction not only from, but to. The news that you intend to write such a book is more exciting than—I can't think when I've been so excited since the news of the Bolshevik revolution. This is funny, no doubt; probably it doesn't make sense, but anyway that's how I feel. And after so many years, for the first time it strikes me that our excitement in those days was, really, a quite personal thing. The news from Russia had a personal meaning to each of us, for it came at last as a confirmation in external reality of our own dreams which we'd cherished so passionately. Cherished so passionately, perhaps, precisely because we didn't quite believe in them? Because they were so far from finding any sanction in realities? Remember how we said and felt, "The sun is rising in Russia!"?

It's a long way from those days to these, and I seem to be saying a great deal about myself in saying that such excitement takes hold of me at the prospect of reading a book, a matter entirely between myself and me. I have, of course, no mind at all for these problems. (It would probably be more exact to say simply that I have no mind. Merely emotional reactions.) The lack of this tool is the reason why I have no point of view whatever on morals, because for years I have wanted one. (I have been heard saying with vigor, here and there, "What we need is *morals.*") It's a dilemma that's important, of course, only because it's the dilemma of so many. But why do I say that? I don't believe it. Not really. That's only the mode, the fashionable way of speaking and thinking nowadays. Is this a hint of your revolution? I hope not.

So, as I was saying, I have thought—or rather felt—with longing of the Catholic Church. Or Islam. It struck me in Damascus, by the way, that the conversion of Englishmen to Islam (not many, but a few) was simply part of the movement into the Roman Catholic church. (I told you I am tired and have no business writing to you.) And the communistic fervor in Tiflis and Erivan[2] was, in a sense, the same thing. No, it does all return to the individual, and the salvation of my soul is important because it is a question of *my soul*—whether or not one single other human being should face my predicament. Yet here I find myself murmuring, and sincerely, that I am not important, that a dilemma is important only if it affects "the majority." I wish to God Rousseau had never been born![3] The world has gone wrong ever since. There's been no room for the human being in it, since Humanity began taking up so much space. When will we learn again that Humanity doesn't exist?

You see, the difficulty is that one *can't* return. It isn't possible to be Victorian. I feel that the problem is essentially, how to contrive to be Victorian while accepting—as at least probable—Eddington's universe.[4] (I would say, Einstein, but I take it for granted that he's far beyond my powers.) And how to find, or to create, the static Being, amid nothing but vibrations? We need a God, and Vibration isn't material for making Him. It's Being we need, not Becoming. Oh, and how we lapped up Bergson![5] Do you remember?

Is it egotism that makes me believe that my own experience proves that it isn't enough to say "There is no God but Lenin, and our heavenly reward is the Cooperative Commonwealth"? Do you remember Shaw's Methuselah; how vigorously he said what I don't believe he ever meant to say, that no man can come to Superman stature by taking thought?[6] Muscular development doesn't really come by faithfully doing the morning calisthenics. It comes by climbing the tree because we want the apple on the topmost bough. What we need is an apple. What we need is an object, an aim, which will compel us to accomplish a purpose by indirection because we somehow never do accomplish a purpose by trying to. After all, it must be admitted that the moral purpose of the Victorian Age was not to produce the Machine Age. (I suppose all my phrases are quaint; it's incredible how long it is since I've seen anyone to talk to. Nearly a year and a half.) I believe that the—what shall I call it?—the communistic idea in ethics is all wrong. The greatest good to the greatest number. Act so that each of your actions might be made a universal pattern of conduct. Do unto others as you would be done by. The brotherhood of Man (unchecked, undisciplined by the Fatherhood of God). It seems to me that it's wrong because (seems to me) it doesn't work, and more importantly because (seems to me) human nature itself rejects it—and not from the greed that's called selfishness either, but from the Self that finds it inadequate. It doesn't work because—maybe this principle of indirection?—no one can serve the Greatest Good to the Greatest Number; he doesn't know what the greatest good for them is, and he can never be in touch with the greatest number. The greatest good to the greatest number will obviously be reached when each individual of the greatest number is doing the greatest good to himself. That's why the Brotherhood of Man is all right, if and when each man is primarily concerned with his own relationship to God. And the hell of it is, we have no God. He's gone completely. We absolutely must make a new one.

You can see that I'm at least perfectly aware of the end of bourgeois morality! And also I'm aware that an end is always a beginning. But a beginning of what? I see nothing but chaos, but you will discern a pattern. Do you wonder that I pant for your book?

Well, I don't know—art? No, of course you're right. But the value of art to the artist is not what it is in itself, but what it is to him. All I was asking for was you, the whole you, freely functioning in your writing. And it seems to me I've got it. *Why Do We Call it Post-War?* and *All the King's Horses*[7] are really you. Nonsense! Hal's remark is amusing and clever, and it says a lot about the SEP, but it's a long way from the whole truth. Everything is done within limitations, (and naturally you are right when you tell Lorimer that you can not write about Russia for him; could you write about a pogrom for the *Christian Science Monitor*?) but there's lots of room within SEP limitations. Hal may be a good trained hack—far from me to dispute him on ground so personal—but if he hadn't been a lot more as well, he'd never have made even the SEP. He knows it, too. Well, well, and why this aspersion cast, anyhow, on a perfectly good horse who may be as thoroughbred as any racer? Not all hacks were short-coupled

Morgans. And at that, Man o' War answered the bit; he'd have been no good if he hadn't.[8] Here's a notion: ask Lorimer sometime if he would have printed, or would now print, were they available, Keynes' views of the economic consequences of peace. Go on; I think it would be amusing. But don't ever let me hear *you* saying "I'm a good trained hack." Not in that tone of voice.

I remember once, when I was first writing newspaper serials, Fremont Older asked me one day if I were really putting everything I had into them. I said "Well, they're getting circulation, aren't they?"

"That wasn't what I asked you," said he.

"What do you want?" I asked him. "Victor Hugo?"

"Yes, that's what I want," he said.

I was dumbfounded. "Do you mean to tell me you'd print in *The Bulletin—Les Misérables,* for instance?"

You know Older, Dorothy. He leapt in his chair, he struck the desk a blow with his fist that almost splintered it and shouted "GOOD GOD, *YES*! Good GOD, if I could get a thing like *Les Misérables*!"

I crept stunned from the office. Some of the best work I've done is in those old *Bulletin* files, and my first novel was a *Bulletin* serial wrenched out of the *Bulletin* by accident and published by Century.[9] Well, you know as well as I do what I'm worth and not worth as a writer. There's nothing to be said about that. But what I'm not is not caused by any imposed limitations. After all, where *are* these famous limitations? This ruthless destruction of The Artist by the mercenary editor? Hal doesn't seem to have been destroyed, really, Edna Millay seems to get along. Hemingway has been heard of, and even Catherine is getting a book published. God bless Hal! Would he like my heart served up as mincemeat, or anything?

This I can do for him. If he has to have one of those teeth extracted—God forbid!—tell him for me to have it done by the Winters method. Tell him to insist upon it, to cry for it till he gets it, to listen to no objections by whomever made, and even to go to McGinnis in Birmingham, Alabama if he must. One tooth out by the Winters method, and he will be as grateful to me as I am to him. But this takes firmness of character, for dentists are as rabid on the subject as doctors used to be about anesthetics in childbirth.[10]

My dear, ever since I have been carrying this frightful financial burden,[11] I've been able to do nothing whatever that I wanted to. Sometimes I think I shall grow old and die in this solitary confinement. You are sweet to want to see me. Somehow, somehow, I will manage to get away from here again, if only I live long enough. It's all I can say. And you know there's never been a time since 1920 that I didn't rush to you when I could. I feel we've never really finished the conversation that we started sitting amid the red satin *couvre-pied*[12] on that bed in an inn in the valley of the Loire.

Here's wishing you the best of voyages and a joyous winter *and* the book, in the Semmering. A kiss for Micky and my grateful love to Hal.

Yours always,

RWL

And *after* you've done the book, do exhaust possibilities of magazine publication. Anything you say is worth saying to as many readers as possible.

---

1. Walter Lippmann, *A Preface to Morals* (New York: Macmillan, 1929).

2. Rose had traveled in Soviet Georgia and Armenia from October to December 1922, according to her diaries for that period.

3. Rose's contempt for the French philosopher Jean-Jacques Rousseau (1712–1778) is a little hard to understand, since his works have provided the seminal arguments for the natural equality of men. Apparently she objected to his myth of a golden age of primitive communal living, from which inferences for modern reform could be drawn: an exaltation of the general will of the people and a tax upon wealth to promote an equality of condition in the social body. Rose was working her way toward a view that accepted the primacy of the individual and a society of dynamic inequality, finally expressed in her *The Discovery of Freedom* (New York: John Day, 1943).

4. According to her diary (June 26, 1930), Rose had been reading Arthur Eddington's *The Nature of the Physical World* (Cambridge: Cambridge University Press, 1928).

5. The French philosopher Henri Bergson (1859–1941), whose work argued that logical and scientific reasoning were inadequate models for understanding reality. Rather, Bergson held, reality has no fixed structure and change is of its essence. Thus, Being is illusory, Becoming the prime reality.

6. Rose seems to confuse here Shaw's *Back to Methuselah* (1921) and *Man and Superman* (1903). The allusion seems to be to a passage in "The Revolutionist's Handbook," appended to *Man and Superman:* see *The Bodley Head Bernard Shaw Collected Plays* (7 vols.; London: The Bodley Head, 1971), 2:775.

7. Dorothy Thompson, "Why Call It Post-War?," *Saturday Evening Post,* July 23, 1932, pp. 205–7; "All the King's Horses," *Saturday Evening Post,* August 6, 1932, pp. 205–9.

8. This vivid argument for the value of disciplined work-for-hire turns, of

course, on the metaphor of the writer as horse hired for an occasion. *Short-coupled* is a term for a horse of a particular muscular configuration of rear legs and body. Man-O'-War was a famous American racehorse in 1919–1920.

9. *Diverging Roads,* serialized in *Sunset Magazine* (Oct. 1918–June 1919) before its book publication by Century Publishers in 1919.

10. Dental problems plagued Rose and her mother during this period; and Rose tended to become well-informed and opinionated on matters of health. The Winters method and Dr. McGinnis no doubt had contemporary significance, but I have not been able to find it.

11. Rose was supporting her own household (with a cook and a hired hand) as well as contributing to her parents' support. She lost a substantial sum in the stock-market failure; thus everything depended on her regular publication of stories and articles.

12. *Couvre-pied:* a coverlet.

Part IV

Letters 36–42 (1938–1939)

Introduction to Part IV

The correspondence falls off significantly after 1932. No doubt letters have been lost, but it should not be surprising that the growing difference in their lives should put a distance between these women. Rose remained tied to the Missouri farm until 1937, when she was able to establish a small independent income for her parents; she then moved to a rural farmhouse near Danbury, Connecticut. In the meantime, Dorothy's career rose, in her own words, like "an ascending comet."[1] In 1931, she visited Germany again and spoke with Hitler; her book *I Saw Hitler* (1932) offered a condescending view of Hitler as the "prototype of the Little Man." She predicted that he would amount to nothing—a colossal error that, nonetheless, made her career. For when she returned to Germany in 1934, she was immediately expelled, presumably at Hitler's personal order. The resulting publicity made her a much-sought-after public speaker and led directly to an offer by the *New York Herald Tribune* to establish her as a regular columnist. "On the Record" ran three days a week, alternating with Walter Lippman's column, and was widely syndicated. Soon she was also given a weekly syndicated radio program by NBC and a monthly column by *Ladies' Home Journal*. In 1939, she appeared on the cover of *Time* magazine, which identified her with Eleanor Roosevelt as the two most influential women in the United States. *Time* estimated her income for 1938 at $103,000.[2]

Neither Dorothy Thompson nor Sinclair Lewis suffered from the stock-market crash of 1929 or from the Depression of the 1930s. Rose, however, lost everything she had in savings, and she wrote heroically to maintain an income sufficient to her family's needs. In 1936, she earned just under $9,000, and earlier years were leaner still.[3] In this period, however, she was doing her own best work—the silent, never-acknowledged coauthorship of her mother's "Little House" books, which were to become children's classics.[4] By 1942, she would have her own newspaper column as well—in an obscure Negro newspaper, the *Pittsburgh Courier*.[5] In the 1930s, both she and Dorothy appeared regularly in the *Saturday Evening Post*, which was hospitable to both writers by virtue of its hostility to the Roosevelt presidency.

In this period, Rose's own political philosophy began to take shape, largely in reaction to the policies of the New Deal. She had lost everything in a disaster—as had her parents in their day and her grandparents in theirs. And she was surviving by her own efforts, as they had. The intervention in people's lives by a government intent on helping them she found an intolerable infringement on personal freedom; and the *Saturday Evening Post* furnished her a forum in which to develop her views, in articles as well as in exemplary tales of pioneer fortitude.[6] During the rest of her life she would continue as a lonely voice against the rising tide of government power, developing a point of view that has in later years come to be called libertarian: in foreign policy, it embraced George Washington's warning against foreign entanglements while correspondingly emphasizing the historical uniqueness of the American discovery of human freedom; in domestic policy, it would reduce government to a peace-keeping function, allowing all other matters to be solved by the dialectic of competition and voluntary cooperation. Needless to say, the central value was the absolute personal responsibility that is the price of absolute freedom.[7]

On domestic affairs, Dorothy shared many of her views. Dorothy's talents alone had raised her from obscurity to fame and prosperity; she opposed Social Security and was suspicious of the Roosevelt presidency in many ways.[8] However, her early love affair with Germany and Austria had made her a determined internationalist and an advocate of American intervention in Europe. But as the war in Europe grew, Dorothy began to see that only Roosevelt could unite the country for the opposition to the Fascist powers that would save Europe. Abruptly, she shifted her support in the 1940 presidential campaign from Willkie to Roosevelt. The change in allegiance cost her many friends and ultimately the sponsorship of her column by the *Herald Tribune.*[9] Her friendship with Rose apparently survived, although the damage must have been considerable.

The period from 1929 to 1937 was in many ways the most painful of Rose's career. Bad health, financial anxiety, rural isolation, and political outrage run as heavy dark lines through her diaries and letters. The contrast with Dorothy's seemingly charmed life must have been frustrating. As she contemplated her misery in one of her darker moments, she noted an uncharacteristic thought in her diary: "Some day, I shall tell this to Dorothy. For her sake, Mickey should die. She needs a taste of suffering."[10] But a reading of the evidence on the other side suggests that Dorothy's successes were tempered by her share of grief. The marriage to Sinclair Lewis had been a troubled one from the honeymoon onward. In time the couple came to separate residences and separate lives. Dorothy was willing to continue the marriage even on these terms, and she resisted Lewis's suggestion that they divorce; but in the end the marriage was dissolved in 1942.[11] Dorothy confided her problems to some of her friends, but not, apparently, to Rose, who renewed her visits with Dorothy after her move to Connecticut in 1937. In a letter to a Missouri friend, she relayed the following anecdote that puts the best possible face on the Lewises' marriage:

> You know how we kept reading from time to time either that the Sinclair Lewises were having trouble, or that the Sinclair Lewises (with pictures) denied any rift within the lute (which made one wonder more than ever.) Well, it started by Winchell's reporting (I imagine in good faith) that they were separating. Dorothy was in Europe at the time. Ships' news reporters met her on her return and asked if it were true. She said, "Oh tell Winchell to go to hell!" (He printed this, under the caption, Run Your Own Errands, Dorothy.) Seems, however, it annoyed him excessively, and thereafter, about four times a year, he reported again that the Lewises were separating. Once printed that she had gone to Reno to get the divorce. Dorothy said, told me, that it got really annoying. She was helpless; a denial often went farther than Winchell's original squib. She could have sued him for libel, but what would that get her but much more publicity, and besides, she said, to have that rotten crowd really aroused and after you is sheer hell; they would probably put detectives on Hal and her and report every time they lunched with women or men. This went on for four years, and then last fall she sailed on the Normandie. A *London Daily Express* man was aboard; the *Express* has a reciprocal arrangement with Hearst; and the second day out he came to her all embarrassed and upset, saying he had a wire from the New York office, he was ordered to ask her a question, he knew she was a fellow journalist and understood that he personally had no choice—etc. Oh well, she said, What is the question? He handed her the radiogram, saying to verify report that Dorothy Thompson had *secretly* sailed on the Normandie to establish residence in Paris and get a divorce from Sinclair Lewis. Then she had the inspiration. Yes, she said, I do have a statement to make about this. I want it sent verbatim, just as I dictate it. A short statement. Will you please take your pencil and write it. Then she dictated: "Mrs. Sinclair Lewis, interviewed on the Normandie by the representative of the *London Daily Express,* confirms the report that she will establish residence in

Paris and divorce Sinclair Lewis; she will name Marian Davies as co-respondent." And she said to the reporter, "Will you please add, that if this question is asked again, I shall give this statement to the A.P." She has never heard one yip from Winchell since. Don't you think it's a honey? Genius, I call it.[12]

1. Sanders, *Dorothy Thompson,* p. 226.

2. Ibid., VI. 4; p. 238.

3. Financial statement from her agent, George Bye, for 1936. Her diaries frequently note annual income in year-end summaries; for 1934 and 1935, she recorded sums of under $5,000.

4. William T. Anderson, "The Literary Apprenticeship of Laura Ingalls Wilder," *South Dakota History* 13 (Winter 1983): 285–331.

5. The *Pittsburgh Courier* column ran from 1942 to 1945.

6. "Credo," *Saturday Evening Post,* no. 208, March 7, 1936, 5–7, 30–35; "American Revolution, 1939," *Saturday Evening Post,* no. 211 (Jan. 7, 1939), 23, 50, 52. Her novels *Let the Hurricane Roar* (1932) and *Free Land* (1938) were both serials in the *Post* before book publication.

7. The thesis of her summary work, *The Discovery of Freedom* (1943).

8. Sanders, *Dorothy Thompson,* VII. 8.

9. Ibid., VII. 1–2.

10. Diary, Jan. 18, 1934.

11. Sanders, *Dorothy Thompson,* pp. 281–82.

12. Rose Wilder Lane to Mary Paxton Keeley, undated letter (Missouri State Historical Society, Columbia, Mo.). Dorothy's tactic was grounded in two facts: that Marian Davies was William Randolph Hearst's mistress, and that Walter Winchell was a Hearst columnist.

Letter 36

R 4 Box 42
Danbury, Connecticut
October 15, 1938

Dorothy dear,

Silently I am sending you (not meaning the alliteration) truly sincere sympathy. From a veteran bearing the scars of the same kind of wounds—destruction of the only republic in the Balkans, and calamities and dangers to our country. Listen, darling. Nobody writing in America seems to have my view of the Munich pact, and I'd therefore think I'm completely wrong, except that it's happened before and events have surprised me by proving me right. Maybe there's something in my view of this thing, and if there be, maybe you'll feel better about it.

I can't see Berchtesgaden-Munich as a British defeat, surrender to force. It looks to me like traditional British diplomacy. What happened was the destruction of France. And subsidiary, a temporary blow to Czechoslovakia's serious trade competition. France is overnight reduced from a major European power, surrounding Germany with her allies, to a negligible third-rater, herself surrounded. Czech trade competition will somewhat revive as German. You remember that the English-French war (far more fundamental than the temporary English-German) revived immediately after 1918; that it became actual fighting in the Near East,[1] that all Europe was lined up, pro-English, pro-French, and that the resurrection of Germany upset the general expectation of an English-French war in this decade. Now France is drastically reduced and completely isolated. I suggest that if the F.O.[2] regarded Germany as the enemy, it would not have destroyed its only allies against Germany on the continent. The British Empire does not commit suicide in fear of being murdered. Really, Dorothy.

Now, IF the British-German alliance be durable, if the Rome-Berlin axis is replaced by a London-Berlin axis, what happens? Then England has made a major shift in world policy by abandoning her tactic of fomenting European wars (the tactic euphemistically known as "maintaining the balance of power") and therefore there will be no more European wars. What we have is a united Europe. United against whom? Russia. The war now rests on an authentic basis of the genuine cleavage between Europe and Asia. It will go east, where Germany wants it to go and where British interests lie and British frontiers can be extended. Germany and England together can make the little nations—Italy, France, Spain—behave very nicely and mind their manners. Germany can have Poland, the Ukraine, the lower Danube and domination of the northern Balkans without endangering British interests. England can advance again as she did in 1920,[3] through Azerbaijan, and this time with German help, she can hold the trans-Caucasus, Baku-Batum, perhaps with some arrangement with Germany about the oil. England can take Persia and recover control of Afghanistan. Turkey can have French Syria, which certainly wants freedom from France, and all noble freedom-loving sentiment would champion the poor Syrians, exploited like hell as they are. Italy can rectify a few French frontiers in north Africa, thus relieving Italian pressure on British interests there. It all hangs together, it all makes sense, IF the British-German alliance holds. And why shouldn't it? Together they can push Russia back into Asia where she belongs, and with so much loot to divide it will be a long time before British and German interests clash or their frontiers collide.

I do not see how a British switch from alliance with Stalin to alliance with Hitler can be any tragic defeat for "democracy." It is a smashing blow to a communist state and to communists as a party and as an international conspiracy—a blow to conspiracy because it will create further dissension in it. But if this alliance is a triumph for Fascism, then the British alliance with the Czar was a triumph for Czarism, and the one with Stalin was a triumph for communism.

What has happened is that England returns to her basic antagonisms—against France, against Russia—from which her attention was only temporarily diverted by the hungry rise of Germany in our generation. As soon as Germany was put down in 1918, England returned to them. Now that Germany proves not to have been defeated, England wastes no more time and energy in attacking Germany, but instead defeats France, adds German strength to her own, and goes on with the real conflict.

If this destroys international law, there never was any international law, for this is nothing but the old pattern of British diplomacy since Elizabeth. I can not see the basis for believing that it is a surrender to force. What would fighting have been, but a surrender to force? Would a pro-French decision by armed force have been any less a decision by force? Force always has decided issues—what won in 1898? in 1905? in 1918?[4] Munich perhaps breaks the awful fact to the American people, who are taught no history in their schools and therefore do not know the simplest historical fact. But I do not think that force won at Berchtesgaden and Munich; I think nothing happened but a commonplace of British (or any other) foreign diplomacy, and that the only important development—if it be durable—is that England abandons her traditional policy of making wars in Europe; therefore war ceases in Europe, the pressure upon us to fight in Europe will relax, and our next war should naturally be in the Pacific, against Japan backed by England and/or Germany.

I do not believe the war-scare from the south,[5] for I think that looting European and Near-Eastern Russia, Persia, Afghanistan and China will occupy England-Germany-Japan for some time. And because Japan will be busy in Asia, I don't think you and I will see America fighting in the Pacific. Hitler's speech[6] was rotten diplomacy, (but the Germans have always been politically inept—the Russians too—because the Roman Empire did not subjugate them and train them to political-mindedness by its political genius), but it seems to me that he was simply stating an obvious fact when he said that an English communist-sentimentalist-liberal defeat of the Chamberlain policy would endanger European peace. I myself would say that, and I mean no threat to England, no attempt to dictate to Englishmen in England. I think that if the Munich pact stands, Europe—and therefore our country—will be peaceful for a long time. It's Asia that all hell will be given to.

The threat to republican government (lack of government) comes really from its own citizens. We let political power entrench itself and expand; and governing power, by its very nature, destroys personal freedom. A man is free only to the extent that he is NOT governed. Eternal vigilance is the price of liberty, etc. etc. etc. In the present state of affairs in our country, with our school-produced ignorance and school-induced leaning toward socialization, and enormous increase of governmental power recently, the death-blow to liberty on earth would be America's fighting any war. This country would instantly be a dictatorship, and no matter how the war ended, it would remain a dictatorship. So would England; so would France. Czechoslovakia would not have been saved by saving her frontiers; modern war IS dictatorship. It seems to me that the hope of saving what you call "democracy" and I would call the ideal of personal liberty, is in getting a little time, warless, for reviving that ideal in America and for teaching Americans what it is, and what it is worth, and what it costs. I would say there is no hope in that, but for the tremendous elasticity of this people, an elasticity like nothing anywhere else on earth, and I believe it comes from the tradition and practice of individual liberty here.

It seems to me that Munich has given us this war-free space of time. For I don't believe that anybody can induce this people to fight for Hitler against Stalin to save "democracy" for the world. And if the old European line-up had stood, this country would have gone pellmell into the resumed European war, in the utterly insane belief that fighting for Stalin against Hitler was vaguely doing something for world "democracy." Just as in 1917 Americans madly fought for Czarist Russia against the Kaiser's Germany in the name of "democracy."

If communists and sentimentalists in England do not hamstring the Chamberlain diplomacy, then we have merely the old ante-Germany lineup: England, Turkey, Japan, against Russia, with the new German strength added and the old enemy, France, eliminated. And the British Empire is saved from its semi-suicidal mistake of 1914. And maybe America can equal our record, unique in world history, of thirty years without a major war. Maybe, with a generation of time to calm down, breathe normally, and perhaps do some thinking, we can save the ideal of individual freedom and even do some more working toward achieving it.

Truly, Dorothy dear, the existence of totalitarian states even as ruthlessly implemented as Hitler's and Stalin's, cannot destroy personal freedom on earth, for when that ideal came into history only a couple of centuries ago, there wasn't anything else. The technical developments that surged up out of free (released from governmental control) enterprise make totalitarian states look much more horribly terrific now; but actually, in relation to their time, they are no more totalitarian, no more ruthless and barbarous and bloody, than the France of the Louis', or than Spain now, or than Pre-Victorian England. These matters are not decided by armaments. Remember that until 1814[7] nobody would have bet anything on this country's surviving. It's a historical miracle that it has survived, and when I think that belief in human rights and individual freedom has survived in it—has even survived enough so that I can write this letter—I swear the fact's incredible. Lenin said once—do you remember?—at a party meeting in St. Petersburg after the November revolution: "Comrades, remember that the Paris commune lasted seventy days. We have already lasted seventy-two."[8] My God, Dorothy, the faith in liberty has lasted on this continent for more than a hundred years. Don't be alarmed, darling.

RWL

---

1. Rose apparently refers to the problems encountered by France and England as they assumed protectorates over large areas of the former Ottoman Empire

and confronted the problem of Arab nationalism. Britain was caught between commitments to both French and Arab interests; in Syria there were some French-Arab skirmishes, the Arab leader finally withdrawing under British protection. A brief account is given in Michael L. Dockrill and J. Douglas Goold, *Peace Without Promise: Britain and the Peace Conferences, 1919–23* (Hamden, Conn.: Archon Books, 1981), chap. 5.

2. British Foreign Office.

3. In the partition of the Middle East, Britain gained control of Mesopotamia, now Iraq. The underlying assumption of this whole paragraph is Britain's need to keep open her sea and land routes to the Far East.

4. Rose perhaps refers to the Spanish-American War (1898) and to the Sino-Japanese War (1905), as well as to World War I.

5. The reference to the south I take to be to the Sudetenland, the German-speaking areas of Czechoslovakia demanded by Hitler at Munich.

6. Hitler had assailed British opponents of the Munich Pact; see the *New York Times,* Oct. 6, 1938, 17:1, 3, 6.

7. The War of 1812, which ended in 1814, marked the end of American dependence on Europe and stimulated a sense of national identity.

8. The Paris Commune, instituted briefly during an insurrection by Paris against the central government at Versailles, lasted from March 18 to May 28, 1871, before it was crushed in a week of bloody battle. In socialist theory it was a legendary event, in which Parisian workers took the first step toward a dictatorship of the proletariat. See Edward S. Mason, *The Paris Commune: An Episode in the History of the Socialist Movement* (New York: Macmillan, 1920). Lenin's speech was on Jan. 24, 1918; see Louis Fischer, *The Life of Lenin* (New York: Harper & Row, 1965), p. 195.

The following exchange of letters revolves around a series of articles in the *Saturday Evening Post* by Walter G. Krivitsky,[1] a general in the Russian military intelligence service who had defected to the United States. The articles reveal details of Stalin's intervention in the Spanish Civil War, his purge of the Russian army's senior staff, his overtures to Hitler, and other insights into the murderous regime that Stalin was creating.

It was a time, of course, of great international tension. Hitler had taken Austria and Czechoslovakia and threatened the rest of Europe. England and France lacked the means and the will to oppose him. The great unknown quantity was Russia, which, by the logic of power-politics and geography, was naturally a counterpoise to Nazi Germany. The atmosphere in the United States was also clouded by the long-established "liberal" view of the Soviet Union as the harbinger of a new and just social order. Dorothy and Rose had themselves come of age in that time when, as Rose had said, "the sun [was] rising in Russia" (Letter 35). The Spanish Civil War had recently enlisted the sympathies of most liberals as a struggle against Fascism; and to the extent that the Spanish Loyalists included Communists within the alliance of groups against Franco, that sympathy afforded Russia a natural reservoir of good will among many American intellectuals. And, of course, there were a number of dedicated American Communists, many of them fervently idealistic. Thus Krivitsky's allegations of Stalin's crimes and his descriptions of the terrors of Soviet Communism in Europe and within Russia would infuriate some and engender skepticism in others. To state, as Krivitsky did, that Stalin secretly admired Hitler and hoped for an understanding was to challenge that special virtue attached to the Russian Communist program since the Revolution. It was also to disquiet those who hoped to preserve European peace by adding Russia to the balance of forces against Hitler. In the immediate future, of course, was the Hitler-Stalin Pact, an event that shook the faith of all but the most dedicated outside admirers of the Russian experiment in a new world order.

Rose's involvement in the Krivitsky affair grew out of her long friendship with Isaac Don Levine, a Russian-born American journalist whose career as an anti-Communist continued from the revolution until his death in 1981. When Krivitsky arrived in the United States, Levine was one of the few persons made privy to his whereabouts: assassination was a daily fear, and his contacts were closely limited. Levine was ideally suited to interview Krivitsky and to assess his revelations; and out of these interviews came the series of articles for the *Saturday Evening Post.* The series bore Krivitsky's name; Levine, however, was the silent coauthor. Rose's part was as intermediary. Much of her recent fiction had been published in the *Post,* and she was well-known there. Her preliminary inquiries paved the way for the acceptance of the articles.

Rose had by this time become staunchly anti-Communist and something of an ideologue; her essential commitment was to a historically unique conception of individual liberty embodied, however imperfectly, in the American experience. Dorothy was always pragmatic rather than ideological (switching her support dramatically from Wendell Willkie to Roosevelt in 1940, for example); and her sympathies were strongly European in many respects. Thus what Rose found in Krivitsky's articles—confirmations of her deepest antipathies—were to Dorothy more problematical. Her natural suspicion of ideologues made Levine himself suspect to her; and Rose's ideological fervor became a test of their friendship.

The controversy began in an address Dorothy made to the International PEN Congress at the New York World's Fair, May 10, 1939. The air was heavily charged with anti-Nazi sentiments; most talks turned on the perilous situation in Europe. In such a setting, Dorothy's remarks on Krivitsky, which she intended as illustrative of the journalist's difficulty in finding truth in a politically charged atmosphere (Letter 41), could easily be interpreted as an attack on Krivitsky's credibility—especially as they seemed to echo a vicious anti-Semitic attack on him by the *New Masses* a few days earlier. A report of her remarks in fact suffered just such a distortion in the *Daily Worker.* At the worst, it seemed as though one of America's leading journalists had been captured by the Stalinists. Rose probably heard of the matter from Levine, and we can reconstruct a telephone conversation in which she challenged Dorothy with this distortion and in which Dorothy spoke with some hyperbole of Levine as a man with an axe to grind. The next stage was a letter from Levine to Dorothy offering arguments for Krivitsky's credibility and suggesting she write a column on the Russian intervention in Spain.[2]

Certainly we can understand Dorothy's irritation at being held accountable for the *Daily Worker*'s version of her remarks and at having her judgment questioned in a matter that she suspected of ideological distortion. On the other side, we can appreciate Rose's concern that Dorothy, like many western liberals, had permitted her revulsion against Hitler to blind her to the threat from Stalin. Isaac Don Levine and Dorothy Thompson were two of her oldest and most valued friends: caught between them, she turns for ideological reasons toward Levine, and all but loses Dorothy. The tensions that shortly would bring about World War II here bring these close friends almost to the limits of their love for each other.

---

1. "Stalin's Hand in Spain," April 15, 1939, pp. 5–7, 115–22; "Why Stalin Shot His Generals," April 22, 1939, pp. 16, 17, 71–77; "Stalin Appeases Hitler," April 29, 1939, pp. 12, 13, 84; "Why Did They Confess?," June 17, 1939, pp. 5, 6, 96–103; "My Flight from Stalin," August 5, 1939, pp. 7, 73–80; "When Stalin Counterfeited Dollars," Sept. 30, 1939, pp. 8, 9, 80–84; "The Great Red Father," Nov. 4,

1939, pp. 12, 13, 66–69, 72–75; "The Red Army," June 1, 1940, pp. 9, 10, 91–96. For an account of Isaac Don Levine's part in this story, see his *Eyewitness to History* (New York: Hawthorn Books, 1973), chap. 9. An account of Krivitsky's defection is by Paul Wohl, "Walter Krivitsky," *Commonweal* 33 (Feb. 14, 1941): 462–68. Krivitsky died in circumstances some considered suspicious in 1941.

2. The letter, and a later one on the same subject, are in the Dorothy Thompson papers in the Syracuse Library: Isaac Don Levine to Dorothy Thompson, May 24 and June 6, 1939.

Letter 37

550 East Sixteenth Street
May 20, 1939

Dear Dorothy,

Don Levine has been my friend since 1921.[1] His wife is my most intimate friend in New York. They are my neighbors in Connecticut.

So you will understand how profoundly your opinion shocks me and the unhappy position in which I am.

To hear such an accusation of a friend and leave him ignorant of it, undefended, is treacherous. To involve you in challenges and annoyances is impossible.

I can no more believe that Don Levine is, or has been, for sale, than I could believe it of myself or of you. Your opinion must be founded on a mistake or a lie.

Apart from personal feeling, there is the fact that American patriots who understand the principles at stake in the world today and who are genuinely devoted to the fight for liberty and human rights are rare. You are one of them. Don Levine is another. Some degree of coherence in mutual efforts is surely valuable; the weakness of individualism against such movements as Communism and Fascism is its essential lack of organization. Another kind of solidarity is imperative. We must know who are the individuals upon whom we can rely.

You spoke from "proof" of Don's veniality. I can not believe the proof. Unless you yourself bought his opinions or were present when they were bought, there is always a possibility of error. Dorothy, can't you tell me how this may be cleared up?

I am returning to town next Friday. My telephone number in the country is Danbury 1684 Ring One Two. Can you come down and meet my tenement neighbors before you go north?[2] If not, do tell me by telephone what may be done to make possible a revision of your judgment of Don Levine's honesty.

With love,
Rose Lane

---

1. Levine is first mentioned in her diary on Jan. 13, 1922, in Berlin. They perhaps had met earlier. In 1937, he helped her find the home in Danbury, Conn., where she would live until 1968.

2. Rose at this time maintained a small apartment in New York City; the letter is written from this address. With some pride she had converted a walk-up slum apartment into attractive, comfortable lodgings; see Emily Genaur, "Little Flats in Old Houses," *New York World Telegram,* July 13, 1939, n.p.

Shortly after her letter of May 20, 1939, Rose dispatched the following telegram, which seems to be the immediate occasion of Letter 38.

New York, N.Y.
May 28, 1939

Mrs. Sinclair Lewis
88 Central Park West NYC
Ten days ago I sent you a note important to me. I send this telegram as insurance that you have received and read the note so that I cannot misinterpret your ignoring it. Perhaps I have become mistaken in being loyal for so many years to my friendship for a Dorothy who in that time may have ceased to exist but I do not accept such a mistake as proved without this effort to verify facts.

Rose Lane

Letter 38

88 Central Park West
New York City
May 31, 1939

Dear Rose,

I had this letter from Don Levine[1] and from it you can perhaps grasp the kind of mind that irritates me and does not seem to me quite honest. When I say this, I want this matter closed. It is not my duty to particularly like Mr. Levine.

He says that I am interested in the "refugee" problem and that he secured information that Krivitsky is under the threat of deportation and that he has good reasons to believe that it is due to Communist pressure.

I was myself responsible for getting Mr. Krivitsky into this country.[2] A man who was intervening on his behalf, and whose name I have forgotten for the moment, telephoned me and told me that Mr. Krivitsky wished to enter the country only for a short time, that he was on his way to Mexico, and that he had an invitation to go to Mexico from President Cardenas. He also had a letter from Léon Blum,[3] I was told, to President Roosevelt. His agent, or friend, or whoever he was, told me that under no circumstances did he wish to remain. He came into this country through the intervention of the Military Intelligence whose interest in him was to put him through the wringer. His permit has expired, and now he must leave. So what is all this talk about his being deported?

It is ridiculous even to raise the question that I might be captured by the Stalinists. I don't know how the *Daily Worker* reported what I said at the P.E.N. Club, and I have not until this morning read what the *Daily Worker* or the *New Masses* have said about Mr. Krivitsky.[4] I am profoundly uninterested in what they say, for whatever they say will be said for a purpose. Because I do not believe what the Communists say, it does not follow that I do believe what Mr. Krivitsky says.

Mr. Krivitsky was, by his own description, for years a secret agent of the Soviet government and a Communist and is now one of the outs. He is a man with an enormous grudge. I think this ought to be taken into consideration. I mean by this that he is not a disinterested witness. But this is not my only reason for doubting some of what he says. My real reason is that I have consulted people who are really disinterested, namely people who are connected with our own Intelligence Service, and their opinion is that to about sixty percent of facts, Krivitsky has added twenty percent guesswork and twenty percent pure lies to support a case of special pleading.

I am not making any case for the Negrín government nor for the Communists in Spain. I am positive that much of what Araquistain writes is correct. Araquistain is doing a piece of special pleading for Caballero, and I have no reason to believe that either Mr. Caballero or Mr. Araquistain are without resentment.[5] After all, after a lost war, it is the custom of the various parties that have participated in it to blame each other for its loss.

I am positive that Stalin has made overtures to Hitler, and I know that groups in Germany have made overtures to the Soviet government. I am convinced that long after Hitler came into power and even possibly up to the present moment there have been exchanges of views and approaches and retreats. This goes on all the time. It is normal diplomatic procedure, which does not mean that Russia will not or has not always been willing and anxious to sign a pact with Britain and apparently has finally done so.[6] I am quite sure that given favorable circumstances she would have signed a pact with Hitler, but apparently the favorable circumstances could not be arranged.

The Comintern is a pain in the neck, and the lie is a regular instrument of Communist policy, but because I think the communists lie does not convince me that all the opponents of the Communists tell the truth. And to take an example: because I do not like Mr. Stalin does not mean that I think Mr. Trotsky[7] is chaste and pure as snow. I distrust *au fond* "revelations" made by outs. Nevertheless, I am sure that Mr. Krivitsky's articles are a contribution to our knowledge of the times. Just how much of a contribution we shall probably never really know.

With much love,

D.T.

P.S. As for the power of the Communists with our Immigration Authorities, excuse me, but I have to laugh. I have had too much trouble with my own refugee friends who at one time have had any connection with the Communist Party to believe this.[8] I think of one who is a composer and wrote some songs—the music—for the Loyalist troops in Spain. He is a nice little man, but he once was congratulated by the *Daily Worker* and called one of their artists, and that was enough to raise hell for him.[9]

P.P.S. Also, I certainly don't like to be told by Mr. Levine what I should write about in my column!

1. Dorothy refers to Levine's letter of May 24, 1939, a copy of which she included. Much of this letter to Rose is repeated from Dorothy's letter to Levine, May 25, 1939.

2. Perhaps in some measure; the extent can not be known, although Dorothy's connections in the government were extensive. According to Levine, the arrangements were made by William C. Bullitt, American ambassador to France; see Levine, *Eyewitness to History,* p. 185.

3. Léon Blum was then the premier of France.

4. In its report of her May 10 talk, the *Daily Worker* misquoted Dorothy's words so as to make them an attack on Krivitsky (May 11, 1939, p. 2). On May 9, 1939, the *New Masses* had seized upon the fact that Krivitsky's real name was Samuel Ginsberg to assert that he was an imposter and his story a fabrication—and to imply that as a Jew he was less than credible (p. 3; see also May 16, pp. 20–21, and May 30, p. 19). Conveniently ignored was that many figures in the Russian Revolution, including Lenin and Stalin, bore *noms de guerre.* The episode reflects the efforts of the American left to deflect Krivitsky's charges against Stalin, the most serious of which predicted his alliance with Hitler (Levine, *Eyewitness to History,* p. 186; *New York Times,* May 9, 18:1; May 10, 20:5; May 11, 23:1; May 12, 19:4; May 14, IV, 8:4; *Nation,* July 8, 1939, p. 32; *Saturday Evening Post,* June 24, 1939, p. 22).

5. Largo Caballero, Spanish socialist leader, had gained power in a coalition Republican government in 1936. According to Krivitsky, Juan Negrín, who was finance minister in the Caballero coalition, made a deal with Stalin's agents to transfer the Spanish gold reserves to Moscow to finance arms purchases. The Stalinists quickly consolidated control of the coalition government; Caballero was forced out, and Negrín succeeded him. See Krivitsky, "Stalin's Hand in Spain." Luis de Araquistain had been the ambassador of Republican Spain to France during the civil war; on April 23, 1939, he essentially confirmed Krivitsky's revelations in a Paris newspaper article. See Levine, *Eyewitness to History,* pp. 186–87, and Levine's letter to Dorothy Thompson, June 6, 1939.

6. There were ongoing negotiations between Russia and England to reach an accord against Germany, but despite reports of a forthcoming pact a final agreement could not be reached. The negotiations continued almost to the point of Stalin's pact with Hitler, which led to the fall of Poland and the beginning of World War II. Dorothy apparently relied on optimistic reports of Anglo-Russian negotiations current in May 1939: see the *New York Times,* May 9, 8:5; May 10, 15:3; May 11, 1:2.

7. Leon Trotsky, nominally Lenin's successor, had been displaced by Stalin and led an opposition from abroad.

8. In a letter of June 6, 1939, Levine states that he is gathering evidence of Communist influence in the Immigration Office. Levine was at this time investigating the Communist presence in the U.S. government; he was, for example, among the earliest journalists to interview Whitaker Chambers, well before the Alger Hiss Case (*Eyewitness to History,* chap. 9).

9. This person was probably Hanns Eisler; see *The Daily Worker,* Jan. 7, 1938, p. 7, and Feb. 1, 1938, p. 7.

Letter 39

Route 4, Box 42
Danbury, Connecticut
June 1, 1939

Dear Dorothy,

My friendship for you has been genuine since 1920. It ends now, not because yours is a pretense, but because you are not the Dorothy I thought I knew and have been defending.

Once you were a fine person, sensitive, intelligent, witty, poetic, ardent for truth and justice, sure in judgments based on moral and humane values. Now you are coarse and stupid. You surround yourself with sycophants and exploiters who would betray you and vanish at a rumor that the by-line[1] was fading; in a crowded evening in your home I find that three decent guests are out of place. I explained that by your being over-worked and hellishly unhappy.[2] I see rotten trick after trick, half-truth and propaganda-slant, in your copy; and explain that by your hurry and ignorance and human emotional biases. Ask yourself if I have tried to serve you. Why did I write you in '36 that Roosevelt, if re-elected, would attack the Supreme Court? Why did I telephone you during the Austrian crisis? Why did I warn you, in time, to be cautious about the Krivitsky revelations?[3] When did I fail you when you asked me for help? When have I, in the slightest degree, exploited you? traded on my knowing you? Did I ask you for help in saving my Albanian son and his family, or my Albanian property?[4] In nineteen years, when have I come to you with an axe to grind? Do you no longer know a genuine thing when you see it, or do you no longer value it?

I do not care why you used a trick to attack the credibility of an expose of Russian-German relations. I was your friend; I believed in your honesty; I guessed you were deceived; I knew you would be embarrassed by coming events; I feared you might become more embarrassingly involved or committed. When I saw you and when I telephoned, you dodged and doubled like a hunted rabbit; you attacked Krivitsky to me, declared you did not attack him in your speech, repeated twice that you got him into this country. Made an atrocious and false accusation against Don Levine and asserted that you have known Don Levine for years. I have known him for years; I know precisely how well you have known him.[5] You know as well as I do how your other statements stand up.

For half your lifetime I have signed notes to you "with love" and meant it. I could not believe what my reason told me. So I appealed to your honesty, your love of justice, and your patriotism; I told you that your charge against Don Levine is a mistake or a lie; I asked for a chance to prove that it is not true. You prefer to discard a genuine friendship.

RWL

---

1. The by-line: Dorothy's regular column in the *New York Herald Tribune.*

2. Dorothy was at this time still trying to salvage her failing marriage to Sinclair Lewis.

3. Rose might have thought Dorothy unduly optimistic about Russia joining an anti-Nazi alliance with France and England; Krivitsky's prophecy of a German-Russian pact would thus embarrass her. See Letter 38, note 6.

4. During her first visit to Albania, Rose had fallen ill during a visit in a remote mountain area; her guide, a twelve-year-old boy, led her to safety. She subsequently adopted him informally, supported him through a Cambridge education, and sent money for him and his wife to build a home for the three of them in Albania. He worked for the Albanian government and was, of course, in danger when Mussolini moved to annex Albania in April 1939. Rose did not seek Dorothy's aid in assuring his safety, but she did appeal later through Herbert Hoover and a friend of Bess Truman. Rose Wilder Lane, *The Peaks of Shala* (New York: Harper, 1923); letter to Herbert Hoover, May 30, 1945; letter to Mary Paxton Keeley, June 27, 1945 (State Historical Society of Missouri, Columbia, Mo.).

5. According to Levine, he had known Dorothy almost as long as Rose had; he mentions her asking his advice prior to her marriage to Josef Bard (Letter to Dorothy Thompson, June 6, 1939).

Letter 40

Route 4, Box 42
Danbury, Connecticut
June 6, 1939

Dear Dorothy,

Since writing you, I have received your letter of May 31.

Certainly the matter is closed. I shall state, however, what is closed. This:

You said to me (it would not matter of whom,) "He is another Sokolsky."[1] "I have known him for years." "I tell you, he is purchasable." "Naturally, I do not make such a statement without proof." I tell you that not one of those statements is true. I asked for your "proof," that I might show you it is false.

That is the matter that you close, at that point. It was only a matter of truth and justice.

Your disliking the man, your doubts of Krivitsky, your having some common sense about communists, had nothing to do with it.

Even allowing for prejudiced dislike, your obtuseness to Don Levine's note is incredible. Obviously to the dullest mind he is indicating to you two important fields of inquiry, and he offers you facts. In writing you at all, he was venturing on unknown ground, and I do not find it dishonest that he speaks by plain implication instead of putting into your hands a dangerously explicit document.[2]

Probably you do not see, either, that his writing you is proof that I was still more loyal to you than to him. Had I warned him of your irresponsible unreliability, he would never have written to you. And I, I am his trusted friend who has been telling him for two years that your honesty and good faith could absolutely be depended upon.

You will hear nothing further from me.

RWL

---

1. George E. Sokolsky was also a columnist with the *New York Herald Tribune.* In his obituary he is referred to as the "high priest of anti-communism" (*New York Times,* Dec. 14, 1962, 16:7). Dorothy apparently identifies him with Levine as another rigid ideologue—hence, to her, an unreliable source.

2. In his letter of May 24, 1939, Levine suggests a column on Stalin's role in Spain and implies that Krivitsky is under threat of deportation due to Communist pressure: these, apparently, are the "two fields of inquiry." His June 6, 1939, letter promises Dorothy evidence of Communist influence in the Immigration Service, but it is not clear that any "dangerously explicit document" was ever sent.

Letter 41

88 Central Park West
New York City
June 6, 1939
(Dictated Sunday, June 4)

Dear Rose,

I do not know how to answer your letter that I got the other day. If that is your opinion of me, there is no answer. You have a right to it.

However, I would like to say that I neglected to answer your letter because I was not well and was greatly overworked and because I wanted to talk to you personally. But I learned from your letter that you wouldn't be in town till Friday, and on that day I went to a sanatorium, from which I have just returned. So I was not dodging you, except in the sense that I was dodging everybody—because I had to have medical treatment and a rest. Meanwhile, I had your telegram and a letter from Don Levine, and I answered both.

There was nothing in my letter to you, Rose, nor has there ever been any suggestion in my mind that you have failed me in anything or in the slightest degree exploited me, or that I have ever found you with an axe to grind.

I think I do know a genuine thing when I see it; I think you are a genuine thing, but I do not know why it is necessary to believe that because you are genuine, Krivitsky and Don Levine are genuine in the same sense.

Now I have finally managed to dig up a copy of the speech I made at the P.E.N. Congress. In it I said this:

"The reporter used to think that all he needed to do was objectively to report events in order to present a fair picture of what is going on in the world. But that is obviously no longer in the least adequate, because the events themselves may be staged and represent quite the opposite of what they seem to represent. This week, for example, an editorial in the *Hamburger Fremdenblatt* attracted worldwide notice. It was first picked up in this country in the *Staats Zeitung,* later in the *Baltimore Sun* and finally got around to appearing in the *Times.*[1] The gist of this article was that with the retiring of Litvinov, the ideological warfare between Russia and Germany might come to an end and both countries return to a policy of realism. The journalist has to ask himself whether that article is not deliberately planted for the purpose of scaring Japan; whether the Russians did not remain quiet on it for the purpose of bringing pressure to bear on England, or whether, even, it might not be doing that most disconcerting of all things—meaning just what it said.

"The journalist has to contend today with the most subtle forms of pressure, as well as with many crude forms. In all countries, his access to the facts depends upon personal connections, and back of each is usually somebody trying to use him. He really lives a large part of his time in the middle of a detective story. Who, for instance, is this Mr. Krivitsky, who affirms that he was head of the Western European Intelligence Division of the Red Army and proceeds to tell millions of readers in the *Saturday Evening Post* the inside story of the relations between the Gestapo and the OGPU? The fact that his name is not Krivitsky is of no importance. But his facts are neither provable nor unprovable. One can only measure them with other facts, most of which are also not provable or unprovable, and see whether they seem to make sense."

This is what was called an "attack" on Krivitsky.

The *New Masses* played up the fact that Krivitsky's name is not Krivitsky.[2] I said in my speech that this is of no importance, which is my belief.

I should not have said to you what I did on the telephone about Don Levine, and I apologise for it. It was a careless and exaggerated way of expressing my lack of confidence in him as a disinterested witness in the Krivitsky matter. When I said I had known Don Levine for years, I meant that I had been acquainted with him and his work for years.

After all, Rose, I think that journalists should be careful of becoming the mouthpieces of ex-secret agents. Several years ago the first Nazi agent in the United States—that was his claim, and there was plenty of evidence to support it, including photographs of himself with Hitler and correspondence with Hitler and other Nazi leaders, as well as the unquestionable fact that he had been the correspondent of the *Völkischer Beobachter* in Washington—asked me to assist him in writing his memoirs.[3] Exactly like Krivitsky, he had escaped a purge, he had been put in a concentration camp at the time of the big purge in 1932, and now that he had escaped he wanted to tell all. I was naturally fascinated and interested and actually started to work with him. But in the course of a month—during which I had many conversations with him and took down his story—I began to distrust intensely a man who had been an ardent Nazi to the extent of being a secret agent of the Nazis. It was perfectly obvious to me that he was writing with an obsession against Hitler personally; despite the fact that I detest the Nazis, I did not want to put myself in the position of having to take responsibility for the words of a man whom I did not trust and whose assertions it was impossible for me to check.

Now Don Levine, as I understand it, takes full responsibility for Krivitsky. I can very well understand that he dislikes the Soviet Government. So do I. But I think it is unwise, and it shows that he has an axe to grind if he is willing to take full responsibility for the words of a man whose statements can be only partially checked.

That has been my whole attitude in this case, and why it makes me a scoundrel I really cannot see; or what it may have to do with who was invited to my party a year and a half ago I cannot see; and why it should be an act of unfriendliness to you I cannot see. I do not see why it is a trick to have sent you a letter in which Don Levine definitely misrepresents a situation, as an example of my reason for distrusting him. This you do not answer.

Why does Don Levine ask me to intervene for Krivitsky as a refugee who is being deported because of "communist pressure"? If I am wrong in this respect, then I would like to be set right; if you can prove to me that I have been deceived about Krivitsky—I gave you my estimate of the article—then I am willing to listen to you, because, believe it or not, I really like to know the truth. But merely asserting that a thing is true does not make it so.

As for my personal qualities, I am the last person in the world able to judge them. Your letter made me unhappy. I have never had anything except a feeling of deep affection and gratitude for you, and that I shall continue to have. I regret that you have changed in your feeling toward me.

I know I have neglected my friends. I have neglected many things that matter to me very much. I really live beyond my means in the work I am doing, but I wish you had told me personally how you feel about me. Had you been in town, I should have tried to see you before I left, but I am leaving town today for the coast, and therefore I must write. I still refuse to believe that a twenty-year friendship is over.

D.T.L.

P.S. Finally, I was grateful to you for having called me up—not ungrateful and not angry.

---

1. See the *New York Times,* May 9, 1939, 8:5, 6. Litvinov was the Russian foreign minister; he had been well known for his views that peace in Europe required collective international effort. His resignation was widely interpreted to signal a Russian retreat into isolationism and hence a blow to hopes for a French-British-Russian alliance. The "realism" would be presumably that of power politics, replacing the "ideological" approaches of Litvinov and Anthony Eden with the calculated self-interest of Hitler and Stalin's new foreign minister, Molotov. Japan would be nervous at any rapprochement between Russia and Germany, for it would free Russia to look to her interests in Asia, where Japan had imperial ambitions. And such tough realism might make the British more accommodating in their negotiations with Russia, who wanted British agreement to a substantial Russian sphere of influence in Eastern Europe.
2. *New Masses,* May 9, 1939, p. 3.
3. I have not been able to identify this figure. The *Völkischer Beobachter* was the paper of the Nazi party.

Letter 42

Route 4, Box 42
Danbury, Connecticut
June 7, 1939

Dear Dorothy,

As you wished, the matter between us is closed. I wrote you so, yesterday. Today I received your letter dated June 6. You ask a question I shall answer. *This question has nothing to do with my relations with you.*

You ask, "Why does Don Levine ask me to intervene for Krivitsky as a refugee who is being deported because of 'communist pressure'?"

He does not. I have not spoken to him about this, I have only read his note that you sent me. It tells you developments regarding Krivitsky, and says, "This is not written for the purpose of soliciting your further aid but just for your own confidential information."[1]

No one but yourself is responsible for your assuming that his words are lies. He could not say more clearly that he does not ask you to intervene. I know that he positively wants no intervention, from you or anyone.

The meaning of that note leaps to the eye; you do not see it.[2] Though I did not know he was writing it, indirectly I was responsible for his doing so. I take it upon myself now to say that you may forget it was written.

I never implied that you "have been deceived" about Krivitsky. Why do you ask me to prove that you have been? My sole, entire object was to warn you to be cautious, as I was concerned for you and feared you did not know the possibilities of embarrassment for you that were developing.[3] I have no interest in Krivitsky.

It is useless to tell your prejudice that Don Levine is an honest and responsible journalist. As such, he does not "take full responsibility for Krivitsky." He is responsible for the *"The Post" articles.* At his own cost, he has had a corps of assistants; he has himself verified with independent corroborative evidence every statement in those articles; he has discarded material he could not thus verify. I take this as a commonplace of this field of journalism, as he does.

I repeat, all this has nothing to do with the issue between you and me, which you wanted closed and which is closed. This is to me a tragedy.

Your letters, so full of irrelevancies and cross-purposes and confusions, seem evidence that hurry and sickness and all the circumstances of your present life control your thoughts and actions more than you do. Perhaps some day the old Dorothy may revive and want to revive a former friendship. In any case, I wish you well.

RWL

---

1. Rose quotes accurately from Levine's letter of May 24, 1939.
2. The meaning does not quite leap to the eye, but the clear implication is that there had been a Communist effort to discredit Krivitsky and to silence him, and that Dorothy's address to the PEN Congress had been distorted to those ends.
3. See Letter 39, note 3.

Part V

Letters 43–44 (1943–1949)

Introduction to Part V

What can be said of the merely two letters in the decade of the 1940s? Simply, perhaps, that they seem to be fragments of a continuing, if intermittent, correspondence. But doubtless it was a less frequent correspondence than before. The distance, in almost every respect, between the two women was greater than ever. Dorothy Thompson moved on the world stage as adviser to statesmen; her voice, on radio and on lecture platform as well as in print, was one of the great rallying cries in the West against the Fascist menace in Europe.[1] Rose, in voluntary isolation in her Connecticut farmhouse, was instinctively aligned with the isolationist tradition in American politics. In her view, European civilization was a spent force; and her voice, with its own vigor and eloquence, was directed through a small newsletter[2] and a voluminous correspondence to the smaller audience receptive to her views. There is little doubt that she saw herself as a member of a saving remnant of the true American tradition that would in time prevail.

It is Rose's voice, then, that we hear in this fragment from a decade of world-shaking events. Dorothy's pragmatic and flexible intelligence, her commanding presence and great powers of persuasion and interpretation, were addressed to such complex problems as the role of postwar Germany and the emergence of the Arab-Israeli dilemma in the Middle East. It is a mark of the capacious terms of her thought that in 1940 one newspaper dropped her column because of outrage from its conservative constituency while in 1947 another dropped it because of outrage from its liberal-Jewish readers.[3] Rose, with the clarity of a radical analysis, could set aside all such issues as old-world problems and write long ideological letters to her few correspondents with the same intensity that Dorothy brought to her column for millions.

1. Sanders, *Dorothy Thompson,* VI. 6.

2. She edited the *National Economic Council Review of Books* from 1945 until 1950, writing most of the copy herself.

3. Sanders, *Dorothy Thompson,* IX. 1–4.

Letter 43

R 4 Box 42
Danbury, Connecticut
May 20, 1943

Dear Dorothy,

I'm sorry we haven't seen each other, and now with June so near I suppose you have even less time. At least I am glad to hear from you, and I'm sure you know that I am sincerely wishing you both a most successful marriage.[1] I still think of you often as the girl I used to know in Paris, and I can't believe that she won't come through everything to her whole finest and best.

Probably I don't know how to be fully just to anyone. I try, but memories of my past efforts don't encourage belief in my present infallibility. But when I said that you are European, my dear, I meant only that it seems to me that many of your unconscious, unexamined, assumptions are European.[2] It seems to me, for instance, that you're basically European in (it seems to me) taking for granted that the government should take over your young people's land corps.[3] You seem to me to be looking at events from the point of view of a European when you speak of fascism, national socialism, and communism as radical, or revolutionary. I think that from an American point of view these movements are not radical, and are reactionary.

Of course, nowadays we all speak in the debacle of the Tower of Babel. We have no vocabulary. Even "American" has no solid meaning. I wish you would read my new book, *The Discovery of Freedom.* If you would read that, and then read Isabel Paterson's (I think badly titled) *The God of the Machine,*[4] perhaps you and I would have a few words that we could speak to each other without merely creating misunderstandings. My book must be around somewhere in your offices or apartments; the publishers sent you a copy.

I do not think that Jefferson can be too much relied upon in 1943. In considering his ideas it is necessary to transpose to the meanings of his time. For instance, when he said "city" he did not mean a modern city, which not only had never existed a hundred years ago, but had not even been imagined. When he said "ownership" he could not have meant the innumerable new forms of ownership which had never existed, nor been imagined, in his time.

The fact is that no one has ever studied capitalism; we have no body of data upon its development, its tendencies, its actual errors and successes, the good and the harm it has so far done. Do you know any scholar or writer, American or European, who does any work of this kind? A little research is done by capitalists, but it is so scattered and fragmentary that I can't even begin to assemble it. Most capitalists have subsidized research which has for its predetermined aim the destruction of capitalism.

It seems to me (and I wish you would please take this phrase as covering all that I say, so I needn't continue repeating it) that what has occurred during the past century is a terrific outburst of human energy, amounting to an explosion. Its center has been in these States. Within even my lifetime and yours, it has altered every assumption and aspect of living. It has literally created a new world. Now the *assumptions* of past thinking do not apply to these unprecedented conditions. You cannot say (it seems to me) that Henry George is an American theorist; his assumption is that social forms rest upon ownership of land. This was true in feudalism. Is it true today, when—for example—Standard Oil may rest upon ownership of oil *leases*? Thorstein Veblen's assumption (one of them) is that there are classes. Is this true in a time when the political-military fate of the world depends upon roughly 1/17th of the world's population, living in a *lack of social order* deriving from an attempt to create a *classless* society resting upon individual freedom and human equality?

How I wish it were possible to introduce Thoreau to George, Veblen, Arnold,[5] and tell him that they are all American revolutionary comrades! Oh dear, it would be a fizzle; he would go home.

When a state of affairs exists, in which a $40-a-month mechanic can become Henry Ford—or Lockheed[6]—how can you say that "unless they take direct action with guns, the people cannot redistribute ownership"? Isn't there an assumption here (a European assumption as old as Athens) that "the people" is an entity? I would call it an American revolutionary assertion that "the people" does not exist; that what does exist is an infinite variety of individual persons, each one endowed by the Creator with inalienable liberty.

From this assertion of reality, and an attempt to base a new *kind* of government and a new society upon it, comes capitalism. The release of every individual's productive energy is so enormous that it not only (for the first time in European-American history) produces enough food to keep everyone (in these States and the British commonwealth) alive, but it accumulates a surplus which is turned back into production. So that we have the first and only instance in western history of a *dynamic* society. Capitalism is a constant process of creating and distributing wealth.

I would question whether, in the dynamics of capitalism, it is true (as Jefferson believed) that it is the distribution of ownership that matters. This is only a question; nobody knows enough about capitalism (so far as I am aware) to answer it. It was true in the times that Jefferson knew, in a feudal society resting upon ownership of land. The man who owned no land was then actually dispossessed. He literally had no right to stand upon the earth. I think myself that the defence of personal freedom depends upon the institution of private property: i.e., the right of every individual to *own* an actual piece of ground upon which to stand. But, assuming that this *right* is firmly established in constitutional law (and vigorously defended against all attacks upon it), then isn't the question of distribution of wealth a question of income?

You know, of course, the record of distribution of income here. I mention it sketchily to refresh your memory. In 1800, a prosperous year, the total income of Americans (called "the national income") was something over 2 billion dollars, a fabulous amount then. Capitalists and landlords got 68%, farmers and laborers 32%. In 1930, of tragic memory, near the bottom of "the worst depression in history", the incomes of all Americans amounted roughly to 75 billions. Of this wage earners (who had increased *in number* 17%) got 64%; entrepreneurs, 20%; capitalists and landlords the remaining 16%.[7]

Now, I do not see (and this may be short-sightedness in my mind's eye) how this record supports a belief in the economic power of capitalists. The capitalists whom I have known (and your passing references to those you know indicate an experience like mine) are the dumbest of human creatures. I don't know of one in American history who has shown the sense that God gave little green apples. Is it conceivable that they have *wanted,* consistently for 80 years, to reduce their share of Americans' income from 68% to 16%? If they have economic power, why have they permitted this? or encouraged it, or *done* it?

I think we need a serious study of capitalism, from actual data, with no *a priori* assumptions. Aren't you simply assuming that "owners (have) economic power in all branches of life"?

Of course it is true that they "seek to capture the state." From the beginning of this Republic, rich men have not only tried to capture the State but to increase the power of politicians in public office, imagining—like the dumb clucks they are—that they could increase a power always greater than their own, and still control it.

I'd like to have a study made of this process, too. That's never been done, so far as I know, and in my opinion, it would be a genuine contribution to genuine American thinking.

You remember, as I do, the muck-raking period. You and I know at first hand a few facts about that. This was the period when the "intellectuals" really got busy at reforming America—Charles Edward Russell, Lincoln Steffens, etc.[8] They made great reputations and lots of money exposing The Shame of the Cities; they publicised with trumpets the tie-up between politicians and vice, the exploitation of "the people" by their elected representatives, the graft, the political holdup of capitalists by office holders. In San Francisco, they put the whole city government, every man, in jail. In every instance, what they revealed was that the politicians, in public office, acted as highwaymen, *demanding* from the capitalists cash bribes in return for granting franchises, usually to build streetcar lines. I know of not a single scrap of evidence that the capitalist *offered* a bribe; the evidence was that he only wanted to build a streetcar line, and would have gone after a franchise in the legal way, bidding against his competitors. Pat Calhoun's purpose (for one example) was not to buy the city government; it was to build a streetcar line, furnishing quicker and cheaper transportation to "the people," and making a profit by pleasing his customers. Instead of honestly doing the job that San Franciscans hired them and paid them to do, the city supervisors refused to give Calhoun a franchise unless he'd bribe them to.[9] I think this is a typical instance. On this evidence, my reasoning at the time, and I think yours, followed that of the country's "intellectuals" and it was: We have proved that men elected to public office in this country are crooks and traitors; therefore, be it resolved that Americans give these men complete control of all public utilities, from which at present they are stealing only a little bit in comparison to the total revenues.

Now this is thinking on European assumptions. (When I say European, I do not mean every individual European. I mean the prevailing, general, philosophic basis of European life.) These assumptions are: that "the people" is an entity having an actual existence; that The State also exists as an actual entity; that there is a "public good" distinguishable from the "good" of any, and all actually living persons; and above all, that government has power to *control.* Speaking for myself—but, I believe, also for you—I simply assumed, in the first place, that public ownership is possible, and secondly, that being "public" it must be "for the good of 'The People'."

I think this instance is fairly typical of a trend in thinking that has been going on here with an increasing momentum for about half a century. I think it is European, and I think that, in our country, it is pernicious.

"Public ownership" is of course a fantasy. "The People," "The Public," do not exist and therefore can't own anything. "Public ownership" is actually destruction of ownership. Where everyone ostensibly "owns" something, nobody owns it. Who owns a "public" park? or a post office? Complete and absolute "public ownership" is communism, in which nobody owns anything and all persons are inevitably slaves, either willingly obeying or compelled to obey an authority residing outside their own wills. The essential to individual liberty (or more accurately, to the *exercise* of the individual's natural self-control and responsibility) is an established legal right to individual ownership of property. Every attack upon "private property" is an attack upon human rights.

You say "Socialism is the alter-ego of modern, advanced capitalism." Here we'll be all tangled up again in words without agreed-upon meanings. If you say this as a comment upon contemporary events, I agree with you. It is historical fact that numbers of capitalists "turn to The State," i.e., bribe men in public office, in order to use police-power for their own purposes; and that multitudes of poorer persons are persuaded, by the "intellectuals" and the politicians, that giving more police-power to men in public office will get for these poorer persons what *they* want. (It will, for example, "soak the rich".)

Obviously, though, both these actions are based upon crass delusions. The American woods are full of examples of how this "turning to The State" works. The Interstate Commerce Commission. The Farm Bureau. The Farm Loan Banks. The income tax. The "Protective" Tariff is the oldest of these. These are merely repetitions of experiences older than the Pyramids. Have you reread recently Buckle's *History of Civilization in England*? If not, do. Buckle was a genuine English liberal; the kind whose passing Spencer laments in *The Man vs. The State.*[10] His mass of data is marvelous and might be collected again today if there were any genuine American liberals.

If, on the other hand, you are quoting Marx in saying that socialism is the alter-ego of modern capitalism, I don't agree at all.

In the first place, we need a definition of "modern capitalism." Everyone defines those words in terms of the static, precapitalist (usually the feudal) world. Capitalism is the way in which men handle their economic affairs when the politicians don't try to control these economic affairs. Nobody has ever learned what this way is; partly because the men who are acting in this way are too busy doing it to think about it, partly because thinking is done by men who get their ideas from books and books naturally report only the past; and, in this country, the past they report is the European past.

So far as is discernible to me, capitalism has no alter-ego, strictly speaking. *In theory,* capitalism is the economics of a society of free individuals. It rests upon the nature of man; this nature being, that each person is a source of human energy, a dynamo *creating* life energy, and self-controlling in action. (Self-control being, of course, responsibility for the action, whatever it may be.) I do not see how there can be an "alter-ego" to this basic reality. One might as well say that there is an alter-ego to the fact that the earth is not flat.

Capitalism develops concentrations of economic power (and redistributes these concentrations, a most important fact to which no one pays any attention.)

The effect of these concentrations of economic power, when

they are first formed, is (so to speak) to create stresses and strains among the dynamic human energies at work. The reaction (the "alter-ego" to these) is more new concentrations of economic power. NOT a resort to political (which is police) power.

For instance: one of these reactions is the labor union movement. This movement, as well as capitalism, must be studied in these United States, not in Europe, where capitalism struggles against the feudal class system and is distorted in that struggle.

The railroads were a concentration of economic power, which (wholly because of the intervention of political power) was in the hands of a few persons. The reaction was the Railroad Brotherhoods, an organization of free men, concentrating the economic power of skilled labor, and the Grange, an organization of free men, concentrating the economic power of farmers. IF such men as Stanford and Fair and Harriman had had the elementary common sense to manage their own affairs instead of imagining that they could get the politicians to give them handouts of the tax-payers' money without giving politicians any control of their affairs, the history of the railroads and the Railway Brotherhoods would be an instance of the working of pure capitalism. They didn't have. The result is that nobody owns the railroads, that railway executives cannot act without permission from politicians, and that the wage-earners who work on railroads can no longer work or stop working or spend their own wages, except as permitted or decreed by the politicians.[11] Briefly, the working lives of men who own and operate railroads in America have been reduced to the semi-servitude of the railway workers of, say, France. They have been transferred from a dynamic, free, society of contract, to the pre-American-revolution, European society of status.[12]

The idea that socialism is the alter-ego of capitalism is an idea of a society of status. It is based on *an assumption* that individuals are not free, that they must be controlled by someone or something outside themselves, in this case, either by The Capitalist Class or by The State.

The American revolution tries to establish a society of contract, based on (I say) *the fact* that individuals are free, i.e., self-controlling and responsible. Men who build railroads by contract-agreements among themselves are *acting* as self-controlling, responsible individuals. Their actions create concentrations of economic power. It is a delusion that their economic interests are opposed to each other; but they had that delusion. (Some of them had it.) The duty of the men in American government was to maintain, by their police power, the human right to ownership of property, the right of every individual to police protection, and the sanctity of free contract. They didn't do it; they used police power to suppress the free labor unions when the workers struck, and now they are using police power to destroy the human right of ownership (private property) and to dictate to every worker. This is reactionary; it is not liberal; it is counter-revolution, not revolution; it is an enforced return to a status society under police control. And when you advocate it, Dorothy, it seems to me that your thinking is European.

There is a vast amount of data in this country which nobody has even made an attempt to collect, data upon the innumerable efforts made, mostly by owners, to develop *new* ways of dealing with the unprecedented, unforeseen, totally unexpected developments of capitalism. My impression is that most of them took the wrong direction because, usually, the bewildered capitalist was seized upon by "social welfare workers," who convinced him that he should act as a benevolent member of an "upper class." Poor Mr. Kohler, and Kohler Village! This wasn't really what he meant. But he didn't know what he meant; it wasn't his business to be a thinker, his business was to make bathtubs. Did you ever know a more heart-broken man? But how instructive it would be, to know something about all the efforts—the bonuses, the profit-sharing, the share-selling-to-employees, the company unions—that employers have made to solve all these totally new problems without any assistance at all from the swarms of American Big Brains. Ford tried raising wages; and who is more hated than Ford? Procter and Gamble tried employee-ownership and employee participation management; do you know how that worked out? I don't. And what has become of the Weyerhaeuser "American plan," do you know? The employees of Western Union were broken-hearted, without exception, when Washington ruthlessly killed their company union; that seemed to me a real solution. I was interested in that, having gone out in the nation-wide telegraph strike of 1906. I remember a girl in the W.U. office in the Cincinnati bus station, breaking down and crying so uncontrollably that she couldn't take my telegram; I thought that her baby had died and her husband left her, at least; but no, she was crying for the company union that they couldn't have any more. I tried to get a bit of information about it, from an old friend in Western Union, but he didn't dare give it to me in writing.[13] Have you any idea of the little terrors in this country, Dorothy?

You should have been here last Saturday; it was funny. And not so funny. Samuel Grafton asked on the radio some weeks ago, for a listeners' vote on the question: do you want the benefits of Social Security extended to those now excluded from them? Of course, I knew what the announced results would be, but just for shucks (and being urged by others here who were doing it) I sent him a postcard saying "no". I signed it Mrs. C. G. Lane (my name) for obvious reasons. Last Saturday, I'm peacefully digging dandelions out of my lawn with a paring knife, when the State Police arrive, in full uniform, complete with gun, and stern and overpowering as hell. The FBI, if you please, is investigating the subversive activities of Mrs. C. G. Lane. Is it true that I sent this postcard? (Copy held accusingly before my eyes.) Is it true that I oppose Social Security? What (in effect) do I mean by it? My sense of proportion completely failed; I rose up in fury, and it's really too bad that only the dandelions heard me. The State Police, really very decent young fellows, tried to explain that they didn't really mean anything by it, that I should give them credit for coming to me instead of going around collecting evidence against me from the neighbors, and that of course if I'm Rose Wilder Lane—all of which only made me madder, naturally.[14] (This isn't connected with my reference to a terror, above. I meant a terror affecting a whole community.)

As to the Russian revolution: from my point of view, it began with the freeing of the serfs in 1860. It was an effort to establish in Russia a constitutional monarchy. It was an extension of the movement begun here in 1660, accelerated by the successful federation of these States and by the impact upon Europe (in the first French revolution; I mean that of 1792.) The increase in small land holdings in Russia was proceeding at an amazing rate of increase under the Czar; I forget the figures exactly, but you probably have them; something like 60% of the arable land was in peasant holdings before 1917—or was it 40%? Anyway, the *rate* of increase in small holdings was rapidly increasing. In 1917, the revolutionary effort culminated in the attempt to establish a

Russian republic, and was defeated by the circumstances, by the personal lack of ability of its leaders, and by the Bolshevik reaction. After all, I think it's silly to call an attempt to resurrect Sparta in the 20th century, a "revolution." The Revolution is an attempt to create a *new kind* of society, based on a (true or not) at least new view of the nature of God and man. There's nothing new in communism. Any effort to reestablish it can't be anything but an effort to return to the past.

Can't you see, Dorothy, that the "ending up" of the communist effort, and the fascist, and the nazi, are inevitable in the nature of things? Can't you see that the New Deal is essentially the same effort as all these, and that its end is inevitably the same end? I do wish you would read my book; then you would at least understand what I mean.

Honest and true, I wasn't saying you're European because of sauerkraut. I sent you the clipping because I think you don't maybe, quite realize the opportunity you have to be a voice for America, which, God knows, so badly needs one. I know you live part of the time on a farm and among Americans (don't you hear the European accent in your word "villagers"?) and you might have written what you did write, in the language that this comparatively unknown person used. Then she would have applauded you.

I wonder, anyway, how much reality there is in this image of the helpless city woman. Millions? That seems to me a large figure. You are a city woman, and I have been. I remember once standing at a window in the Waldorf-Astoria Towers and saying something to Mr. Hoover about the marvelous incredibility of Park Avenue; how amazing that this has risen, in half-a-minute of history, from Manhattan's island. He said he hated it; it makes people helpless. Yet there we were standing, he as able to plow a field of corn as anybody, and I having baked six loaves of bread that day.[15]

How thoroughly have you studied compulsory insurance in Germany? And why do you believe that it will work here otherwise than it worked there? I would really like to know. My own opinions haven't ripened yet. So far, I am opposed to so-called "Social Security" principally because I am opposed to tyranny; I think it is tyranny to take my money, money earned by my labor, and to spend it *for* me—in any way whatever—instead of allowing me to spend it for myself. But so far as I have learned, and thought, about this use of tyranny in Germany since Bismarck established it, I'm inclined to believe that it *can't* work otherwise than as disastrously as it worked there. When a free person buys insurance from a private company, the company has a profit-motive in remaining solvent, and the government uses its police power properly to enforce the carrying-out of the terms of contracts freely entered into. But when government uses police power to compel a person to buy government insurance, there is no profit motive, and there is no third party existing, to enforce the terms of the contract. It seems to be a most precarious venture, at best.[16]

Yes, I wish we could talk. I wish you were here now; I have just taken from the oven two beautiful rhubarb-cream pies topped with perfect meringue, if I do say so as I shouldn't; and, earlier, three impeccable loaves of bread, one pan of rolls, one pan of cinnamon buns, and two applesauce coffee cakes. I am happy, hoping you are, and ever will be, the same,

With love,
Rose

---

1. Dorothy was divorced from Sinclair Lewis in January 1942. She was married to painter Maxim Kopf in June 1943. Sanders, *Dorothy Thompson,* pp. 281, 304.

2. Rose echoes an insight by Dorothy's good friend Vincent Sheean, *Dorothy and Red,* p. 241.

3. In 1942, Dorothy had written about a volunteer "land corps" of high school workers who came from the cities to live and work with the farmers of Vermont and New Hampshire, thus replacing the men lost to military service: see "Education and Independence," *Ladies' Home Journal* 59 (Sept. 1942): 6, 79; "Patriotism of Work," *Survey Graphic* 31 (May 1942): 233–34. Her letter to Rose presumably suggests a national Land Corps under government sponsorship.

4. *The Discovery of Freedom* (New York: John Day, 1943) was an elaboration of the argument of this letter. Isabel M. Paterson was a close friend of Rose's; she had been editor of a book review column in the *New York Herald Tribune* when Dorothy's columns appeared there. *The God of the Machine* (New York: Putnam's, 1943) is a witty and idiosyncratic study of political theory, very close to Rose's in its assumptions and argument.

5. Henry George (1839–1897) advocated a "single tax" based on land value—essentially, common ownership of all land, mediated by government tax policy. *Progress and Poverty* (1879) was his great work. Thorstein Veblen (1857–1929) was the author of *The Theory of the Leisure Class* (1899). By "Arnold," Rose probably refers to Sir Arthur Arnold (1832–1902), author of *Social Politics* (1878) and *Free Land* (1880), a book on land tenure in England that Rose might have encountered in

researching her own novel of homesteading, *Free Land* (New York: Longmans, Green, 1938).

6. The original Lockheed Aircraft Company was founded in 1916 by Allen and Malcolm Lockheed (Loughead); their work was known for advanced design. See Tre Trycare, *The Lore of Flight* (Gothenburg, Sweden: Cagner & Co., 1970), p. 375.

7. Rose used these figures again in a similar argument in the *National Economic Council Review of Books* 2 (Oct. 1949): 1–2; there she claims to have taken them from the national census.

8. Charles Edward Russell (1860–1941), journalist, author, socialist, and President Wilson's special envoy to Russia in 1917. Lincoln Steffens (1866–1936), identified with "muck-raking" journalism from his days with *McClure's Magazine* in the decade before World War I; *The Shame of the Cities* (1904) was reprinted from *McClure's*.

9. Rose draws here on her days as a newspaper writer (1915–1918) under Fremont Older, the crusading editor of the *San Francisco Bulletin*. Older's *My Own Story* (New York: Macmillan, 1926) recounts much of the history Rose refers to, including the role of Pat Calhoun, in chaps. 4–17.

10. Henry Thomas Buckle (1821–1862), *History of Civilization in England* (1857–1861); Herbert Spencer (1820–1903), *The Man versus The State* (1884).

11. Rose's argument assumes much that is no longer common knowledge. Briefly, she refers to the government subsidy of the building of the western railroads by means of land grants along the rights-of-way. Leland Stanford (1824–1893), president of the Central Pacific Railroad, and Edward H. Harriman (1848–1909), president of the Union Pacific Railroad, were solicitors and major benefactors of this government largesse. (The reference to Fair is obscure; Rose perhaps had in mind James G. Fair [1831–1894], a mining speculator who amassed a fortune from the Comstock Lode: he invested with Collis P. Huntington of the Central Pacific and Southern Pacific and later served in the U.S. Senate with Stanford during the time that the Interstate Commerce Act was debated and passed.) By the 1870s, the abuse of power by railroad monopolies had so enraged midwestern farmers, who depended on the lines to ship their produce, that they sought political relief; the National Grange of the Patrons of Husbandry became an important vehicle for expressing their demand for government regulation of the railways. The Interstate Commerce Act of 1887 was subsequently so broadened as to regulate the railroads as closely as Rose describes. Railroad workers, likewise abused, organized into five occupational "Brotherhoods" in the 1880s and 1890s, which eventually became organizations for collective bargaining. (I draw here on standard encyclopedia accounts and the *National Cyclopedia of American Biography.*)

12. "Society of contract" and "society of status" Rose borrows from Paterson's *God of the Machine,* chap. 5. The distinction is between an open society in which relationships are negotiated and fluid and a closed society in which relationships are fixed in a hierarchy.

13. Kohler Village received much attention in the 1920s as a model town—planned and financed for employees by the Kohler Manufacturing Company. When large layoffs came in the 1930s, the company became the target of a long and violent strike. Walter J. Kohler was widely portrayed as the archetype of the employer as paternalistic despot. For contrasting views, see Gunnar Mickelsen,

"Kohler Myth Dies," *Nation,* no. 139 (August 15, 1934), 187–88, and Garet Garrett, "Section 7-a at Sheboygan," *Saturday Evening Post,* no. 207 (Oct. 27, 1934), 5–7, 77–83. A balanced view is by Walter H. Uphoff, *Kohler on Strike: Thirty Years of Conflict* (Boston: Beacon Press, 1966). Henry Ford's five-dollar-a-day wage was legendary in the early years of the auto industry, but equally legendary were the violent conflicts with the union movement in the 1930s. See Allan Nevins and Frank Hill, *Ford: The Man, the Times, the Company* (New York: Scribner's, 1954), chap. 20; Nevins and Hill, *Ford: Decline and Rebirth, 1933–1962* (New York: Scribner's, 1962), chap. 2. Rose had interviewed Ford in 1915 for a series of stories in the *San Francisco Bulletin,* subsequently published as *Henry Ford's Own Story* (New York: E. O. Jones, 1917). Procter & Gamble Company offered employee stock-ownership in 1903 and guaranteed employment in 1923; it held to these plans at great loss through the 1930s. See Frederick Tisdale, "99.44% Security—and Efficiency," *Reader's Digest* 30 (May 1937): 105–7; Herbert Feis, "Workers as Capitalists," *Review of Reviews,* no. 77 (April 1928), 400–404. The "American Plan" was essentially an argument for an "open shop" labor policy, based on assumptions of maximum personal freedom for both employer and employee. The term was coined by a manufacturers' association and gained currency in the 1920s and 1930s as various manufacturing and trade associations tried to organize opposition to the union movement. The Weyerhaeuser Timber Co. was presumably an endorser of the plan, although I have found no indication. See *New York Times,* Sept. 17, 1922, VIII, 1:5; Oct. 1, 1922, VIII, 5:3; Aug. 23, 1933, 2:5. But Rose might also have had in mind the 4L Union (Loyal Legion of Loggers and Lumbermen), an employer-employee union organized by the War Department to guarantee timber production during wartime. The union had strong patriotic overtones, and Weyerhaeuser was a signatory. See Ralph W. Hidy, *Timber and Men: The Weyerhaeuser Story* (New York: Macmillan, 1963), pp. 344–47. On November 1, 1939, the National Labor Relations Board acted on a petition by the American Communications Association of the CIO and found the Western Union Company guilty of unfair labor practices. At issue was the "company union" (Association of Western Union Employees), which had been established in 1918 as a counter to the union movement. It provided significant benefits for employee members, but in light of the company's long history of discrimination against employees' attempts to form rival unions, the association was found to be an illegal company-dominated union under the Wagner Act and was ordered to be disbanded. See *Decisions and Orders of the National Labor Relations Board,* 17:34–144. Such government intervention was anathema to Rose, even though her own participation in a labor strike in 1906 (she was a telegrapher from 1904 to 1909) ended in failure: see R. F. Hoxie, "Failure of the Telegraphers' Strike," *Journal of Political Economy* 15 (Nov. 1907): 545–47.

14. Samuel Grafton was at this time associate editor of the *New York Post.* For a dramatic published version of this anecdote, see "What Is This—The Gestapo?," *National Economic Council Review of Books* reprint, 1943.

15. Rose's correspondence with Herbert Hoover began with her *The Making of Herbert Hoover* (New York: Century, 1920). She apparently visited him several times after his presidency.

16. Rose refused to register with Social Security. She refused even to accept a number, let alone payments, although she lived to the age of eighty-one. See her

letters to Jasper Crane, *The Lady and the Tycoon,* ed. Roger Lea MacBride (Caldwell, Idaho: Caxton, 1973), pp. 151, 202–3, 285.

Letter 44

Route 4, Box 42
Danbury, Connecticut
July 11, 1949

Dear Dorothy,

I'm glad to have your note and to know that you are happy and (until October) resting, I hope principally with only two old friends: Dorothy and her husband. I have always thought that if ever you had time you would find Dorothy superlatively worth knowing.

In separate cover I send you the *NEC Reviews*[1] since May, deducing from your note that I sent you the May one. The *Review* is the smallest fraction of what I have been doing since I stopped writing fiction in 1936. Nothing and no one was more influential than you in convincing me that (even if I were, as then appeared, the solitary American surviving from an extinct species) my life depended not on earning a living but on being a voice in the wilderness. The echoes that came from one little yell[2] were astonishing and wonderful; I was working 16 hours a day before the opportunity to do the *Review* came along two or three years ago and further reduced the time for sleep.

Thank you for asking me to Twin Farms. Please believe that I would like to come, very much, and that I can't possibly. There is far too much to be done and too little of it is transportable. If ever you should travel by earth again between Vermont and New York you'd be passing not far from my little house, and I would be delighted if you would stop. It really is the most amazing news, that Mickey-Mike is 6′4″ and to be a star of stage and screen,[3] though I did report to you his lengthening at its beginning. Living is certainly a fantastic occupation, isn't it?

Every good wish to you always,

RWL

---

1. Rose took over as editor of the National Economic Council's monthly *Review of Books* on the death of Albert Jay Nock, a respected conservative theorist, many

of whose views closely paralleled her own. From 1945 to 1950 it provided the main forum for her views.

2. The "one little yell" was perhaps her book *The Discovery of Freedom.*

3. Michael Lewis had entered the Royal Academy of Dramatic Art in London (Sanders, *Dorothy Thompson,* p. 331).

Part VI

Letters 45–51 (1960)

Introduction to Part VI

No letters survive from the decade of the 1950s. For Dorothy, this period saw—quite naturally—a decline in her great energies, but also a gradual loss of sympathy with the postwar world. Hers had been a voice for the great causes that presumably had triumphed at the end of World War II, and the complexities of the period following found her note wavering and uncertain—she was "pawing the air," as one of her editors put the case. Life with her third husband provided a domestic tranquility absent in her earlier marriages; and the arrival of grandchildren focused her attention on family matters to a degree unknown before. She began to reduce her commitments and to simplify her life.[1]

Her public career effectively ended with the death of her husband, Maxim Kopf, in 1958. In the month following, she ceased her newspaper column. The only regular writing she continued was her monthly essay for *Ladies' Home Journal.* In the last summer of her life, she produced for the *Atlantic Monthly* what is probably her finest occasional essay, an appreciation of Sinclair Lewis, dead by then since 1951. She projected an autobiography, but it was never completed beyond her childhood years. The report of her intentions, however, was widely circulated, and it apparently prompted Rose to return to her a batch of letters from their earlier correspondence.[2] The renewed contact produced the nostalgic reminiscences of these last few letters.

Of Rose in these years, little can be said except that her life continued much as it had since 1937. Content with a small circle of local friends and a large correspondence, she continued her private effort to illuminate the idea of individual freedom and its implications. It may fairly be said that she was obsessed with the metaphysical status of *freedom* and its social and political manifestation as *liberty.* A sampling of her letters on the subject may be found in her correspondence with Jasper Crane of the DuPont Company.[3] There is, of course, a strong drift of this obsession through her last letter to Dorothy Thompson.

---

1. Sanders, *Dorothy Thompson,* IX. 4, 5; X. 1.

2. Ibid., X. 2, 3; "The Boy and Man from Sauk Centre," *Atlantic Monthly,* no. 206 (Nov. 1960), 39–48.

3. *The Lady and the Tycoon,* ed. Roger Lea MacBride (Caldwell, Idaho: Caxton, 1973).

Letter 45

R1 King Street
Danbury, Connecticut
September 4, 1960

Dear Dorothy,

The letters from you, enclosed, have been for years in my safety deposit box in an envelope addressed to you, with instructions to my executor to forward it to you unopened. Legally they are your property, I believe.[1] Anyway, though I destroy all answered letters, I had kept these a long time. Now I hear that you are writing an autobiography, so they may have some practical value to you.

If wishes came true, nothing would be as it is—though perhaps much worse—but I hope that so many of yours are realized that you don't need mine for your good health and contentment, which I'm sending you as always.

Rose Lane

1. Legally, the copyright remained Dorothy's; the letters as tangible property were Rose's.

Letter 46

Twin Farms
South Pomfret
Vermont
September 21, 1960

Dear Rose,

How extraordinarily kind of you to send me back my letters! I am sure they are *not* "legally" mine, but they throw an enormous light on how I felt and thought in the twenties. We all make, I think, traitors of our memories (to credit our own lies). I see that in my personal outlook on life I have changed enormously since then. Impersonally, less so—but there's waving, forward and back.

I wrote you some time ago but never received a reply. I wish I could see you! I shall be here until around October 15th. Then I am going for a few days to New York and then to 2101 Connecticut Avenue, N.W., Washington. My telephone no. here is Bethel, Vermont, 4–4591. I'd love it if you'd call me!

As for good health and contentment, the former is all right, but I have had many cares and sorrows since I lost my beloved Maxim in the summer of 1958. Nothing has gone well since then.

With love,
Dorothy Thompson Kopf

Letter 47

Route 4, Box 42
Danbury, Connecticut
September 25, 1960

Dear Dorothy,

Thank you for your note. My kindness is ordinary. Anyone would send you letters that might be useful to you, but later it did strike me that the action could be misunderstood. Mary Margaret McBride expected to please me by putting my name in her autobiography where it didn't belong,[1] as of course it doesn't in yours. I am glad that you remember me more accurately.

I wish our friendship were revived, but how can it be, after so many years? We aren't what we used to be. If you recall the cause of our only discord (to me, it was your disregarding my hurt pleas for any substantiation of your remark that Don Levine could be bought), I should tell you now that I may have been wrong. After thirty years of absolute mutual loyalty, he made me the victim of the most total treachery; I didn't try to verify a confidential report that he got $1500 for it, which was much too little, but he would not deny nor admit it, and evaded any explanation.[2]

I have not received a letter from you that I did not answer. Oh come, Dorothy, really. You know that you cram-jammed your days with people and ideas that have nothing to do with me, and you've had no time nor need for our exchanging letters. I wrote you once, and for some months I sent you copies of my very effective little *NEC Review* and wrote again asking you if you wanted them. Since now you believe that you ever wrote me, I believe that you had a letter in mind, but the cablegram came, the telephone rang, the car was waiting, and you'd be late. You've done what you wanted to do and got what you wanted to have; I wanted none of it for myself, but ever since we went walking in the valley of the Loire I've wanted for you whatever you wanted. So that's all right.

All lives are tragic. I WISH yours had not been, and we know that that is wishing that you had not lived, so I take it back quickly and so do you. I am glad your health is good—so is mine—and I truly wish that all things go better for you soon and always.

Rose Lane

---

1. Mary Margaret McBride, hostess of a long-running nationally syndicated radio talk program, was in her own way as well known as Dorothy Thompson in the 1930s and 1940s: Yankee Stadium was filled for her fifteenth anniversary show in 1949. Rose apparently met her in New York in 1920, when McBride was still a struggling newspaper writer. Their letters in the late 1920s reveal Rose's efforts to help her with her writing. Mary Margaret McBride, *Out of the Air* (New York: Doubleday, 1960), p. 13, and *A Long Way from Missouri* (New York: Putnam's, 1959), pp. 176–77.

2. At issue here is an article by Isaac Don Levine, "The Strange Case of Merwin K. Hart," *Plain Talk* 4 (Feb. 1950): 1–9. Hart was the founder of the National Economic Council, an organization dedicated to private enterprise and human freedom; he was Rose's good friend. In December 1949, he published a Council letter titled "Is Christianity to Die?," which warned of a Zionist threat to Christianity and implicitly linked the Zionist movement with the Communist threat to freedom. Levine's article identifies Hart's paranoid style of argument with Hitler's anti-Semitic strategy. Hart, by all accounts a sincere and dedicated man, seems to have fallen into a not-uncommon aberration of the fundamentalist Christian. Rose, caught between two friends, and herself no anti-Semite, apparently sided with the one attacked.

Letter 48

Dear Rose,

Yes, I *did* write you, largely to ascertain whether you were still alive. Perhaps I got the address wrong.

There was a time when I was so swamped with "success" and so surrounded by secretaries and others interested in keeping me at the wheel, that I never saw half my mail, let alone answer it! Your description of my life is only too accurate. But *I did see* some of your NEC Reviews, and although they seemed to me then like a last stand, I appreciated both your guts and your presentations.

I do not think that I *ever* really did what I wanted to do—except to be well-known and admired. And I was always afraid of poverty and loss of independence. (The latter shows in my letter to you, long, long, ago.) In this American civilization, one either succeeds as a writer (or anything else) or, by self-choice, chooses *der Waldgang.*[1] I have certainly been a child of my time, which is the only reason for writing an autobiography—if I can.

I don't believe old friendships cannot be revived.

I remember *most vividly* the walk in the Loire. But I cannot remember the name of the village and the little inn (really a cafe) where we stayed overnight in a pouring rain, and ate a strange, sweet soup and, I think, hare or rabbit or squirrel prepared by the hosts, who normally didn't serve meals. Do you remember the place?

Affl'y

This letter survives as a handwritten draft on the margin and back of Letter 47. Rose no doubt received a copy typed by Dorothy's secretary.

1. *Der Waldgang:* the path of romantic self-indulgence.

Letter 49

R 1, King Street
Danbury, Connecticut
October 19, 1960

Dear Dorothy,

I remember (I believe) every detail of that walk along the Loire, including the little refuge from the rain, the strange sweet soup, and I-Hope-Not-Cat dish, and the three of us[1] sitting, wrapped in blankets on one bed while our clothes dried in the kitchen and—of all things!—I told my adventures and Berta's in the haunted house on Jones Street, Greenwich Village, NYC.[2] But I do not remember the name of the place. I remember all those little villages three or four miles apart, at each of which we stopped to sit down while villagers marveled at our drinking water and none of them knew how far to the next village, never having been there, of course. Can you recall at all WHAT we were wearing, that was so soaked in that rain? I can't.

My view of "this American civilization" is not at all yours. So far as any generality more-or-less applies to groups of persons, Americans (as I see them) don't think about "success" one way or another: Europeans do. Americans want quite other things, and go after them and get them. But this statement requires more supporting evidence than I'll bombard you with now.

If only I'd known that you bothered to glance at those NEC Reviews. I would have been glad to send you more and other things. What I have been doing, including those Reviews, required no guts whatever and was always so far from a last stand. Really, it was one of the little ripples that begin the turning of an ebb tide and forecast the coming Wave of the Future, as I hope you see by now?

I wonder whether I could interest you at all in the little Freedom School?[3] Not publicly, I suppose, but personally perhaps? It is a detail of a current American phenomenon; if you could spare a summer day I could arrange for your welcome to a class as a sight-seeing guest. Bob and Loy Lefevre and three young women started the school four years ago with their current wages and their hands. They bought, with borrowed first payment and mortgage, some acres of forest in the Rampart Range, with a deserted shack on it, and worked together, weekends, to make the shack habitable. Bob Lefevre is editor of the *Colorado Springs Gazette;* he was then a feature writer for it. His wife is a trained concert singer, young and charming and then a "success." The others are a trained nurse and secretaries. They lived in the shack and tents and contributed their salaries to the school; also did its clerical work. Loy did the housework and cooking. Bob worked half days on the paper and taught the classes afternoons and evenings through the summers. They still do, though others now help with the teaching. I did, the second and third years. And they now employ a wrangler who takes care of horses and of students who may want to go riding in the mountains in the mornings. They have built a central house—living-classroom-library, diningroom, kitchen—and several cabin-dormitories (with baths) of logs cut on the place. It is all very comfortable, and Loy is an inspired cook: wonderful food. Bob is a remarkable teacher, too. In the second year, when I was there first and by pure accident discovered that they couldn't meet the mortgage payment and had to lose the place and close the school, I thought it worth saving with all the money I had, except fare home.[4] It is thriving now; they have just sent me, for my information, a form-letter letter giving details, which I'll enclose. It isn't asking more money from me, and I'm not asking for any of yours. I think that you might find the school interesting to see in action; that is all. I hope I haven't bored you. As I said, this school is only a detail of a current all-States American phenomenon, that gets no headlines in the *New York Times*.

With best wishes to you and yours,
RWL

1. Writer Kate Horton was the third party on this memorable trip.

2. Berta Hader, with her husband Elmer, was author and illustrator of many children's books. They had been Rose's friends in San Francisco. For the winter of 1918, while Elmer Hader was in the army, the two women shared a house at 31 Jones Street, New York City.

3. The Freedom School, also known as Ramparts College, was one of the libertarian projects Rose supported enthusiastically. The school offered summer seminars in libertarian thought.

4. For her emergency donation to the school, see her letter in *The Lady and the Tycoon,* pp. 208–9.

Letter 50

R-1, King Street
Danbury, Connecticut
November 18, 1960

Dear Dorothy,

I am so sorry. How futile, but what can I say? All my own griefs, tragedies, suddenly new again with news of yours. O Dorothy, *you* were to have none, they never should have happened to you.[1]

We—everyone—must somehow get back to, stay on, an equilibrium. Other persons beat against us so, all the time, unbalancing us. We've just GOT to be steady on our own—each on his-her own—base. Do you remember, once you said to me you couldn't live if . . . and I said, "Oh, yes you will," because I had, and I knew you well enough to know you would. And when the dreaded did happen, you did.[2] We survive, Dorothy, you and I and our like. In spite of hell and high water, we are the survivors. Whatever the purpose of the whole thing—of human life—is, the first essential is survival, and we survive; the gates of hell do not prevail against us. It's American; it's a great life if you don't weaken.

I wish you could arrange to have, perhaps, an endurable housekeeper or caretaker in a separate house, and stay at home. I am not so far from neighbors, but I almost never see them, and it really makes no difference to a telephone whether it rings next door or some miles away. I have (I don't legally own, but complications are too many to bother to explain) 1200 acres at Halifax Center, Vermont, where I think I'll live when this town gets unbearably crowded.[3] It was sweet farming country when I bought this place; now it's New York City suburban. My woodlots and evergreens planted along the road keep an illusion of country and privacy in summer, but when trees are bare the "developments" sit on the hills all around and summer and winter, the cars make the road so dangerous that my puppies must be fenced in. Vermont, with static population, or Arkansas with almost, allure me. I would love to live alone in the middle of 1200 acres. And maybe be snowed-in for Christmas. Which sounds so misanthropic, when in fact I am anything but. It's only that I keep me so busy and interested, and like space and silence to be busy in.

Berta was Berta Hoerner, who is Berta Hader of The Haders who write—or used to write—children's books and illustrate them. They spent forty years building, with their own hands, a castle or palace or mansion overlooking the Hudson, on a hill in Grandview, Nyack, New York. Stone, with 60′ x 40′ living room, little theater, studio, and by me uncounted bedrooms, bedroom suites and baths, all Swedish-carved woodwork—Elmer Hader being of Swedish ancestry. I haven't seen or heard of them for years; they were guiltless "innocents", artists and fringe-intellectuals, so in the 1930's their handiwork was a nest of comrades dearly beloved, and no place for me.[4]

In 1918 I was in New York on my way home (San Francisco), and Bessie Beatty (SF newspaperwoman, on her way back from Ten Days That Shook the World)[5] urged me to stay in the great metropolis, cultural center of the USA, so I telegraphed my resignation of my $90-a-week San Francisco job. Simultaneously Berta arrived to say goodby to Elmer, her fiancée, who had been drafted; he was shipped before she arrived. She had no money; I had $100, so we leased an empty house on Jones Street (we didn't know it was in The Village) and were shocked when the landlord demanded $100 in advance, 2 months' rent, to guarantee the lease. We borrowed $25 from Bessie Beatty and lived that winter on 50 cents a day: split-pea soup, nothing else, and I still love split-pea soup. We slept, heaven knows why, on a bedsprings (which someone gave us) on the floor, under newspapers and all our clothes, and woke in the mornings deeply impressed, like waffles, by the bedsprings. No heat. The place seemed infested by rats at night, but we soon discovered that it was a ghost. We had a grand good time and many delightful adventures. By day, Berta worked at her drawing board and I at my typewriter, wearing all the clothes that could be superimposed and frequently warming our hands in our armpits. And I wrote the tender and touching story of the carrier pigeon that saved (the remnant of) The Lost Battalion and blithely took it to Philadelphia and handed it to Mr. Bok.[6] He read it then and there, said he'd take it, and urged me to write more for LHJ; I said thank you, no, I wanted to go back to San Francisco; he argued that I could do that and still write for LHJ; I could, he said, commute. I said no, I did not like New York, I thought the Atlantic far inferior to the Pacific. Think it over, think it over, he said, as we parted. Berta and I discussed for a couple of weeks, and even dreamed on the bedspring about how much LHJ would pay for that piece; we decided $50, and privately I thought $75 but suppressed the thought to prevent being disappointed. (Floyd Dell[7] always said that I hedged my bets.) The envelope came. With flopping hands, while Berta held her breath, I opened it. Check for $750. My God, we were so rich that I didn't write another word all that spring. So much for memories of youth's sweet scented mss.

Look, Dorothy, Spengler and Toynbee and Social Science are cockeyed.[8] A "civilization" is not an organism, it is not biological, it is not an entity at all. "Civilization" does not exist; what exists is living individual persons, each one endowed by his Creator with life energy and with liberty, which is his own control of his own actions (kinetic life energy). There is no inevitability whatever in history. Certainly, a collectivist "system" will break down, as socialized Rome did, as all "governments" antique and ancient and modern have broken down, when a majority of living persons believed the socialist fallacy: that there is a Human whole of which persons compose the cellular mass. People who believe that will act *as if* the Whole were a reality, *because* it isn't, i.e. because each person is endowed by his Creator, etc., and therefore controls his actions according to his concept (true or false) of reality.

Now, IF a majority of Americans truly hold that reactionary notion, you are right; they will go on collectivizing themselves (as you say), and their actions will wreck the economy, all their institutions, and destroy this political structure; like Rome, France, Bismarck's Germany, the British Empire, these USA will "fall." This is simply saying that attempts to make a perpetual-motion machine fail because they are attempts to do the impossible. But it is not inevitable that anyone try to make one; persons are not fated to try to do that.

So much, I think, is simple statement of fact, self-evident from any point of view. The rest is belief and opinion, and I'm not a prophet. But I do not believe that anything like a majority of Americans are looking for security; I do not believe that the groups of young radicals in the colleges and all over this country are in a "flight" from socialization. I think they are furiously rebelling against it and determined to abolish it. I believe that their revolt is founded solidly on reality, as the similar socialist revolt of our youth was not; and I believe that they will succeed in overturning the status quo (as the socialists did) and end this century as Americans ended the 18th, in a great surge of liberalism, this time world-wide. I mean genuine liberalism. Since the socialists have stolen that good word, true liberals flounder all over the place, calling themselves "libertarians" and even "conservatives," but the accurate word, individualists, seems to be gaining ground lately. What a genius Lenin was: "First, confuse the vocabulary."[9]

The Communists (Russians, Chinese, you say, but all Communists) are easily "more logical" because their fallacy and the logical development from it have existed since Plato. (The fallacy earlier, but Plato developed the theory in terms of political structure superbly in his *Politicus*. The whole line of European secular thinkers to Hegel, Rousseau, Marx, Lenin have contributed to the intellectual tradition.)[10] There have been a few individualists ever since whoever formed the Ten Commandments, but they have been as obscure as the few heliocentrist astronomers since—what's the name of the fellow? 200 years before Ptolemy?[11]—I forget. The Founding Fathers have the relation to Plato that Galileo had to Ptolemy; they didn't recant, they made this federalist political structure instead, but they had no intellectual followers until now. Since Brook Farm,[12] American intellectuals have been European, while active men have been "too busy to think," transforming this continent (which the Spaniards thought not worth having) into the New World. Individualism hasn't had a Plato yet. I'm betting that the oncoming youngsters will produce one. Have you seen, an example occurring to me off hand, the magazine *Insight and Outlook*[13] that they're publishing in the University of Wisconsin? I think it compares favorably, more than favorably, with the *New Republic, Nation, Masses,* that nourished us. The group in Yale[14] isn't stupid either. Oh well, however this century ends, you and I won't be here to see it. I do so wish that you were happier, Dorothy dear. At least don't despair of our country, of the future, of the somehow meaning of it and the somehow getting better endlessly. I suppose you are a Christian; I am not, but who with eyes can avoid seeing that purpose is intrinsic in life and that nothing in the visible universe is wasted?

Affectionately,
Rose Lane

P.S. Yes, from Blois to Amboise.[15] Please give my regards to Fodor and still continuing best wishes. I liked him. But last I heard from you about him was in the 1920's.

A letter from Dorothy appears to be missing; it probably questioned Rose about Berta Hader and her own early career.

1. The source of Dorothy's new grief is not clear; a letter is missing. Probably the reference is to the breakup of the marriage of Michael and Bernadette Lewis, which Dorothy felt keenly. And Dorothy was in ill health, having recently suffered a heart attack (Sanders, *Dorothy Thompson,* pp. 367, 369).

2. The reference here is probably to Dorothy's divorce from Josef Bard.

3. Rose was by now relatively prosperous with the income from her late mother's books. She had turned her financial affairs over to Roger Lea MacBride, an attorney she had known since his schoolboy years. Recently she had informally "adopted" MacBride as grandson in a relationship marked by affection on both sides. MacBride's home at this time was in Vermont; Rose overstates her claim to ownership, although the understanding was that his home was to be hers as she should wish or need.

4. The Haders' house is less grand and more charming than Rose describes—-

really more a chalet than a mansion. It was the social center for many writers and artists in the 1920s and 1930s. For another account, see Mary Margaret McBride, *A Long Way from Missouri,* pp. 131–39.

5. Bessie Beatty was Rose's earliest friend on the *San Francisco Bulletin.* She traveled Russia during the Revolution; her *Bulletin* reports on that trip were published as *The Red Heart of Russia* (New York: Century, 1918). *Ten Days That Shook the World* (1919) was the famed account of the Revolution by John Reed.

6. "A Bit of Gray in a Blue Sky," *Ladies' Home Journal* 36 (August 1919): 33, 98. Edward W. Bok was the editor.

7. For Floyd Dell, see Letter 27, n. 2.

8. Oswald Spengler (1880–1936), *The Decline of the West* (first published 1926–1928); Arnold Toynbee (1889–1975), *A Study of History* (10 vols.; 1934–1954). Both of these important historians treat "civilization" as an entity with a life of its own.

9. I have not been able to trace this quotation to Lenin, who seems to stress the need for clear and accurate language (*Lenin on Language,* ed. P. N. Denisov and N. A. Kondrashov [Moscow: Raduga Publishers, 1983]). Rose perhaps has in mind some later Agitprop theorist: propaganda by deception became a deliberate Communist tactic after 1935 (Philip Selznick, *The Organizational Weapon: A Study of Bolshevik Strategy and Tactics* [Glencoe, Ill.: Free Press of Glencoe, 1960], p. 145).

10. The line of thought from Hegel to Marx and Lenin is well established in the history of Communist theory. Rose's attempt to find the roots of the fallacy leads her to Plato's seldom-read *Politicus,* perhaps the earliest treatise on constitutional government. She could object to Rousseau for this fallacy as well as for others; see Letter 35, note 3.

11. Rose perhaps refers to Hipparchus (fl. 146–127 B.C.), the most important astronomer before Ptolemy.

12. The Brook Farm communal experiment flourished near West Roxbury, Massachusetts, from 1841 to 1847. Much of its inspiration came from the work of the French socialist Charles Fourier.

13. *Insight and Outlook* was published only in 1959.

14. Rose refers to the conservative group of students at Yale who took their inspiration from William F. Buckley's *God and Man at Yale* (Chicago: Regnery, 1951).

15. The route of their walking trip along the Loire.

Letter 51

December 8, 1960

Dear Rose,

Thank you for your delightful letter of November 18. It came as I was just coming down with the flu, and I am more down than up with it yet.

I don't think I'm up to living alone in the midst of 1200 acres, although I infinitely prefer the country to the city. The work for the *Journal* takes a lot of time and involves a great deal of research and correspondence, and even my book is not compatible with living miles from a good library.[1] And in summer I have my grandchildren, though what will happen next summer I am not really sure.

Without being able to go into it now, I agree with you wholly about the Socialist fallacy, but I don't think I do agree with you about "civilization." At any rate—even according to your definitions, I am sure that it is more organic and biological than it is mechanical and organizational. Did I suggest to you a book I think you would find very stimulating? It is *The Failure of Technology,* written by Friedrich George Jünger and published by Henry Regnery, Hillsdale, Illinois.[2] The title, as usual, is mistranslated. The author called it *The Perfection of Technology.* It is ruining everything that is vital, human, and free in man. His thesis that it is also not labor-saving is very interesting. Before I had read the book, I wrote a piece in the *Journal* called "The Remarkable Inefficiency of Efficiency,"[3] which would, I think, have amused you. But technology leads to collectivism, I am afraid, inexorably.

I wish you could come to Vermont next summer and stay with me for a little while. Conversation is much more pleasant than correspondence and more illuminating.

Affectionately, as always,

---

1. Dorothy had by now sold the large establishment at Twin Farms. She was living in a small apartment in Hanover, New Hampshire, and doing some work on her autobiography at the Dartmouth library (Sanders, *Dorothy Thompson,* pp. 359, 362). She was continuing her monthly column for *Ladies' Home Journal.*

2. Jünger's book, translated by F. D. Wiek, was published in 1949.

3. *Ladies' Home Journal* 76 (Sept. 1959): 11, 136.

Epilogue

Would Rose have made the visit to Vermont in the summer of 1961, as invited? Probably not. Each had in late years issued the other such invitations and had them declined. The years had drawn them apart, and the honored past was, perhaps, better saluted in letters than in embarrassing meetings. Dorothy Thompson died in January 1961 while on a visit to Portugal, at age sixty-seven.[1]

Rose Wilder Lane had still ahead of her one of her most remarkable accomplishments. Although she had not been abroad since 1927, she went in 1965 to Vietnam to gather material for a special article for *Woman's Day* magazine. She was then seventy-eight years old. Her report was a moving and vigorous account of the country, its people, and the U.S. presence in that land in the years before the war there had become a national crisis for the United States. Its perspective was militantly anti-Communist.[2]

In 1968, at the age of eighty-one, Rose planned her first trip to Europe in more than forty years. While in the process of closing her Connecticut home in preparation for the trip, she died in her sleep in October of that year.

1. Sanders, *Dorothy Thompson,* X. 4.
2. "August in Vietnam," *Woman's Day,* Dec. 1965, 33–35, 89–90, 92–94.

Index